THE
HOUSE
BY
THE
MEDLAR
TREE

GIOVANNI VERGA

THE
HOUSE
BY
THE
MEDLAR
TREE

TRANSLATED BY
RAYMOND ROSENTHAL

WITH A NEW INTRODUCTION
BY GIOVANNI CECCHETTI

UNIVERSITY OF CALIFORNIA PRESS
Berkeley   Los Angeles   London

University of California Press
Berkeley and Los Angeles, California
University of California Press, Ltd.
London, England
(c) 1964 by Raymond Rosenthal
Giovanni Cecchetti's introduction (c) 1983 by the
Regents of the University of California
Printed in the United States of America

First published in 1964 by The New American Library
as a Signet Classic

Library of Congress Cataloging in Publication Data

Verga, Giovanni, 1840–1922.
  The house by the medlar tree.

  Translation of: I Malavoglia. I. Title.
PQ4734.V5M33 1983   853'.8   83–3466
ISBN 0–520–04846–6
ISBN 0–520–04850–4 (pbk.)

This translation is for my wife, Haidy, whose acute and sensitive knowledge of two languages, Italian and English, has been of inestimable help to me in this and other translations.

—*R.R.*

INTRODUCTION

Like all works of genius, *The House by the Medlar Tree* is rich in permanent significance. Its being again made available in English must be saluted as a literary event. Although it first appeared more than a hundred years ago, it is still extraordinarily fresh. Its main themes and more so the novelty of its narrative technique identify it as one of the first, if not the first, of the most "spontaneous," and most strenuously sought, narrative forms developed and mastered by the greatest European and American writers of our own century. In Italy it is a classic, and as a classic it deserves to be read in the context of modern literature.

Critics no longer marvel at Verga's "leap into genius." Some find its seeds scattered in various passages of his early novels and others are satisfied with the great works of his maturity without attempting to account for their origins. The components of genius are many: among them are a profound awareness of human destiny; a knowledge of social truths reached through observation, meditation, and reading; and, not least, an expressive medium, through which characters, springing from the private realm of memory, claim independent life on the page and relate their inner vicissitudes effortlessly in words so full of implications that each one of us can recognize himself in them. These are the apparent components of Verga's genius— as suggested by our perception of his works and by the scanty documentation he has left us.

We can say with a measure of certainty that, like others before him, Verga attained the stature of a great writer by relentlessly pursuing a literary ideal. After publishing a number of undistinguished novels of passion, he became convinced that his generally bourgeois characters and the social milieu within which they moved were false at the roots and that he needed to return to the fundamentals of human existence to find a voice free of the redundancies which do not contain life but distort it. In *Eros*, the last, the most complex, and the most thought-provoking of his early novels, he wrote: "The whole science of life consists in simplifying human passions and in reducing them to their natural proportions." Thus he was implicitly rejecting the artificiality of the late romantic narratives, including his own, and proclaiming the necessity for renewal by focusing on the fundamentals of life.

It was certainly as a result of this insight that in 1874, at the age of thirty-four, he interrupted the composition of *Eros* to write a short story, "Nedda," in which for the first time he let his memory lead him back to Sicily, the land of his youth, to relive in his imagination the unglamorous trials and tribulations endured by an illiterate peasant girl. Although chronologically a pivotal work, "Nedda" is not a masterpiece; it is at times marred by saccharine compassion and by unreticent social polemics at the expense of objective narrative. But it is a beginning, the moment at which the writer turned his attention to the type of character and social milieu that would become the living feature of all his mature works and masterpieces.

Verga himself must have realized the significance "Nedda" had for his literary career. Shortly after completing it, he began to write a longer story framed in a similar Sicilian environment, in which the characters belonged to generally the same social class and were moved by equally elemental passions and by the same impulses for sheer survival. In 1875 he wrote to his publisher, Emilio Treves of Milan: "Soon I'll send you *Padron 'Ntoni* (Master 'Ntoni), a novelette about fishermen." But the novelette never reached the publisher, due to Verga's dissatisfaction with it. It was repeatedly rewritten over the next six years, until it was turned into one of the great novels of the century, *I Malavoglia* (The House by the Medlar Tree).

During those six years Verga broadened his vision of life

and of society and deepened his search for an appropriate narrative style. He read Balzac, Flaubert, and the first volumes of Zola's *Rougon-Macquart*; and he followed as closely as he could the development of French naturalism and the many discussions reported in French literary journals; he also read Darwin. He participated in some of the debates on the need for a new literature that took place in Milan within the group of writers and artists who called themselves *Scapigliati* (The Disheveled) and who may be defined as the "Lost Generation" of nineteenth-century Italy. Revolutionary in the arts as well as in their manner of life, they paid heed to the ideas coming from beyond the Alps, just as they found inspiration and revelatory power in the music of Wagner.

Verga was profoundly interested in those same ideas. He accepted the Flaubertian theory of impersonality, but also felt it was no great discovery, since he had always tried to be objective by putting himself, as he would say later, "under the skin of [his] characters, trying to see with their eyes and speak in their words." But he rejected the basic principles of French naturalism, especially the positivistic theory of heredity, the treatment and analysis of characters as "clinical cases," and the deliberate exploration of city slums. After considering the visions of other writers and welding some of their beliefs onto his own, he planned a cycle of five novels, each one presenting a successive stage in the human effort to gain financial well-being and then to assert it in an ever-widening social context. The plan became clear to him in the early spring of 1878, when he wrote to his friend Salvatore Paola: "I am thinking of a work that I consider great and beautiful—a sort of phantasmagoria of the struggle for existence, extending from the rag picker to the cabinet minister and to the artist—taking all forms, from ambition to greed, and lending itself to a thousand representations of the great human tragicomedy."

The phenomenon of a cycle of novels, as that which Verga planned after the examples of Balzac and of Zola's work in progress, developed in Europe along with the concept that common people could slowly rise to wealth and power and thereby reach a social level previously exclusive to the privileged few. The French Revolution, which declared the rights of all citizens and resulted in the ascent of the bourgeoisie, and the subsequent wave of socialist thought, which focused on the cause of the proletariat during the first sixty years of the nineteenth century, were instrumental in nourishing such a concept and in drawing the attention of writers to it. Whether or not Verga's thinking was influenced by widespread social theories, it appears that he had always been convinced that the accumulation of wealth is an essential prerequisite for respectability and power, because wealth rules the world (as one of his main characters, Mastro-don Gesualdo, likes to repeat). The poor are subjected to all kinds of adversities and abuses simply because they are poor. Yet they keep trying to better their condition in the hope of reaching financial security. Verga called this effort "struggle for existence," thus applying the Darwinian theories of the survival of the species and natural selection to human society.

The "struggle for existence" was to be explored within the framework of the society of Sicily, the society he knew best. But he also equated it with the motivating force of human activity, which produces the current of progress. He saw it as a movement that appears grandiose if regarded from a distance and as a whole. In the glory of its totality, Verga says in the preface to *The House by the Medlar Tree*, are lost all the anxieties, the ambitions, the greed, the selfish compulsions that prompt it on an individual level. Like a great tide, it sweeps everyone away. The novelist is nothing more than an observer, himself carried away by the flood; he may be interested in those who fall by the wayside, in the doomed who raise their arms in despair and bend their heads under the brutal steps of those who are hurrying on—the victors of today, who will be the doomed of tomorrow. Such is Verga's vision of mankind's march toward progress. There are no winners, only losers. Through Verga's eyes, the Darwinian struggle for survival turns first into a struggle for progress and then into a universally devastating effort to realize one's own greed and one's own ambitions. The five novels were to be collectively entitled *I vinti* (The Doomed). Verga completed only two of them: *I Malavoglia* (The House by the Medlar Tree), which concentrates on "the struggle for the bare necessities," and *Mastro-don Gesualdo,* which deals with a middle-class character fatefully driven by an irresistible compulsion to accumulate wealth through all the means at his disposal, so that his children and grandchildren can enjoy the power that wealth assures. Although they were designed as parts of a series, these novels may be considered independent masterpieces. Of the third, *La Duchessa de Leyra* (The Duchess of Leyra), Verga was only able to draft the first two chapters.

The foregoing should not suggest that Verga conceived his novels as sociological dissertations, but rather that he gave himself an ideological platform on which to stand and from which to report the actions and reactions of the people he was "observing." He devised a somewhat massive, and yet elastic, frame merely because he initially felt that to give purpose and direction to his work he should not lose sight of a comprehensive human landscape. He never let his characters elaborate on the logic or nonlogic of the human condition, but simply let them live it; he never let them analyze their impulses, but simply let them be driven by them.

The preface to *The House by the Medlar Tree* was written in January 1881, when the text of the novel was being printed. It was sent to the publisher together with an alternate preface; of the two, Emilio Treves was to select the one he thought more appropriate. Treves's choice stands to prove the exceptional literary insightfulness of a nineteenth-century publisher. The preface he chose has become indispensable for the understanding of the novel and of Verga's intentions in writing it. The opening paragraph defines *The House by the Medlar Tree*:

> This story is the sincere and dispassionate study of how the first anxious desires for material well-being must probably originate and develop in the humblest social conditions, and of the perturbations caused in a family, which had until then lived in relative happiness, by the vague yearning for the unknown and by the realization that they are not so well off and that they could indeed be better off.

Although this passage appears saturated with a specific social purpose, there are phrases—such as "anxious desires," "relative happiness," and "vague yearning for the unknown"—that betray the writer's effort to look inside the individual members of the family and bring their emotional complexities to light with the greatest possible objectivity. Such an effort is also expressed in the first two adjectives, "sincere" and "dispassionate." Further on Verga states that his goal can be achieved by leaving the picture "its clear, calm colors and its simple design," thus insisting on the means through which he can realize his purpose. He is obviously referring to what he calls "form," that is to say, to narrative style and to language: "one must be truthful in order to present the truth, since form is as inherent a part of the subject as each element of the subject itself is necessary to the explanation of the general argument."

Verga must have conceived and developed the fundamental concept of the oneness of characters and style over the years he spent writing *The House by the Medlar Tree.* He soon translated it into the principle that the writer should limit himself to the essential by eliminating all that is superfluous and all that could be suggested between the lines, thereby charging every word with nuances and implications that open vast horizons before the reader's eyes. Much later he told a Roman journalist the following anecdote:

> I had published some of my first novels. . . . I was planning others. One day I happened to lay my hands on a logbook. It was a rather ungrammatical and asyntactical manuscript, in which the captain related certain difficulties his ship had faced—in a sailor's style, without a word more than necessary, briefly. It impressed me. I re-read it. It was what I had unconsciously been looking for.

We do not know the time of this incident; we do not even know if it really took place. I would conjecture that it indicates no more than a point of consciousness, the moment when the writer clearly realized that to be himself he had to abandon the romantic forms—the authorial intrusions; the endless descriptions for the sake of description—so that the characters would narrate themselves.

Almost one year before completing *The House by the Medlar Tree,* Verga sent a journal a piece entitled "L'amante di Gramigna" (Gramigna's Mistress), prefacing it with a letter to the editor in which he tried to justify the extreme compression of the narrative:

> Here is not a story, but the sketch of a story. It will at least have the merit of being short and of being factual—a human document as they say nowadays. . . . I shall repeat it to you as I picked it up along the paths in the countryside, with nearly the same simple and picturesque words

characterizing popular narration, and you will certainly prefer to find yourself face to face with the naked, unadulterated fact, rather than having to look for it between the lines of a book, through the lens of the writer.

This time, by means of a complex terminology of which we can detect the source, Verga reveals his slow search for a narrative style. "Factual" and "human document" are further developed when he mentions the "science of human passions" and "the perfect novel of the future," whose "every part will be so complete that the creative process will remain a mystery . . . its manner and its reason for existing [will be] so necessary that the hand of the artist will remain absolutely invisible [so that] the work of art will seem to have made itself." Some of these statements, as well as their terminology, resemble fairly closely some of the tenets of French naturalism as assimilated and modified by the writers of the Italian *verismo* "school," of which Verga is thought to be the greatest exponent. This is especially true of the emphasis put on impersonality, that is to say, on the absence of embellishments and personal intrusions by the narrator. But the "science of human passions" repeats what Verga had stated several years before in *Eros*. Still greater emphasis falls on the essentiality of the story and on the elimination of the superfluous, reminding us of the prose of the logbook ("without a word more than necessary"). Verga had discovered the power of the words left unsaid.

During the same period, he tested his literary convictions in a number of short stories (soon to be collected in the volume *Vita dei campi* [Life in the Fields], which must be rated among the best produced in Europe in the last century). One of them is "Cavalleria rusticana," which was later turned into a one-act play and won universal acclaim due to Pietro Mascagni's opera. This story is very probably the reelaboration of an episode expunged from an early draft of *The House by the Medlar Tree*. Others, such as "La lupa" (The She-Wolf), "Rosso Malpelo," and "Ieli," are equally celebrated. Although not all marked by the same narrative compression, all are governed by a tempo born of the world of their protagonists and retain some of the features of "popular narration," as Verga understood it.

In Verga's day popular narration of folklore was considered by many a fresh and powerful manifestation of human creativity that could serve as an unparalleled model and an inexhaustible source for writers. This romantic tenet was widely accepted in Italy during the second half of the nineteenth century and it became a logical component of the *verismo* principles. Verga's interest in popular narration was awakened and nurtured through his friendship with Luigi Capuana and through the works of the greatest contemporary Italian scholar in folklore, Giuseppe Pitrè, who collected the oral traditions of Sicily. It is a matter of record that the stories of "L'amante di Gramigna," "La lupa" (The She-Wolf), and possibly "'Cavalleria rusticana" and "Rosso Malpelo" were told again and again by the people of the area in which Verga spent his youth. When Luigi Capuana wanted to pay his highest tribute to "L'amante di Gramigna," he claimed that its author had recreated the events with an "artistic power rivaling popular narration." It is also possible that some of the events occurring in *The House by the Medlar Tree* are based on fact. But what must be kept in mind is that through a specific social view, by amalgamating fact and vision and by pursuing his ideal of the oneness of form and subject matter, Verga created extraordinarily powerful works.

Either in 1878 or in 1879, when the project for *The House by the Medlar Tree* became clear in his mind, Verga prepared a detailed outline of the action, including definitions of the main characters and a chronology. The novel is set in the period immediately following the conquest of Sicily by Garibaldi (1860) and the subsequent annexation of the island to the Kingdom of Italy, after centuries of feudalism under the Spaniards and the Bourbons. With the new government, most Sicilians looked forward to radical social reforms, but they saw very little accomplished and felt cheated in their expectations. *The House by the Medlar Tree* does not go directly into these problems. Occasionally, there is a feeling of suspense between the old and the new: on one side the nostalgia for the good old days and on the other the hope for a more just society. (This theme was to be dealt with much more visibly nearly a century later by Tomasi di Lampedusa in *The Leopard,* although from a totally different angle.) In *The House by the Medlar Tree* the characters—with the exception of the pharmacist—do not discuss politics as such. Even when they are personally affected rather than thinking of a political and social system, they normally take a fatalistic attitude, as though stricken by a mysterious power, which at most is identified with "the king." Young 'Ntoni feels the need for change, but exclusively in personal terms.

Verga presents the effects without debating the causes; otherwise the narrative would not be born of the world of the characters. One of the springs of the action resides in the Kingdom of Italy's institution of compulsory military service; this and other new laws weigh heavily on a village of fishermen. Even though the head of the Malavoglia family and the other villagers believe in earning their daily bread according to their traditional ways and would not think of rebelling, no one can remain immune to external forces. Historical events that may appear remote have a decisive effect even on the inhabitants of an obscure village of fishermen on the eastern coast of Sicily.

The chronology of *The House by the Medlar Tree* encompasses approximately thirteen years, from 1864 to 1877. But Verga mentions only one date: he writes in the first chapter that in "December 1863 'Ntoni, the eldest of the grandchildren," had been called up "for service in the navy." Shortly thereafter he tells us that it is the following September. Some other dates are merely suggested. Toward the center of the novel, for instance, we can infer that it is 1866 because the family is informed that Luca was killed in the battle of Lissa (fought between the Italians and the Austrians on July 20 of that year). While *The House by the Medlar Tree* hinges on a set of dates, it is not a historical novel. The dates are nothing more than points of reference intended to place the narrative within a believable temporal frame, simply because every human being is grounded in time.

The story of the Malavoglia family is also the story of the community in which they live. Hence the great number of minor characters and the apparent complexity of the plot. This has led many critics to assert that the real protagonist is the entire village, rather than just one family. I do not think that such a view can be shared. The Malavoglias live in a well-defined environment and constantly interact with their friends and neighbors. It could not be otherwise. The villagers thus exert a distinct influence on the Malavoglias' destiny, which necessarily makes them an integral part of the story. The village itself, less than ten miles north of

Catania, is never described; yet we feel familiar with its every corner. From the very beginning we are immersed in its atmosphere, as if we had moved there and were not merely spectators, but villagers ourselves.

The novel is also the story of the house by the medlar tree—a house that symbolizes the family's very roots and its unity—and of how it was lost. Together with the house there is the fishing boat—the *other* house, the home away from home, which makes survival possible. If the village is the world in which the Malavoglias move and express themselves, the house and the fishing boat are the more intimate parts of this world; they are a source of comfort, nourishment, and rest; they are essential, for they represent life itself. The house and the boat make the Malavoglias respected in the village.

The patriarchal grandfather, Master 'Ntoni, is the skipper. He is firmly planted in tradition, and when he speaks he utters proverbial maxims, because old sayings never lie. He knows that whatever is done now has been done an infinite number of times in the past, that life is but the perennial repetition of the same gestures in the constant purpose of survival, that in our voyage we can travel no other path than that marked from time immemorial, and that whoever tries to change paths will reap sorrow and perhaps even death. Such truths are found only in the words that have always contained them.

Yet at one point in his life this solidly conservative man, so fond of repeating "Stick to your trade, you may not get rich but you'll earn your daily bread," gives in to the natural yearning to be better off: he risks a speculation on a cargo of lupins, which he buys on credit from the village usurer. This deviation from tradition is ostensibly motivated by the fact that the eldest of his grandchildren is in the navy and Master 'Ntoni is trying "to find ways to make ends meet"; but it is a deviation nonetheless. The speculation brings disaster, with his son, Bastianazzo, dead and the fishing boat wrecked. It is the beginning of a series of grave losses, all of them spawned by that first step outside the established path. Maruzza too will try to change trades so that she may contribute to the meager finances of the family. She will take advantage of the outbreak of cholera in Catania to sell eggs to those who have fled to the haven of the countryside; but she will catch the disease herself and die of it. Like the heroes of ancient Greek tragedies, she too seems to do everything possible to aid the hand of destiny.

Master 'Ntoni is extraordinarily resilient. He fights against the disaster he has brought upon himself: he returns to his normal trade and tries to rally the family, but he is not able to put together enough money to pay his debt. True, Uncle Crocifisso's lupins were nearly rotten and therefore worthless; yet Master 'Ntoni never gives this fact any serious consideration. For him what counts is the obligation he has incurred, which is a matter of conscience; the rest is not his business, but Uncle Crocifisso's. Against the advice of the lawyer, Scipioni, he mortgages the house to buy time. But the house will be lost, and so will the boat together with all the fishing implements. The latter loss brings Master 'Ntoni intense physical suffering, for he has identified with them: "but when they carried off the lobster pots, the nets, the harpoons and poles and everything else, Master 'Ntoni felt as though they were ripping the guts from his belly." Even after taking a job on someone else's boat, he keeps fantasizing about the house by the medlar tree, of how they will buy it back, and of how they will put together a dowry to settle the girls. He is indeed Verga's hero. His entire world collapses around him, yet he stands like a giant, indomitable in his courage, unbending in his confidence. Only one thing will crush him. When disgrace befalls a member of the family, everything is lost, and Master 'Ntoni is finished, for poverty can be lived with and overcome through hard work, but disgrace cannot. Thus he will invoke death as liberation.

Different from his grandfather is young 'Ntoni, who has been in Naples and has seen people who wallow in luxury and never have to break their backs working. He complains about being a poor devil and cannot accept Master 'Ntoni's philosophy. After the first third of the novel, he acquires enormous relevance. Grandfather and grandchild become antagonists representing two widely different generations with a gigantic gap between them—both of them doomed to defeat. Young 'Ntoni is a hero too, the one who embodies the beginnings of what Verga calls "progress."

In spite of a deviation which confirms the rule, Master 'Ntoni is basically the same throughout the story and like tradition he does not need to be explained. Young 'Ntoni, however, is very carefully prepared and developed. He is fundamentally good, attached to his family and understanding of their needs. What he cannot understand is the passive acceptance of an unrewarding and hopeless life. He believes that it is possible to find fortune in the world. He fancies opportunities but does so nebulously, without a specific program and without realizing that even to catch opportunities requires ability and hard work. In him we recognize the determining power of "the vague yearning for the unknown." His inner motivations are essentially the same as those of many restless poor, who rebel against the establishment because they can no longer stand the straitjacket in which they are confined, only to end up as social outcasts precisely because society does not tolerate those who threaten to usurp material benefits rather than earn whatever benefits are to be had by following the rules.

The episode of young 'Ntoni's leaving home to seek his fortune elsewhere is possibly based on Verga's observation. Sicily, traditionally a land of extreme poverty for the many, has seen her children leave in large numbers. The late 1870s and early 1880s was the time when the great migrations to the New World began. A few of the emigrants later returned, generally well off and ostentatious with their wealth, but most were never to be seen again. This theme had already entered the romantic literary traditions of several countries, especially in northern Europe, where mass migrations had begun much earlier. In Italy, Alessandro Manzoni, although referring to less remote lands, had noted it in *I Promessi Sposi* (The Betrothed); later, in England, Emily Brontë had given it great relevance in one of the most celebrated novels to deal with the theme, *Wuthering Heights*. As a rule, the hero realizes his dreams by returning rich. Young 'Ntoni, on the other hand, comes back home shoeless and in rags, poorer than when he left. Here, as throughout the narrative, Verga follows the stringent logic of human reality, which can be neither deflected nor modified, because it coincides with the substance of the character. For him it is another way to abandon romantic artificiality and pursue facts rather than dreams.

Young 'Ntoni carries his destiny within himself; at times he may ignore it, even negate it, but ultimately he will not be able to resist it. Circumstances will, of course, favor it, but he will always take the fatal steps. Yet the reader cannot help being moved by both compassion and admiration

for a man who, in his own way and within the serious
limitations of his background, could feel in his bones a
manner of life that would be attainable only many decades
later. It was to be men like him—though much better prepared, with much more practical objectives and with a much
clearer vision—who over a long period of years were to
make reality out of his aspirations.

Verga himself must have had the indistinct perception
that with young 'Ntoni he was creating a man projected
toward the distant future. At the end of chapter 10, the
pharmacist speaks of his favorite subject, social revolution, and adds that "new men" are needed to carry it out.
The town clerk rebukes him by drowning in sarcasm the
names of some of these "new men," especially 'Ntoni
Malavoglia, whom he judges irresponsible and inept.
Through the town clerk Verga voices his conservative con-
viction that one should stick to one's trade without being
seduced into unproductive fantasies. But that "new man"
label suddenly, if sarcastically, attached to young 'Ntoni
may indeed signify Verga's historical perception of his
character. It was precisely this aspect of young 'Ntoni's
personality that Luchino Visconti developed and empha-
sized in his 1948 film version of *The House by the Medlar
Tree*, entitled *La terra trema*.

Young 'Ntoni's belief that society overflows with injustice, complicated by his desire to make money without hard
work and by his natural restlessness, causes him to ignore
tradition and to choose a way of life that clashes with it.
As a result, he becomes instrumental in his sister's disgrace
and ends up in jail for five years. During that time he learns
about himself, about the roots he has forsaken, and about
why he cannot replant himself in the village. At the end of
that last chapter, where Verga so masterfully concludes the
stories of all his characters, young 'Ntoni reappears in the
village, only to leave it forever. He walks the deserted
streets for the last time, "now that he knows everything,"
and when at dawn he sees life continue with the same voices
and the same gestures, as if nothing had ever happened, he
picks up his bundle and walks away, alone with his alienation. It is the end of *The House by the Medlar Tree*. There
is no house and no family for the one who has ostracized
himself from them. We are left with the feeling that young
'Ntoni is embarking on a long and mysterious journey, as

if he were not leaving just his village but the planet itself, to wander forever in the vacuum he has created. But he will remain with us, not only as the personification of the "vague yearning for the unknown," but also as an intensely complex human being who has been destroyed by his own unbridled and untimely aspirations, and above all as the first, and certainly one of the best, examples in Western literature of the alienation of modern man.

Of the other characters that are an integral part of the mechanism of the novel, Uncle Crocifisso is the first to come to mind. He is the ultimate symbol of the dire economic realities by which everyone is governed. A known usurer and an exploiter, he has a definite function in the village, for in times of need he can be of help, although in his own way. Everyone respects him, not only because he is rich, but also because he "sticks to his trade" and does a good job of it. In a society ruled by the struggle for survival, the one who manages to acquire money and property is both understood and admired. Uncle Crocifisso is solid and does not let himself be fooled. However, such people as Master 'Ntoni and the Malavoglia family, who have allowed themselves to plummet from near prosperity to near indigence, must be avoided like lepers. That Master 'Ntoni has done all in his power to pay his debt and has been brought to a desperate pass only because of his unflinching honesty is irrelevant; and so is the fact that Uncle Crocifisso has acquired the house and the boat by totally unscrupulous means. What counts is that Uncle Crocifisso has won and that Master 'Ntoni has been trapped. And since the Malavoglias no longer have property with which to protect themselves, no lasting relationship can be established with them —this is what Master Cipolla, who breaks his son's engagement with Mena Malavoglia, accusing Master 'Ntoni of having cheated him into agreeing to the marriage, tells the old man; and what Barbara will tell young 'Ntoni.

But Uncle Crocifisso too carries his pecular destiny with him. To pick up a plot of land, he marries Vespa, who in turn is after his money and soon gains control of everything he owns. Thus he is punished by the very greed that has guided his life. Uncle Crocifisso is the prototype of the protagonists of two other Verga works: Mazzarò of "La roba" (Property) and especially Mastro-don Gesualdo, the extremely complex man who falls victim to his compulsive desire for wealth.

The sexual mores of the characters significantly determine the course of some events. During young 'Ntoni's trial, the lawyer tries to justify his client's knifing of don Michele as an attempt to restore the honor of the family after don Michele had supposedly "seduced" young 'Ntoni's sister Lia. It is a common line of defense in Sicily; the lawyer utilizes it, whether it corresponds to the truth or not, for he knows that such a motivation will be not only accepted but expected. As a consequence Lia, although innocent, has to leave town and in order to survive must become a prostitute in the city. In such a society, a girl is supposed to guard her virginity until she is allowed to give it to a husband; any appearance of distraction or of looseness is blown out of proportion and equated with prostitution. Don Michele had been seen entering the Malagvoglia cottage one evening to tell the girls to urge their brother 'Ntoni to steer clear of the smugglers. This, added to the lawyer's "defense," is enough for the villagers to believe that Lia had indeed behaved like a prostitute. The girl's reputation is permanently ruined and she has no choice but to leave. Thus, in order to avoid the appearance of dishonor, she is actually forced to become a prostitute by the same people who abhor prostitution. It is one of the paradoxes of human interaction: in its blind intransigence, society often creates for the individual the very destiny it vehemently condemns.

Lia's plight also deeply affects her sister's future. Some of the most beautiful passages in the novel are devoted to the intensely lyrical, tender, and sad story of the love between Mena, Master 'Ntoni's older granddaughter, and Alfio Mosca. In the last chapter, when he returns to the village, Alfio is no longer poor and can marry Mena, who is still in love with him. But she has to refuse because of what has happened to Lia. And he must agree with her; all he can do is curse fate. The disgrace of a woman weighs heavily on her close female relatives. It is a remnant of the tribal system, under which the sins of one member were visited on the entire tribe, and even on future generations. Should Alfio marry Mena, the villagers would say that his wife is a prostitute's sister, one who must have the same inclinations in her blood, and he would be ridiculed and despised by the very group in which he has his roots.

The entire novel is constructed with a supreme sense of equilibrium. Each chapter is magnificent in itself but cannot be separated from the whole, very much as Master 'Ntoni's five fingers cannot be separated from his hand. The interaction between events and style is prodigiously effortless. Reading is like following the rhythm of life as it reaches into the most intimate, capillary ramifications of the village. Everything seems obvious; but it is the highly difficult "obvious" that only great artists can attain. The transitions from one character to another and from one chapter to the next are accomplished by means of association: a name occurs in the narration, and soon the corresponding person is before us in action. The dialogue has the crucial function of revealing events, thoughts, and emotions.

As already indicated, Verga's effort to place himself "under the skin of his characters" so that he could "speak in their words" and his fascination with some of the features of "popular narration" led him to narrate in the words of the characters. Previously even the most poignant stories had carried in every sentence the visible imprint of the author, and the reader had to look at characters "through the lens of the writer." Verga's texts often sound as though they were related by a popular narrator who belongs to the same social milieu as the characters and who has been witness to the events. More often the very thoughts and words of the individual characters are audible in the narrative stream. We are under the impression that the characters are painting their own portraits. This feature has caused some critics to speak of "dialogued narration" and of "free indirect speech." In reality we are confronted with an embryonic form of interior monologue. In our age, after Joyce and Faulkner, when even the stream of consciousness seems to have been surpassed, this narrative technique may not sound so noteworthy, but in 1880 it was a remarkable achievement indeed.

In addition to narrating in the words of his characters, Verga's desire for objectivity led him to the creation of a language that was to be the most "real" for them. As Sicilians they would express their emotions in dialect, in expressive patterns that could not carry the same weight if translated into the existing literary language. Verga refused

to let his Sicilian peasants and fishermen speak the shallow
bourgeois idiom of the time, but he had to write in Italian.
Thus he created a linguistic medium by which those poor,
illiterate people could live with all their emotional fresh-
ness: he adopted many local expressions and grafted them
onto the old trunk of standard Italian. With very few ex-
ceptions, every word in the works of the mature Verga can
be found in a common Italian dictionary. As a matter of
fact, he uses a rather limited vocabulary, and yet every
word sounds new and original. However, the cadences and
the rhythms evoking emotions and environments are often
unusual, not quite Italian; they may sound translated. Of
course this observation does not concern *The House by
the Medlar Tree* in an English version. But it carries some
significance if we consider that such an expressive texture
makes translating any Verga work a particularly difficult
undertaking.

Besides speaking in the words of his characters, Verga
also tried to "see with their eyes." Hence his avoidance of
all descriptions per se, contrary to the modes of the romantic writers and of his own contemporaries. For him the
outside world is not a mere construct of the author, but an
integral part of the characters' lives. It therefore should be
presented through their reactions and their feelings, not
through the writer's eyes. In *The House by the Medlar Tree*
we learn of the landscape, of the weather, of the sea, of the
houses, and of the village only from the people who live in
them. The first sea storm, in which Bastianazzo perishes,
is suggested through an atmosphere created by the reactions
of the villagers; it is never described directly, for none of
those who suffer its consequences had personally experi-
enced it. Thus it is much more tragic. The second storm is
depicted through the eyes of the survivors; it is not cheap-
ened with a bravura description by the writer.

Indeed Verga never forgets "the naked and unadulterated fact," and his novel does appear "to have made itself." But because of its language, because of the associa-
tional method applied in every page, and because of its
extraordinary evocative power, *The House by the Medlar
Tree* is also a work of poetry, as William Dean Howells
asserted in 1890. As in a poem, certain recurring images
run through the entire text and stay with the reader. In the
theoretical introduction to "L'amante di Gramigna" Verga

implied that he aimed at "the perfect novel of the future." With *The House by the Medlar Tree* he came as close to this ideal as seems humanly possible.*

—*Giovanni Cecchetti*

* For a more detailed discussion of the various aspects of Verga's narratives, and especially of *The House by the Medlar Tree,* I take the liberty of referring the reader to my book, *Giovanni Verga* (Twayne Press, Boston, 1978), pp. 41–97.

The best and most representative of Verga's short stories are available in English under the general title, *The She-Wolf and Other Stories,* and so is his second great novel of *I vinti* (The Doomed), *Mastro-don Gesualdo.* The two volumes are published by the University of California Press and both are in my translation.

SELECTED BIBLIOGRAPHY

WORKS BY GIOVANNI VERGA
in recent editions, chronologically according to
first appearance

I carbonari della montagna. Sulle lagune. Milan: Vita e
Pensiero, 1975.

Una peccatrice e altri racconti. Milan: Mondadori, 1943ff.

Eros. Il marito di Elena. Milan: Mondadori, 1946ff.

Tutte le novelle. Milan: Mondadori, 1979.

I Malavoglia. Milan: Mondadori, 1972ff.

Mastro-don Gesualdo. Milan: Mondadori, 1972ff.

Teatro. Milan: Mondadori, 1972.

In English
(recent translations)

Cavalleria rusticana. Translated by Eric Bentley. In *Modern
Theater*, 1. New York: Doubleday, 1955.

The She-Wolf and Other Stories. Translated by Giovanni
Cecchetti. Berkeley and Los Angeles: University of
California Press, 1973. (The best and most representative
of Verga's short stories.)

Mastro-don Gesualdo. Translated by Giovanni Cecchetti.
Berkeley and Los Angeles: University of California
Press, 1979.

BIOGRAPHY AND CRITICISM

Alexander, Alfred. *Giovanni Verga*. London: Grant & Cutler, 1972.

Cattaneo, Giulio. *Verga*. Turin: UTET, 1963.

Raya, Gino. *Bibliografia verghiana*. Rome: Ciranna, 1972.

Santangelo, Giorgio. *Storia della critica verghiana*. Florence: La Nuova Italia, 1962.

Bergin, Thomas G. *Giovanni Verga*. New Haven, Conn.: Yale University Press, 1931. Reprint. Westport, Conn.: Greenwood Press, 1969.

Bigazzi, Roberto. *I colori del vero*. Pisa: Nistri-Lischi, 1969.

Cecchetti, Giovanni. *Giovanni Verga*. Boston: Twayne Press, 1978.

———. *Il Verga maggiore*. Florence: La Nuova Italia, 1968ff.

Chandler, S. B. "The Primitive World of Giovanni Verga." *Mosaic* 5 (1972): 117–128.

Debenedetti, Giacomo. *Verga e il naturalismo*. Milan: Garzanti, 1976.

De Roberto, Federico. *Casa Verga*. Florence: Le Monnier, 1964.

Luperini, Romano. *Pessimismo e verismo in Giovanni Verga*. Padua: Liviana, 1968.

———. *Verga e le strutture narrative del realismo*. Padua: Liviana, 1976.

Mariani, Gaetano. *Storia della scapigliatura*. Caltanisetta-Roma: Sciascia, 1967.

Masiello, Vitilio. *Verga tra ideologia e realtà*. Bari: De Donato, 1972.

Navarria, Aurelio. *Lettura di poesia nell'opera di Giovanni Verga*. Messina-Florence: D'Anna, 1962.

Ragusa, Olga. *Verga's Milanese Tales*. New York: S. F. Vanni, 1964.

Russo, Luigi. *Giovanni Verga*. Bari: Laterza, 1947ff.

Scrivano, Riccardo. *La narrativa di Giovanni Verga*. Rome: Bulzoni, 1977.

Spitzer, Leo. "L'originalità della narrazione ne *I Malavoglia*." *Belfagor* 11 (1956): 27–53.

CAST OF CHARACTERS

The Malavoglia:
Master 'Ntoni
Bastianazzo (Bastiano), his son
Comare Maruzza, called La Longa,
    wife of Bastianazzo
Master 'Ntoni's 'Ntoni ⎫
Comare Mena (Filomena),   ⎪
    called Saint Agatha   ⎪
Luca   ⎬ their children
Alessi (Alessio)   ⎪
Lia (Rosalia)   ⎭

Uncle Crocifisso (Crucifix), also called Dumbbell,
    money lender
Comare La Vespa (Wasp), his niece

Don Silvestro, town clerk
Don Franco, pharmacist
La Signora (The Lady), his wife
Don Giammaria, the priest
Donna Rosolina, his sister
Don Michele, customs sergeant
Don Ciccio, doctor
Dr. Scipioni, lawyer

Mastro Croce Callà, called Silkworm and Giufà (puppet), mayor and mason
Betta, his daughter

Master Fortunato Cipolla, owner of vineyards, olive groves, and boats
Brasi Cipolla, his son

Comare Sister Mariangela, called Santuzza, tavern keeper
Uncle Santoro, her father

Nunziata, later Alessi's wife
Turi, one of her brothers

Compare Alfio Mosca, carter

Mastro Turi Zuppiddo (Lame), caulker
Comare Venera, called La Zuppidda, his wife
Comare Barbara, their daughter

Compare Tino (Agostino) Piedipapera (Duckfoot), middleman
Comare Grazia Piedipapera, his wife

La Locca (The Madwoman), sister of Uncle Crocifisso
Menico (drowned with lupin boat), her older son
La Locca's son, her younger son

Cousin Anna
Rocco Spatu, her son
Mara, one of her daughters

Comare Tudda (Agatuzza)
Comare Sara (Rosaria), her daughter

Compare Mangiacarrube, fisherman
La Mangiacarrube, his daughter

Mastro Vanni Pizzuto, barber
Massaro Filippo, farmer
Mastro Cirino, sexton and shoemaker
Peppi Naso, butcher
Uncle Cola, fisherman
Barabba, fisherman
Compare Cinghialenta, carter

THE
HOUSE
BY
THE
MEDLAR
TREE

AUTHOR'S PREFACE

This story is the sincere and dispassionate study of how the first anxious desires for material well-being must probably originate and develop in the humblest social conditions, and of the perturbations caused in a family, which had until then lived in relative happiness, by the vague yearning for the unknown and by the realization that they are not so well off or that they could indeed be better off.

The motive force of human activity that propels the current of progress is here caught at its source, in its most modest, material expressions. The mechanism of the passions acting as determinant in these low spheres is less complex and can therefore be observed with greater precision. All one need do is leave the picture its clear, calm colors and its simple design. Gradually, as that search for material well-being by which man is tormented grows and expands, it also tends to rise and pursue an ascendant course through the social classes. In *I Malavoglia* (The House by the Medlar Tree) it is still only the struggle for the bare necessities. Once these are satisfied, the search turns into greed for riches and in *Mastro-don Gesualdo* is personified by a middle-class character framed in the still-narrow confines of a small provincial town, though here the colors will begin to be more vivid and the design broader and more varied. Then it will become aristocratic vanity in *La Duchessa de Leyra* (The Duchess of Leyra), and ambition in *L' Onorevole Scipioni* (The Honorable Scipioni), to arrive finally at *L'uomo di lusso* (The Man of Luxury), who

3

gathers in himself all those yearnings, all those vanities, and all those ambitions, embracing them and suffering from them, feeling them in his blood and being consumed by them. As the sphere of human activity widens, the mechanism of the passions becomes more complex, and the characters certainly appear less original, but they are also more peculiar due to the subtle influence of their upbringing on their personalities and also due to the large dose of artificiality inherent in civilized manners. Even their language tends to grow more individualized, enriched by all the half-tones of ambiguous sentiments, all the artifices of speech, which serve to give prominence to ideas in an age that imposes, as a rule of good taste, flat and common formality to conceal the uniformity of emotions and ideas. If the artistic reproduction of such milieus is to be precise, one must scrupulously follow the norms of this analysis; one must be truthful in order to present the truth, since form is as inherent a part of the subject as each element of the subject itself is necessary to the explanation of the general argument.

The fateful, incessant, often difficult and feverish course that humankind travels to achieve the conquest of progress is grandiose in its results when seen as a whole, from a distance. The glorious light accompanying it obliterates the anxieties, the greed, the selfishness, all the passions, all the vices that are turned into virtues, all the weaknesses that aid the tremendous task, all the contradictions from whose friction the light of truth is generated. The resulting benefit for humankind covers whatever is mean-spirited in the personal interests that produce it; it justifies them as necessary means to stimulate the activity of the individual who unconsciously works for the benefit of all. Every impulse of such universal activity, from the search for material well-being to the loftiest ambitions, is legitimated by the simple fact that it contributes to attaining the goal of the incessant movement. When one knows where this immense current of human activity is headed, one certainly does not ask how it gets there. Only the observer, he too swept along by the flood, has the right to be interested, as he looks around, in the weak who fall by the wayside, in the weary who let themselves be overtaken by the waves in order to end the struggle sooner, in the doomed who raise their arms in despair and bend their heads under the brutal steps of those who are pressing on—the victors of today, who are also in a hurry and eager to arrive and who themselves will be overtaken tomorrow.

I Malavoglia (The House by the Medlar Tree), *Mastro-don Gesualdo, La Duchessa de Leyra* (The Duchess of Leyra), *L'Onorevole Scipioni* (The Honorable Scipioni), and *L'uomo di lusso* (The Man of Luxury), are all people who are doomed and whom the current has strewn along the banks, after having swept them away and drowned them, each one bearing the stigmata of his sin, which should have been the emblazoned splendor of his virtue. Each one of them, from the lowliest to the most highly placed, has had his part in the struggle for existence, for material well-being or for ambition: the humble fisherman; the newly rich; the intruder into the upper classes; the man of talent and robust will, who feels he has the strength to dominate other men and to seize that portion of public esteem which social prejudice denies him because of his illegitimate birth and who has now the power to make laws—he who was born outside the law—and finally the artist, who believes he is pursuing his ideal, though he is actually pursuing another form of ambition. The one who observes this spectacle does not have the right to judge it; it is already much if he can draw aside from the field of struggle for an instant, to study it without passion and to render the scene clearly and with appropriate colors, so as to offer the picture of reality as it was, or as it should have been.—*Milan, January 19, 1881*

—*Trans. R. R. and G. C.*

CHAPTER ONE

There was a time when the Malavoglia were as thick as the stones on the old Trezza road. You could find them even at Ognina and Aci Castello, all seagoing folk, good, upright, the exact opposite of what you would think from their nickname. And this is as it should be. In the parish register they were in truth called Toscano, but that didn't mean a thing, for ever since this world was a world they'd been known from father to son as Malavoglia at Ognina, Trezza, and Aci Castello, and they had always had their own boats in the water and their own roof tiles in the sun. But now at Trezza all that was left of them was Master 'Ntoni's branch of the Malavoglia, who lived in the house by the medlar tree and kept the *Provvidenza* moored on the beach below the wash shed, alongside Uncle Cola's *Concetta* and Master Fortunato Cipolla's big trawler.

The squalls that had driven the other Malavoglia here, there, and everywhere had passed over the house by the medlar tree and the boat moored below the wash shed without doing too much damage; and Master 'Ntoni, to explain the miracle, used to lift his clenched fist, a fist made like a chunk of walnut, and say: "To pull an oar the five fingers must work together."

He also used to say: "Men are made like the fingers of a hand: the thumb must act like a thumb, and the little finger must act like a little finger."

7

And Master 'Ntoni's family was truly set out like the
fingers of a hand. First came the old man himself, the
thumb, who commanded when to feast and when to fast;
then his son Bastiano, called Bastianazzo, because he was
as big and burly as the St. Christopher painted under the
arch of the fish market in the city of Catania; and big
and burly as he was, he'd put about directly when ordered, and wouldn't even blow his nose without his
father's say-so. In fact he had taken Maruzza for a wife
when he'd been told to take her. Then came Maruzza
herself, or La Longa, a tiny woman who kept busy weaving, salting anchovies, and bearing children, like a good
housewife. And last the grandchildren, in order of age.
'Ntoni, the eldest, a loafer of twenty, who was still getting clouts from his grandfather, and then a few kicks
lower down to straighten him out when the clout had been
too hard. Then Luca who, his grandfather always said, had
more good sense than his older brother; and Mena, short
for Filomena, who was nicknamed Saint Agatha because
she was forever at the loom, and you know what they say:
Woman at the loom, hen in the coop, and mullet in January! After Mena came Alessio, Alessi for short, a little
snot-nose who was the spitting image of his grandfather;
and finally Lia, short for Rosalia, who was not yet fish,
flesh, or fowl. On Sundays, when they walked into church
one behind the other, it looked like a procession.

Master 'Ntoni also repeated certain sayings and proverbs which he had heard from the old folks, because, as
he put it, "the sayings of the old folks never lie." For
instance: "Without a man at the tiller the boat can't
sail."—"You've got to be a sexton before you can be the
Pope."—Or: "Stick to your trade, you may not get rich but
you'll earn your bread."—"Be satisfied to be what your
father made you, if nothing else you won't be a rascal."
And many other wise maxims.

That's why the house by the medlar tree prospered, and
Master 'Ntoni was considered a man with his head screwed
on right, and they would have made him a councilman if
Don Silvestro, the town clerk, who was a shrewd fellow,
hadn't preached that he was a rotten reactionary, one of
those who supported the Bourbons and plotted for the re-

turn of King Bomba's son, so that he could tyrannize the village just as he tyrannized his own house.

But Master 'Ntoni wouldn't have even known King Bomba's son if he saw him, and minded his own business, and used to say: "The man who runs a household can't sleep whenever he wishes," because "he who commands must give an accounting."

In December, 1863, 'Ntoni, the eldest of the grandchildren, was called up for service in the navy. And then Master 'Ntoni ran to see all the bigwigs in the village, who can help us poor people. But Don Giammaria, the parish priest, replied that it was just what he deserved, and that it was all due to that revolution out of hell which they'd made by unfurling a tricolor kerchief on the church tower. On the other hand, Don Franco, the pharmacist, began snickering behind his big beard and rubbing his hands, and vowed that if they ever managed to put together some kind of a republic, all the people in charge of taxation and military service would get a parting kick in the behind because there wouldn't be any more soldiers and sailors, and if the need arose, the whole country would go to war. When he heard this, Master 'Ntoni begged and pleaded with him for the love of God to make his republic soon, at least before his grandson 'Ntoni went off to the service, as though Don Franco had the republic in his pocket; and he pleaded so much that finally the pharmacist went into a rage. Later Don Silvestro, the town clerk, had a big laugh over this conversation, but at last he said that if Master 'Ntoni slipped a wad of money into the palm of the right person, whom he happened to know, the government might be able to find a defect in his grandson and declare him unfit. But as luck would have it the boy was built without a flaw, as they can still make them at Aci Trezza, and the conscription doctor, when he saw that hulking young man in front of him, said that his only defect was to be planted like a pillar on those huge feet which looked like cactus blades. But in nasty weather feet shaped like cactus blades are better than tight little boots for holding the deck of an ironclad, so they took 'Ntoni without even saying: "Do you mind?" When the conscripts were marched to the barracks at Catania, La Longa trotted breathlessly to keep up with her son's long strides, and kept advising him always to wear the scapular of the Madonna on his chest, and to send back the news when some acquaintance from their parts returned to the village and they'd mail him the money for writing paper.

His grandfather, being a man, didn't say a word, but he had a lump in his throat too, and avoided looking his daughter-in-law in the face, as though he were angry with her. So they walked back to Trezza in silence, their heads bowed. Bastianazzo had hastened to strip down the *Provvidenza* so that he could go and wait for them at the end of the road. But when he saw them appear like that, so crestfallen, carrying their shoes in their hands, he hadn't the heart to open his mouth all the way home. La Longa immediately darted into the kitchen, as if she were in a great hurry to be alone with her old pots and pans, and then Master 'Ntoni said to his son: "Go and talk to the poor woman; she's at the end of her rope."

The next day they all went to the station at Aci Castello to see the conscripts' convoy go by on its way to Messina, and they waited for more than an hour, crushed in the crowd behind the fence. At last the train arrived, and they saw all those poor boys waving wildly, their heads sticking out of the windows, like cattle being taken to the fair. And what with the singing, the laughter and the tumult, it was just like the feast day at Trecastagni, and in the crush and noise you even forgot that ache you had in your heart.

"Goodbye, 'Ntoni!" "Goodbye, Mother!" "Goodbye, and remember what I said, remember!" Nearby, at the side of the road, stood Comare Tudda's Sara, cutting grass for the calf, but Venera Zuppidda went around whispering that Sara was there to wave goodbye to Master 'Ntoni's 'Ntoni, with whom she was carrying on over the garden wall, she'd seen them herself, with her own two eyes, may the worms devour them! And the fact is that 'Ntoni waved to Sara, and she stood there, clutching her sickle, watching the train until it left. To La Longa it seemed that that wave had been stolen from her; and for a long time afterwards, whenever she met Sara in the piazza or at the wash shed, she would turn her back.

Then the train left, whistling and snorting so much that it swallowed up the singing and the last farewells. And after that the people who had come out of curiosity went away, and the only ones left were a few housewives and some poor devils who clung to the rails of the fence without knowing why. Gradually, they too began to stray off, and Master 'Ntoni, sensing that his daughter-in-law had a bitter taste in her mouth, bought her two cents' worth of lemon water.

To comfort La Longa, Comare Venera Zuppidda kept telling her: "Now put your heart at rest, because for five years you've got to act as if your son were dead, and just forget about him."

But they never forgot about him for a moment in the house by the medlar tree. First because every time La Longa set the table she would find that extra soup bowl in her hand. And then because of a certain double loop which 'Ntoni knew how to tie better than anyone else to hold the sail in place; or when they had to stretch a line as taut as a violin string, or haul in the mooring, which really called for a winch. His grandfather, panting as he pulled, would cry: "Here's where 'Ntoni came in handy!" Or: "Do you think I've got the wrist that boy has?" His mother, when she shifted the comb in the loom—one! two! three!—remembered the engine's boom-boom when it had snatched away her son, and it had stuck in her heart in that great moment of dismay and bewilderment and still pounded in her breast—one! two! three!

His grandfather came out with peculiar arguments to console himself and the others. "Anyway, do you want to know what I say? A little soldiering will do that boy some good; he enjoyed swinging his arms more on a Sunday stroll than using them to earn his bread." Then he'd add: "After he's tasted the bitter bread they eat elsewhere, he won't complain about the soup he gets at home."

At last 'Ntoni's first letter arrived from Naples and set the whole neighborhood in an uproar. He said that the women in those parts swept the streets with silk skirts, and that on the quay there was a puppet show, and they sold pizzas for two centesimi, just the kind the rich folk ate, and that without money you couldn't live there; for it wasn't like Trezza, where unless you went to Santuzza's tavern, you wouldn't get to spend a penny. "So we're to send that glutton money to buy pizzas, eh?" Master 'Ntoni grumbled. "But it's not his fault, that's the way he's made. Like the mullet, who gulp even at a rusty nail. If I hadn't held him in these arms of mine at his christening, I'd say that Don Giammaria put sugar in his mouth instead of salt!"

When Comare Tudda's Sara was at the wash shed, the Mangiacarrube girl always said: "Sure! the ladies dressed in silk were all just waiting for Master 'Ntoni's 'Ntoni, so they could grab him. They'd never seen a cucumber in that part of the world before!" And the other girls laughed so much their sides hurt, and from then on the girls who were sour because he'd passed them up called 'Ntoni the "cucumber."

'Ntoni had sent his photograph too, and all the girls at the wash shed had seen it, for Comare Tudda's Sara passed it around hidden under her apron while the Mangiacarrube girl was so jealous she could have choked. He looked like the Archangel Michael in the flesh, with those feet planted on the carpet and that drapery above his head, just like the drapery above the Madonna of Ognina, so handsome, so licked and polished that even his own mother wouldn't have recognized him; and poor La Longa couldn't stop gazing at the carpet and the drapery and that squat pillar against which her boy stood stiff as a ramrod, one hand tickling the back of a fine armchair; and she thanked God and all the saints who had put her son amid all those elegancies. She kept the picture on the dresser beneath the glass bell together with the Good Shepherd, so that she said her Hail Marys to it and, so Venera Zuppidda went around saying, she figured that she had a special treasure on her dresser, but Sister Mariangela La Santuzza had another exactly like it, as everyone could see, which Mariano Cinghialenta had given her, and she kept it nailed up over the tavern counter, behind the glasses.

But after a while 'Ntoni got hold of a comrade who knew how to write, and he reeled off his complaints about the miserable life aboard ship, and the discipline, and the officers, and the soft rice and the hard shoes. "A letter which wasn't worth the twenty centesimi to mail!" Master

'Ntoni growled. La Longa took it out on that scrawl on the paper there, which looked like a mess of fishhooks, and certainly couldn't be saying anything good. Bastianazzo shook his head to signify no, that's not the way to act, and if it had been up to him he would always have put cheerful things on that paper, to make everybody's heart glad—and he pointed a finger thick as the pin of an oarlock at the letter—if for nothing else out of pity for La Longa, poor woman, who never stopped worrying and looked like a cat who's lost her kittens. Master 'Ntoni went on the sly to have the letter read to him by the pharmacist, and after that by Don Giammaria, who was in the opposing camp, so he could hear it from both sides, and when he was finally convinced that this was really what was written there, he went home and said to Bastianazzo and his wife:

"Haven't I always been telling you that that boy should have been born rich, like Master Cipolla's son, so he could sit there scratching his belly and not do a blessed thing!"

Meanwhile it was a lean year, and now that Christians had learned to eat meat on Friday too, like so many Turks, the fish had to be practically given away as alms for the souls of the dead. The men who had remained in the house weren't enough to run the boat, and sometimes they had to hire La Locca's son Menico by the day, or somebody else. You see, that's what the King did—he took the boys for service as soon as they were big enough to earn their bread; but as long as they were a burden, the family had to raise them so that they could make good soldiers and sailors. Besides, they had to start thinking about Mena, who'd just had her seventeenth birthday and had begun making the young men turn and stare when she went to Mass. "Man is fire and woman is straw," so the saying goes, "and the devil comes and starts blowing." So they had to work as hard as they could to keep the boat of the house by the medlar tree running.

So Master 'Ntoni, trying to make ends meet, had put through a deal with Uncle Crocifisso, nicknamed "Dumbbell," to buy some lupin beans on credit and sell them at Riposto, where Compare Cinghialenta said there was a ship from Trieste taking on cargo. To tell the truth, the lupins were a bit spoiled; but they were the only ones you could get at Trezza, and that foxy old Dumbbell also knew that sun and water were uselessly eating up the *Provvidenza,* tied up below the wash shed, completely idle; so that's why he kept on pretending that he was a little dense. "What's that?" he said. "You think it's too much? Don't take them! But I can't do it for a cent less, on my conscience, because I have a soul that must meet its Maker!"—and he swayed his head, which really looked like a bell without a clapper.

All this was said in front of the church door at Ognina, on the first Sunday in September, which was the feast day of the Holy Virgin and had brought a great throng of people from all the nearby villages; and Compare Piedipapera was there too, and with his joshing got them to agree on two onze and ten a *salma,* to be paid at so much per month. That's how it always ended, Uncle Crocifisso said—they'd talk and talk until he gave in, because he had the accursed weakness of not being able to say no. "Sure, you can't say no, especially when there's something in it for you," Compare Piedipapera jeered. "You're like the whores, that's how you are."

When La Longa heard about the lupin deal, after dinner, while they were chatting with their elbows on the table, she was dumbfounded, as if that huge sum of forty onze had hit her in the stomach. But women are too fearful and Master 'Ntoni had to explain to her that if the deal went well there'd be bread for the whole winter, and earrings for Mena, and Bastianazzo would be able to get to Riposto and back in a week, together with La Locca's son Menico. Meanwhile Bastianazzo snuffed the candles without saying a word. So that was the way the lupin deal and the voyage of the *Provvidenza* was settled. She was the oldest boat in the village, but the name she bore was a good omen. Maruzza still felt her heart sink, but didn't open her mouth, because it wasn't her business, and silently set about preparing the boat for the voyage, storing the fur-lined coat, the fresh bread, the jar full of olive oil, and the onions under the footboards and in the locker.

But all that day the men had to wrangle with that usurer, Uncle Crocifisso, who had sold them a pig in a poke, because the lupins were rotten. Dumbbell said that he hadn't known about it, as true as there's a God above! "A fair bargain is not a trick," he cried, and went on to say that he didn't dare break it, because his soul was meant for heaven, not for the pigs; and Compare Piedipapera was raving and cursing like a man possessed to get them all to agree, swearing up and down that he had never seen the like in all of his natural life. Then he would thrust his hands into the pile of lupins and show them to God and the Holy Virgin, calling on them as his witnesses. Finally, red in the face, panting, beside himself, he made a last desperate proposal, which he flung right at Uncle Crocifisso, standing there like a fool, and the Malavoglia, who were holding their bags in their hands. "Here! What about this? Instead of paying so much a month, pay up at Christmas, and so you'll save a tarì for every salma! Will that make you stop, holy devil!" And he started filling the bags. "In the name of God," he cried, "there's one bag that's filled."

The *Provvidenza* left on Saturday, towards evening, and it must have been after vespers, although the bell hadn't been rung because Mastro Cirino, the sexton, had gone to deliver a pair of new shoes to Don Silvestro, the town clerk. At that hour the girls were fluttering like a flock of sparrows around the fountain, and the evening star was already shining bright and beautiful, looking like a lantern hanging on the *Provvidenza*'s boom. Maruzza, with Lia clinging to her neck, stood on the shore without saying a word, while her husband loosed the sail, and the *Provvidenza* bobbed like a duckling on the waves that were breaking against the Fariglioni rocks. "When north is dark and south is clear, you can put to sea without fear," Master 'Ntoni chanted from the shore, as he looked towards Mount Etna, completely black with clouds.

Locca's Menico, who was on the *Provvidenza* with Bastianazzo, shouted something which was swallowed by the rush of the sea. "He says that you can give the money to his mother, La Locca, because his brother isn't working," added Bastianazzo, and those were the last words of his they heard.

CHAPTER TWO

All through the village they were talking about the lupin deal, and when La Longa returned home with Lia in her arms all the women came to their doors to watch her go by.

"You couldn't make a better deal!" Piedipapera bellowed, hobbling quickly on his twisted leg after Master 'Ntoni, who had gone to sit on the church steps, next to Master Fortunato Cipolla and Menico della Locca's brother, who were enjoying the cool evening breeze. "Uncle Crocifisso screamed as though we were ripping out his quill feathers; but don't mind that—the old boy has plenty of feathers! Oh, we had our work cut out for us—you can say that too, can't you, Master 'Ntoni?" Yet for Master 'Ntoni's sake, Piedipapera went on, he would have thrown himself off the Fariglioni rocks, as true as there's a God! And Uncle Crocifisso listened to him, because he was the ladle that stirred the pot—a big pot in which more than two hundred onze a year were on the boil! Why, Dumbbell wasn't even able to blow his nose without his help!

Locca's son, hearing them talk of the wealth of Uncle Crocifisso, who was actually his uncle since he was La Locca's brother, felt his breast swell with a great tenderness for his kin.

"We're relations," he said. "When I hire out by the day

he gives me half pay, without wine, because we're relations."

Piedipapera sneered: "He does it for your own good, so you won't get drunk and so he can leave you more money when he croaks."

Piedipapera enjoyed gossiping about everybody, as it popped into his head, just like that, straight from the heart and without malice, so that nobody could really take offense. "Massaro Filippo has already walked past the tavern twice," he said, "waiting for La Santuzza to give him the sign to join her in the stable, so they can say a rosary together."

Then he said to La Locca's son: "Your Uncle Crocifisso is trying to steal the plot of land from your cousin La Vespa. He wants to pay her half of what it's worth, making her believe that he'll marry her. But if La Vespa can get the old man to steal something else from her, then you can spit out your hope for an inheritance, and besides you'll lose the wages he didn't pay you and the wine you didn't drink."

At this they started to argue, for Master 'Ntoni claimed that after all Uncle Crocifisso was a Christian and wouldn't throw his good sense to the dogs by marrying his brother's daughter.

"What has Christian got to do with it, or Turk either?" Piedipapera retorted. "He's crazy, you should say! He's as rich as a pig, while La Vespa only owns that plot of land no bigger than a nose-rag."

"You're telling me, I have a vineyard right at the edge of it," Master Cipolla said, swelling like a turkey.

"You call those four cactus plants a vineyard?" Piedipapera hooted.

"Among all those cactus plants there are plenty of vines, and if Saint Francis sends us a good rain, then you'll see what wine it will yield. Today the sun went down in a sack, which means rain or wind."

"When the sun goes down in a sack, you can expect a west wind," added Master 'Ntoni.

Piedipapera couldn't stand the high and mighty way that Master Cipolla delivered his opinions. Just because he was rich he thought that he knew everything, and that he could make poor people lap up any sort of nonsense.

"Some want it hot and some want it cold," Piedipapera concluded. "Master Cipolla wants rain for his vineyard, and you want the west wind behind the *Provvidenza*'s sails. You know the proverb: 'White caps at sea, a fresh wind there'll be.' Tonight the stars are shining, and at midnight the wind will change. Can't you feel the gusts?"

They could hear carts going by slowly on the road.

"Whether it's night or day, there are always people traveling about the world," Master Cipolla remarked.

Now one couldn't see either the sea or the countryside, it seemed that there was nothing in the world but Trezza, and each man was thinking about where those carts could be going at this time of the night.

"Before midnight the *Provvidenza* will have passed the Capo dei Mulini," Master 'Ntoni said, "and by then the fresh wind won't bother her."

Master 'Ntoni couldn't think of anything but the *Provvidenza,* and when he wasn't talking about his own affairs he kept quiet; so he took as much part in the conversation as a broomstick.

That's why Piedipapera finally told him: "You ought to join the people at the pharmacy, who are discussing the King and the Pope. You'd make out fine there, too. Don't you hear them yelling?"

"That's Don Giammaria," La Locca's son said. "He's arguing with the pharmacist."

The pharmacist was holding the usual palaver at the door of his shop in the cool of the evening, with the parish priest and a few other people. Since Don Franco was an educated person he read the newspaper and made the others read it too; and he also had the *History of the French Revolution,* which he kept handy under the glass mortar, and so, to kill time, he quarreled all day long with Don Giammaria, the parish priest, and they both made themselves sick with bile, but they couldn't have lived through a day without seeing each other. Then on Saturday, when the newspaper arrived, Don Franco went so far as to burn a candle for half an hour or even a whole hour, at the risk of being bawled out by his wife, and he did it so that he could reel off his ideas, and not go to bed like a brute, as Uncle Cipolla and old Malavoglia did. Besides, in the summer he didn't even need a candle, for he could sit at the doorway under the street lamp, when Mastro Cirino lit it, and sometimes Don Michele, the sergeant of the customs guard, joined them; and also Don Silvestro, the town clerk, coming back from his vineyard, stopped by for a while.

At such times Don Franco rubbed his hands and declared that they looked just like a small parliament, and then he posted himself behind the counter, combing his big beard with his fingers, with a certain sly grin on his face, as if he intended to eat somebody for breakfast; and sometimes he would rear up on his short legs and let slip one or two significant little words under his breath, right out in the open; and it was obvious that he thought he knew more than everybody else. Until Don Giammaria could no longer bear him and, dying of rage, spat a string of big Latin words in his face. As for Don Silvestro, he was greatly amused, watching them poison their blood, trying to square the circle, and without even making a cent out of it. He at least wasn't as rabid as they were, and that's why, people in the village said, he owned the most beautiful plots in Trezza—where he'd arrived, Piedipapera would always throw in, without shoes on his feet. In any case, the town clerk egged them both on and then laughed till he nearly split his sides—with a loud cackle that made him sound just like a hen.

"There it goes. Don Silvestro's laying an egg," La Locca's son said.

"Don Silvestro lays eggs of gold, down at the Town Hall," Piedipapera replied.

"Hmm!" Master Fortunato Cipolla spat out. "Stuff for beggars! Venera Zuppidda refused to give him her daughter."

"Which means that Mastro Turi Zuppiddo prefers the eggs of his own hens," Master 'Ntoni replied.

And Master Cipolla nodded his head in agreement.

" 'Bone, bone, bone, stick to your own,' " old Malavoglia said.

Then Piedipapera retorted that if Don Silvestro had been content to stick to his own, he'd still be wielding a hoe and not a pen.

"Now, tell me, would you give him your granddaughter Mena?" asked Cipolla, turning to Master 'Ntoni.

" 'Each man minds his own business, and the wolf tends the sheep,' " said Master 'Ntoni.

Cipolla continued to nod his head, all the more since between him and Master 'Ntoni there had been some talk of marrying Mena to his son Brasi, and if the lupin deal went well, Mena's dowry would be paid in cash and that deal would also be quickly settled.

"The girl is as she has been brought up, and the hemp is as it has been spun," Master 'Ntoni finally said; and Master Cipolla agreed that everyone in the village knew that La Longa had brought up her daughter just right, and all who passed through their lane at that time of night, hearing the beat of Saint Agatha's loom, said that Comare Maruzza didn't waste her candle wax.

After she had come home, La Longa had lit the lamp and had sat down with her winder on the landing, to fill the bobbins she needed for the week's warp.

"You can't see Mena, but you can hear her. She sits at the loom night and day, like Saint Agatha," the neighbors said.

"These are the habits a girl should get, instead of sitting at the window," Comare Maruzza replied. "You know the saying: 'A girl who at the window stays should never get praise.' "

"But some girls just by sitting at the window manage to hook a husband, out of all the men who pass by," said Cousin Anna, from the door across the way.

Cousin Anna knew what she was talking about, because that lout of a son of hers, Rocco, had let himself be hauled in by the skirts of the Mangiacarrube girl, one of those girls who sit at the window, as brazen as they come.

Comare Grazia Piedipapera, hearing the talk in the street, came to the door too, her apron bulging with the broad beans she was shelling, and started cursing the mice that had riddled her bean sack like a colander. From the way she talked you'd think that they'd done it on purpose, as if the mice had the cunning of Christians. Then they all began talking about it, because those excommunicated little beasts had done as much damage to Maruzza's house. And Cousin Anna's house was full of them, ever since her cat had died—a creature worth his weight in gold, and he had died from a kick Compare

Tino had given him. "Gray cats are best for catching mice; they'd creep into a needle's eye to snatch them." But you shouldn't open the door at night for cats, because that's how an old woman at Aci Sant'Antonio got murdered. Thieves had stolen her cat three days before, and then they brought him back half dead of hunger to meow at her door; and the poor woman, not having the heart to leave the creature on the street at that hour, had opened it, and so the thieves had slipped into her house.

Nowadays the thieves think up all sorts of tricks to do their dirty work; and you saw faces at Trezza which had never been seen before, out on the rocks along the sea, people who pretend they're going to fish and then, if they get the chance, grab the laundry laid out to dry. That's how they'd stolen a brand-new bedsheet from poor Nunziata. The poor girl! to steal from her who had to give bread to all those little brothers left on her hands when her father deserted her to seek his fortune in Alexandria, Egypt!—Nunziata was just like Cousin Anna, whose husband had died and left her with that houseful of children, and at that time Rocco, the eldest, hadn't even reached to her knee. And now, after all the trouble of bringing him up, the lazy lout, she had to watch the Mangiacarrube girl steal him from under her very eyes.

In the midst of all this gossiping, La Zuppidda, the wife of Mastro Turi, the caulker, suddenly popped up. She lived at the end of the dirt road and always appeared unexpectedly, to speak her piece like the devil in the litany, because nobody could ever tell what hole she'd sprung from.

"Anyway," she started to grumble, "your son Rocco never helped you either. Because whenever he gets hold of some money, he immediately rushes to the tavern to drink it up."

Venera Zuppidda knew everything that happened in the village, and that's why, they said, she went roving about all day in her bare feet, spying on people, pretending she was working her spindle, which she held high in the air to keep from twirling it against the stones. She always spoke the truth, like the Gospel, that was her vice, and so people who didn't like to have the truth flung in their faces accused her of having a tongue out of hell—the kind that leaves a slimy track. A bitter mouth spits gall; and she really had a bitter mouth, because of that Barbara of hers, whom she hadn't been able to marry off, the girl was so arrogant and rude; but with all this, nobody less than the son of King Victor Emmanuel was good enough for her.

"A fine piece, that Mangiacarrube girl," she went on, "a brazen hussy, who'd let the whole village walk past her window." "A girl who at the window stays should never get praise," and Vanni Pizzuto brought her the prickly pears he stole from Massaro Filippo, the vegetable gardener, and they ate them together in the vineyard under the almond tree—she'd seen them with her own eyes. And Peppi Naso, the butcher, after he became jealous of Mariano Cinghialenta, the carter, used to go and throw all the horns of the beasts he slaughtered in her doorway, so that everybody said that he went to comb his hair under the Mangiacarrube window.

But Cousin Anna, who had such a kind heart, took it all with a smile and said: "Don Giammaria says that it's a mortal sin to speak evil of one's neighbor."

"Don Giammaria should save his preaching for his sister, Donna Rosolina," Zuppidda answered, "and not let her play the flirt with Don Silvestro when he walks by, and with Don Michele, the sergeant. You know why she does it? With all those years and flesh she carries around, poor thing, she's in a fury to land a husband!"

"It's up to God!" Cousin Anna said. "When my husband died, Rocco was no taller than this distaff and his sisters were all smaller than he was. Did I lose heart? Trouble makes its own callus, and besides, it helps us to work hard. My daughters will do just as I did, and as long as there are slabs in the wash shed we'll make a living. Why, just look at Nunziata, she has more sense now than an old woman, and she manages to bring up those little ones as if she'd given birth to them herself."

"Where is Nunziata? Why haven't we seen her yet?" La Longa asked a cluster of ragged kids, who were whimpering in the doorway of the small house opposite. As soon as they heard their sister's name they all began wailing in chorus.

"I saw her going up to the lava field to gather a few

sheaves of broom," Cousin Anna said. "And your son Alessio went along with her."

The children listened for a moment and then they started to squeal all at once, and after a while the biggest child, perched on a large rock, answered: "I don't know where she is."

The neighbors had come out like snails after a rainstorm, and all down the road you heard the continuous murmur of people talking from doorway to doorway. Even Compare Alfio Mosca, who drove the donkey cart, opened his window and a great cloud of burning broom smoke came streaming out of it. Mena had left her loom, and she too came out on the landing.

"Oh, here's Saint Agatha!" they all cried, and made a big fuss over her.

"Why don't you start thinking of marrying off your Mena?" La Zuppidda asked Comare Maruzza in a low voice. "She'll be eighteen at Easter. I know, because she was born the year of the earthquake, like my Barbara. But whoever wants to get my Barbara has to please me first!"

Just then a rustle of leafy boughs was heard down the road, and there came Alessi and Nunziata. They were so small the big sheaves of yellow broom they were carrying hid them completely.

"Oh, Nunziata!" the neighbors exclaimed. "Weren't you afraid to go up to the lava field so late at night?"

"I was there, too," Alessi replied.

"I stayed late with Cousin Anna at the wash shed, and then I had no wood for the fire."

The girl lit the lamp and began briskly getting everything laid out for dinner, while her little brothers trailed after in the room, so that she looked like a hen followed by her chicks. Alessi had put down his sheaf of broom and stood at the door, his hands in his pockets, watching her with a serious expression.

"Say, Nunziata! after you put the pot on to boil, come and stay with me a while," Mena shouted from the landing.

Nunziata left Alessi to watch the fire and hurried out to perch on the landing next to Saint Agatha, so she could enjoy her rest too, her hands lying idly in her lap.

"Compare Alfio Mosca is cooking broad beans," Nunziata said after a bit.

"He's just like you, poor fellow, because both of you have nobody in the house to make the soup for you in the evening when you come home tired."

"Yes, it's true, and he also knows how to sew and do his wash and darn his own shirts." Nunziata knew everything her neighbor Alfio did and his house was as familiar to her as the palm of her own hand. "Now he's going to fetch the firewood," she said. "Now he's grooming his donkey." And so it was—you could see his lantern bobbing around the yard and under the shed. Saint Agatha laughed, and Nunziata said that all Compare Alfio lacked was a skirt to be exactly like a woman.

"So when he marries," Mena said, "his wife will go around with the donkey cart and he'll stay home to raise the children."

The mothers, clustered on the road, were also talking about Alfio Mosca, whom even La Vespa hadn't wanted for a husband, La Zuppidda said, for La Vespa had her fine little plot of land, and if she wanted to marry she wasn't going to take someone who owned nothing but a donkey cart. A cart can carry you to your grave, the proverb says. But La Vespa, that schemer, has set her eyes on her uncle, Dumbbell!

But the girls, among themselves, took Mosca's side against that nasty Vespa woman; and Nunziata felt her heart ache because of the scorn they were pouring on Compare Alfio, simply because he was poor and had no one in the world, and all of a sudden she said to Mena: "If I were grown-up, I'd take him myself if they gave him to me."

Mena was just going to say something, too; but then she quickly changed the subject: "Are you going to the city for the Feast of the Dead?"

"No, I'm not. I can't leave the house alone."

"We're going if the lupin deal turns out well. Grandfather said so."

Then she mulled this over, and added: "Compare Alfio usually goes too, to sell his walnuts."

Then they both fell silent, thinking about the Feast of

the Dead, where Compare Alfio usually went to sell his walnuts.

"Uncle Crocifisso, with that innocent way of his, can put La Vespa in his pocket!" Cousin Anna went on.

"That's just what she'd like!" La Zuppidda came right back at her. "La Vespa wouldn't want anything better— that he put her in his pocket! She's always hanging around his house, like a cat, with the excuse of bringing him something good to eat, and the old man doesn't refuse, especially since it doesn't cost him anything. She's fattening him up like a pig for the slaughter. I tell you, La Vespa wants to get into that pocket!"

Each of the women had something to say about Uncle Crocifisso, who was always whimpering and moaning like Christ between the thieves, and all the while he had piles of money, because one day when the old man was sick, La Zuppidda had seen a chest as big as that under his bed.

La Longa felt that lupin debt of forty onze weighing in the pit of her stomach and she changed the subject, because ears aren't closed by the darkness, and you could hear Uncle Crocifisso talking with Don Giammaria as they walked up and down the piazza close by. Even La Zuppidda broke off her tirade against him to say good evening.

Don Silvestro cackled like a hen, and that irritating laugh of his put the pharmacist into a frenzy. What's more, the pharmacist had never had much use for patience; he left it to the dunces and to all those who didn't want to make another revolution.

"That's right, you never had any use for it, because you wouldn't know where to put it!" Don Giammaria shouted; and Don Franco, who was a small man, was stung to the quick and sent curses after the priest which, in the dark, echoed all over the piazza. But Dumbbell, hard as a rock, shrugged his shoulders and made a point of repeating that he didn't give a hang and minded his own business. "But what about the business of the Confraternity of the Good Death, isn't that yours? The fact that nobody pays a cent anymore," Don Giammaria said to him. "When it's a matter of pulling money out of their pockets, they all become a gang of Protestants, worse than the pharmacist, and they let you keep the chest of the Confraternity just so the mice can dance in it! It's a dirty shame!"

From his pharmacy Don Franco jeered loudly at their backs, trying to imitate Don Silvestro's laugh which drove people crazy. But the pharmacist was a Mason, everybody knew that; and Don Giammaria shouted to him from the piazza:

"You'd find the money if it were for schools and street lamps!"

The pharmacist shut up, because his wife had appeared at the window. And when he was far enough away to be sure that Don Silvestro, who also picked up a nice fat salary as a schoolteacher, couldn't hear him, Uncle Crocifisso repeated:

"I don't give a hang. But in my day there weren't so many street lamps or schools—and nobody crammed learning down the dunces' throats and we were all better off."

"You didn't go to school, and yet you know how to handle your business," Don Giammaria said.

"And I know my catechism," Uncle Crocifisso added, to balance accounts right away.

In the heat of the dispute, Don Giammaria got off the path, on which he could have crossed the piazza with his eyes shut, almost broke his neck, and nearly let slip a curse, God forbid.

"At least they ought to light them, those lamps of theirs!"

"Nowadays a person must mind his own business," Uncle Crocifisso summed up.

There in the dark in the middle of the piazza, Don Giammaria kept tugging at the sleeve of his jacket, berating the lot of them—the lamplighter who stole the oil, and Don Silvestro who closed an eye to it, and the mayor, that puppet on a string, who let himself be led around by the nose. Mastro Cirino, now that he was on the township's payroll, did his sexton work like a Judas, ringing the Angelus bell when he had nothing else to do, and for the Mass he bought the kind of wine the crucified Christ drank on the cross, which was a real sacrilege. Dumbbell, out of habit, kept nodding his head, although they couldn't see each other, and Don Giammaria, as he mentioned them one by one, said: "This one is a thief.—That one is a scoundrel.—And that other one is a Jacobin. Do you hear Piedipapera talking with Master Malavoglia and Master Cipolla? There's another Mason, a rabble-rouser, with that crooked leg of his!"—And whenever the priest saw Piedipapera hobble through the piazza, he gave him a wide berth and watched him suspiciously, trying to figure out what he was plotting with that twisted walk of his. "He has the devil's cloven hoof," Don Giammaria growled. Uncle Crocifisso shrugged and went on repeating that he was an honest man and wanted to stay out of it. "And Master Cipolla," Don Giammaria continued, "another idiot, a bag of wind, who lets Piedipapera pull the wool over his eyes . . . and even Master 'Ntoni was going to fall into his trap. . . . These days one shouldn't be surprised at anything!"

"If you're honest, you mind your own business," Uncle Crocifisso repeated doggedly.

Meanwhile Master Tino Piedipapera, sitting on the church steps like the president, was laying down the law: "Listen to me—before the revolution it was altogether different. Now the fish have become shrewd, I tell you!"

"Not at all," said Master 'Ntoni. "The anchovies feel the northwest wind a day before it gets here. It's always been like that. The anchovy has more brains than the tuna. These days, beyond Capo dei Mulini, they sweep the tuna out of the sea all at once with their fine nets."

"I'll tell you what it is!" Master Fortunato Cipolla said. "It's those damned steamers going back and forth, churning up the water with their paddle wheels. What do you expect? The fish get a fright and they don't show up again. That's what it is!"

La Locca's son listened, his mouth agape, scratching his head. "Sure!" he said. "That way, there wouldn't be any fish at Syracuse or Messina either, where all the steamers go. But they bring them in from there by the ton, on the railroad."

"Then you figure it out!" Master Cipolla cried angrily. "I wash my hands of it. I don't give a rap. I have my properties and my vineyards which give me my bread."

And Piedipapera hauled off and smacked La Locca's
son, to teach him some manners. "Idiot!" he yelled. "Keep
your mouth shut when your elders say something."

Then the big oaf ran away, beating his head with his
fists and screaming that everybody treated him like a fool
just because he was La Locca's son. Master 'Ntoni sniffed
the breeze and said: "If the northwest wind doesn't rise
before midnight, the *Provvidenza* will have the time to turn
the cape."

Slow, resounding tolls of the bell fell from the church
tower. "The first hour of the night," Master Cipolla
observed.

Master 'Ntoni crossed himself and said: "Peace to the
living and rest to the dead."

"Don Giammaria is having fried spaghetti for dinner
tonight," Piedipapera declared, sniffing in the direction of
the parish house windows.

Don Giammaria, passing by on his way home, greeted
all of them, even Piedipapera, because, times being what
they were, you had to keep on the good side of even such
troublemakers; and Piedipapera, whose mouth was still
watering, shouted after him: "Say, Don Giammaria, fried
spaghetti tonight, eh!"

"Hear that! Even what I eat!" Don Giammaria muttered
through his teeth. "They even spy on God's servants to
count every mouthful they take! And all because of their
hatred for the Church!" And just then he bumped into
Don Michele, the sergeant of the customs guard, who
strolled about with his pistol strapped to his belly and his
pants stuffed into his boots, looking for smugglers, and
Don Giammaria said: "But they don't count what these
fellows eat, oh no!"

"I like these fellows!" Dumbbell answered. "They guard
honest people's property, and so I like them!"

"If they paid him, he'd become a Mason, too," Don
Giammaria said to himself, as he knocked at the door of
his house. "They're all a gang of thieves!" And he went
on grumbling, the door knocker in his hand, suspiciously
watching the sergeant, who disappeared into the darkness
in the direction of the tavern, and wondering why he was
going to the tavern to guard honest people's property.

But Compare Tino Piedipapera knew why Don Michele

went to the tavern to guard honest people's property, because he had spent whole nights hiding behind the elm tree nearby to find out; and he used to say:

"He goes there to exchange notes on the sly with Uncle Santoro, Santuzza's father. Whoever eats the King's bread must be a spy and must know everybody's business in Trezza and everywhere else. And Uncle Santoro, as blind as he is, so that he looks like a bat in the sun when he sits near the door of the tavern, still knows all that happens in the village and can tell each one of us just from our walk. The only time he doesn't hear is when Massaro Filippo goes to recite the rosary with Santuzza, and then he's an angel of a guard, better than if he were blindfolded."

When Maruzza heard the bell strike the first hour of the night, she scampered into the house to spread the cloth on the table. Little by little the women in the street had thinned out and, since the whole village was going to sleep, you could hear the sea snoring close by, at the end of the road, and every so often it groaned, like someone tossing and turning in bed. Only down at the tavern, where you could see the red lamp, the din continued, and Rocco Spatu, who turned every day into a holiday, was still roaring away.

"Compare Rocco is always happy," Alfio Mosca said after a while from his window, though it looked dark and empty.

"Oh, you're still there, Compare Alfio!" said Mena, who had stayed on the landing to wait for her grandfather.

"Yes, I'm here, Mena. I'm here eating my soup; because when I see all of you at the table under the light, I no longer feel so lonely, so lonely that I don't even want to eat."

"Aren't you happy?"

"Ah, a man needs so many things to be happy!"

Mena did not reply, and after a short silence Compare Alfio said: "Tomorrow I'm going to Catania for a load of salt."

"Are you going again for the Feast of the Dead?" Mena asked.

"God knows! This year the few walnuts I've got are all rotten."

"Compare Alfio is going to Catania to look for a wife,"

Nunziata broke in from the door across the way.

"Is that true?" Mena asked.

"Ah, Mena, if that's all you had to do to find a wife, there are plenty of good girls right in my own village, without going far away to search for them."

"Look at all the stars sparkling up there," said Mena, after a pause. "They say that they're souls from purgatory on their way to heaven."

"Listen, please," Alfio said to her, after he had gazed at the stars too, "you, who are Saint Agatha, if you dream of some good numbers for the lottery, tell me and I'll stake my shirt on them, and then maybe I'll be able to think of taking a wife. . . ."

"Good night!" Mena replied.

The stars were sparkling more brightly, almost as if they were catching fire, and the Three Kings, with their arms outstretched like Saint Andrew on the cross, glittered above the Fariglioni rocks. The sea snored softly at the end of the road, and at long intervals you heard the creak of some cart passing in the dark, jolting over the stones, traveling about the world which is so large that even if you could walk and walk forever, day and night, you'd never get to the end of it. And yet there were people going about the world at that hour who knew nothing about Compare Alfio, or the *Provvidenza* out at sea, or the Feast of the Dead—so Mena thought as she waited for her grandfather on the landing.

Before locking the door for the night, her grandfather came out on the landing several times to look at the stars, which were brighter than they should be, and at last he muttered: "Bitter sea!"

Rocco Spatu was braying at the tavern door before the lantern. "A man who has a happy heart can always sing," Master 'Ntoni observed.

CHAPTER THREE

After midnight the wind had begun to make a devil of a racket, as if all the cats in town were howling on the roof, and it blew so hard the shutters rattled. You could hear the sea bellowing around the Fariglioni rocks, and it sounded like all the oxen for the fair at St. Alfio had been gathered there, and the day came up blacker than the soul of Judas. In short, an ugly Sunday in September, that treacherous September which suddenly hurls a storm at you, like an unexpected shot when you're out alone in the cactus grove. The village boats were pulled up on the beach and tied securely to the big rocks below the wash shed. The boys had great fun yelling and whistling whenever they saw a tattered sail in the distance, tearing through the wind and mist as though the devil himself were chasing it. But the women crossed themselves, as if they could actually see the wretched men on board.

Maruzza La Longa didn't say anything, as was only right, but she couldn't remain still for a moment and kept walking here and there, through the house and the yard, like a hen about to lay her egg. To watch the rain, the men were at the tavern, or in Pizzuto's barbershop, or under the butcher's shed, gawking up at the sky. The only ones on the beach were Master 'Ntoni, because of that cargo of lupins he had at sea on the *Provvidenza,* not to mention his son Bastianazzo; and La Locca's son, who had nothing to lose, for all he had at sea in the lupin boat was his brother Menico. Master Fortunato Cipolla, while getting shaved at Pizzuto's shop, said that he wouldn't give two pins for Bastianazzo and La Locca's Menico, together with the *Provvidenza* and her cargo of lupins.

"These days everyone thinks he can be a merchant and make a lot of money!" he said, shrugging his shoulders. "And then, after they've lost the donkey, they start looking for the halter!"

Sister Mariangela la Santuzza's tavern was packed. That drunkard Rocco Spatu was on hand, bawling and spitting enough for ten men; and Compare Tino Piedipapera, and Mastro Turi Zuppiddo, and Compare Mangiacarrube, and Compare Mariano Cinghialenta, and Don Michele, the sergeant of the customs guard, with his pants stuffed into his boots and his pistol dangling at his belly, as if he were going to hunt smugglers in that foul weather. Full of good spirits, Mastro Turi Zuppiddo, that elephant, went about among his friends handing out clouts that would have felled an ox, as if he were still holding his caulker's mallet, and when he got one, Compare Cinghialenta started shouting and cursing, to show that he was a carter and a man of guts.

Uncle Santoro huddled under that scrap of a shed at the door, his hand outstretched, waiting for someone to pass to ask for alms.

"Between the two of them, father and daughter," Compare Turi Zuppiddo said, "they must make plenty of money on a day like this, with so many people coming to the tavern."

"Bastianazzo Malavoglia is worse off than Uncle Santoro right now," Piedipapera replied. "And Mastro Cirino can ring for Mass until his hands drop off, but the Malavoglia won't go to church today. They're angry at the Lord Almighty, because of that cargo of lupins they have at sea."

The wind sent dry leaves and skirts flying, and Vanni Pizzuto, with his curly hair as shiny as silk, held his cocked razor and his customer's nose in one hand, and propped the other on his hip as he kept turning to watch the passers-by. The pharmacist stood at the door of his shop, beneath that hat of his, so huge it seemed he was wearing an umbrella, and pretended to be engaged in an important discussion with Don Silvestro, the town clerk, so that his wife wouldn't force him to go to church. He laughed in his beard over the subterfuge, and winked at the girls who were skipping through the puddles.

"Today," Piedipapera was saying, "Master 'Ntoni has decided to be a Protestant, like Don Franco, the pharmacist."

"If you so much as turn to look at that impudent rascal Don Silvestro, I'll give you a smack right where we are," Venera Zuppidda warned her daughter as they crossed the piazza. "I don't like that fellow!"

At the last toll of the bell, Santuzza left her father to watch the tavern and went to church, dragging her customers along with her. Uncle Santoro, poor man, was blind and therefore it wasn't a sin if he didn't go to Mass; so business went on as usual at the tavern, and though he couldn't see, Uncle Santoro could keep an eye on the counter, for he knew all the customers, one by one, just from the sound of their step when they came for a glass.

"Santuzza's stockings," remarked Piedipapera, as Santuzza tripped past on the tips of her dainty shoes, like a kitten, "Santuzza's stockings, no matter how much it rains or blows, have never been seen by anyone but Massaro Filippo, the vegetable gardener. This is the truth."

"The devils are loose today!" said Santuzza, crossing herself with holy water. "It's a day to breed sin."

Next to her, Venera Zuppidda sat on her heels and chattered Hail Marys, all the while flashing fierce glances right and left, as if she were angry with the whole village, and to anyone who would listen to her she'd say: "Comare La Longa doesn't come to church, yet she has a husband at sea in this storm! Then afterwards people wonder why God punishes us!" Even Menico's mother was in church, though all she could do was stare at the flies buzzing about.

"We've got to pray for the sinners, too," Santuzza replied. "That's what good souls are for."

"Oh sure, just like the Mangiacarrube girl is praying, with her nose hidden in her shawl, and God only knows what ugly sins she drives the young men to!"

La Santuzza shook her head and said that while you're in church you should not say bad things about your neighbor. "The tavern owner must have a smile for everyone,"

Venera Zuppidda retorted. Then she whispered into La Vespa's ear: "La Santuzza doesn't want people to say that she sells water for wine; but she'd do better to worry about keeping Massaro Filippo, the gardener, in mortal sin. And he with a wife and children!"

"As for me," La Vespa replied, "I've already told Don Giammaria that I refuse to be in the Daughters of Mary if they let Santuzza stay on as a superior."

"Then that means that you have found a husband!" La Zuppidda said.

"No, I haven't," La Vespa snapped, stinging right back. "I'm not the kind who drag men after them even into church, polished shoes and all, not to speak of those fellows with big fat bellies."

The fellow with the big fat belly was Brasi, Master Cipolla's son, the darling of all the mothers and their daughters, because he owned vineyards and olive groves.

"Go and see if the trawler is tied up well," Brasi's father told him, as he crossed himself.

All those there couldn't help but think that that rain and wind spelled solid gold for the Cipolla family. That's how things go in this world; now that they had the big trawler safely moored, the Cipolla could rub their hands contentedly at the sight of the storm, while the Malavoglia went white and tore their hair because of that cargo of lupins which they'd bought on credit from Uncle Crocifisso.

"You want to hear what I think?" La Vespa declared. "The real misfortune is Uncle Crocifisso's, giving those lupins on credit. He who gives credit without security, loses his wits, his friends, and his property."

Uncle Crocifisso was kneeling at the foot of the altar of Our Lady of the Sorrows, holding on to his rosary for dear life and intoning the verses in a nasal voice which would have touched the heart of the devil himself. Between one Hail Mary and another they all talked about the lupins and the *Provvidenza,* which was out at sea, and La Longa, who was left with five children on her hands.

"Nowadays," said Master Cipolla, with a shrug, "nobody is satisfied with what he's got and everyone sets out to defy heaven."

"There's no doubt," Compare Zuppiddo pronounced, "that this will be a dark day for the Malavoglia."

"I wouldn't like to be in Bastianazzo's shoes," Piedipapera added.

Evening came down sad and cold. Now and then the north wind blew a bitter gust, bringing with it a spray of fine, silent rain: one of those evenings when, if your boat is drawn up safely, its belly dry on the sand, it is a pleasure to watch the steaming pot, holding your child between your legs and hearing your wife's slippers shuffling behind you about the house. The loafers preferred to spend that Sunday—which gave signs of lasting into Monday—at the tavern, and even the doorposts were tinted gaily by the flames from the fireplace, and Uncle Santoro, posted out there with his chin on his knees and his open palm, had moved a trifle closer to warm his back.

"He's better off than Compare Bastianazzo, right now!" Rocco Spatu repeated, lighting his pipe in the doorway. And without another thought, he dug into his pocket and forgot himself to the extent of giving him two cents of alms.

"You're wasting your alms, thanking God you're safe," Piedipapera said to him. "There's no danger of you ending up like Compare Bastianazzo."

They all laughed at the joke, and then stared silently from the doorway at the sea, black as the lava field.

"Master 'Ntoni has been running around all day," one of them said, "as if he'd been bitten by a tarantula." And the pharmacist had asked him if he'd been taking a tonic, or was out for a stroll in that dirty weather. He'd also said: "Some Providence, eh, Master 'Ntoni?" But the pharmacist was a Protestant and a Jew, everybody knew that.

La Locca's son, who stood outside the tavern door with his hands in his pockets because he didn't have a cent to spend, chipped in: "Uncle Crocifisso has gone with Piedipapera to look for Master 'Ntoni, to make him admit before witnesses that he gave him the lupins on credit."

"That means he also sees them in danger, *Provvidenza* and all."

"My brother Menico's on the *Provvidenza,* too, together with Bastianazzo."

"Bravo! This is just what we were saying. If your brother Menico doesn't come back, then you'll become the lord of the manor."

"He went because Uncle Crocifisso paid him half a day's wage when he sent him out on the trawler, but the Malavoglia pay him a whole day," answered La Locca's son, who hadn't understood a thing, and when they started to jeer at him, he was stunned.

At dusk Maruzza and her children had gone to wait on the lava field, from which you could look far out to sea; and when she heard the sea howl like that, she cringed and scratched her head but didn't say a word. The little girl was crying, and those poor creatures, standing forlorn on the lava field at that hour, looked like souls in purgatory. The baby's wailing gave the poor woman a pang in the pit of her stomach, for it seemed almost a bad omen. She couldn't think of anything to calm her and sang to the baby in a tremulous voice, which sounded as though she were crying, too. The women, on their way back from the tavern with a jar of oil or a bottle of wine, stopped to chat with her, as if nothing out-of-the-way had happened, and some friends of her husband Bastianazzo, Compare Cipolla or Compare Mangiacarrube, going past the lava field to take a look at the sea and find out in what mood the old grumbler was going to sleep, went over to La Longa and asked after her husband, and stayed for a while to keep her company, silently smoking their pipes or talking quietly among themselves. Dismayed by this unusual attention, the poor woman stared at them with consternation and clasped her baby to her breast, as if somebody wanted to steal it. At last, the most hard-hearted, or perhaps the most compassionate, took her by the arm and led her home. She went along meekly, saying over and over again: "Oh, Holy Virgin! Oh, Holy Virgin!" The children followed her, clutching her skirt as if they too feared that somebody might steal something from them. As they passed the tavern, all the customers gathered at the smoke-filled door and silently watched her go by, as though she were already a thing apart.

"*Requiem aeternam*," Uncle Santoro mumbled. "That poor Bastianazzo always gave me something, when Master 'Ntoni let him keep a few cents in his pocket."

And poor La Longa, who did not know that she was a widow, stammered again and again: "Oh, Holy Virgin! Oh, Holy Virgin!"

A group of neighbors were waiting for her in front of the landing of her house, chattering in low voices. When they saw her in the distance, Comare Piedipapera and Cousin Anna came to meet her, their hands folded on their bellies, without a word. Then La Longa dug her nails into her hair with a desperate scream and ran into her house to hide.

"Oh, what a tragedy!" said the people on the street. "And the boat was loaded! More than forty onze worth of lupins!"

CHAPTER FOUR

The worst of it was that they'd bought the lupins on credit, and Uncle Crocifisso was not satisfied with "fine words and rotten apples." That's why they called him Dumbbell, because when people tried to pay him with talk he was deaf in that ear and he'd say: "The creditor worries about the debt." He was a good-natured old devil and lived by lending money to his friends. He had no other trade, and so he stayed all day long in the piazza, his hands in his pockets, or leaning against the church wall, wearing that tattered jacket, so you'd have thought he was penniless, but he always had enough money to lend to everyone, and if somebody went to him for twelve tarì, he lent them right away, but with security, because "he who gives credit without security, loses his wits, his friend and his property," and also with the understanding that he'd have them back by Sunday, in good solid silver and a carlino extra, as was only right, because "there are no friends in business."

He also bought up all the fish at a discount, when the poor devil who'd caught them needed cash immediately; but then they had to weigh them on his scales, which were as false as Judas—so the people said who find fault with everything—with one long arm and one short, like Saint Francis di Paola. And if they asked him, he would lay out the wages for the crew and take back only the money advanced and two pounds of bread for each man, plus half a pint of wine, and he didn't ask for anything else, because

38

he was a Christian and what he did in this world he would have to account for to God in the next. In short, he was providence itself for all those who were in bad straits, and he had also thought up a hundred ways of rendering help to his fellowmen, and though he wasn't a seagoing man himself, he had boats and gear and everything for those who didn't have them, and lent them out, content to take a third of the catch, plus the boat's share, which was equal to that of a man in the crew, and also a share for the gear, if they wanted to borrow that too, and in the end the boat ate up all the profits, so that the people called it the devil's boat. And when they asked him why he didn't go and risk his neck like everybody else, he'd reply: "Fine! And what if I have an accident at sea, God forbid, what if I leave my bones out there, who will take care of my business?" He minded his own business, and he was ready to lend the shirt off his back; but then he wanted to be paid without all that whining; and there was no point in telling him the whys and wherefores, because he was deaf and, what's more, a little dense, and all he could say was: "A fair bargain is not a trick," or "You can tell the good payer on payment day."

Now his enemies laughed in his face because of those lupins which the devil had grabbed; and, with all that, when they held the funeral service, he had to be there to recite the *De profundis* for Bastianazzo's soul, together with the other brethren of the Confraternity of the Good Death, his hood pulled over his face.

The windowpanes of the little church glittered and the sea was smooth and gleaming, so that it no longer looked like the same sea which had stolen La Longa's husband; and now that the weather had turned fine again, the brethren were in a hurry to get through the service and go about their business.

This time the Malavoglia were there, sitting on their heels in front of the coffin, and crying so much that their tears flooded the pavement, as if the dead man were really between those four boards, holding in his arms those lupins which Uncle Crocifisso had given him on credit because he had always known Master 'Ntoni as an honest man; but if they intended to swindle him out of his property, on the excuse that Bastianazzo had drowned, they were swindling

Christ, as true as there's a God! because that credit was as sacred as the sacred Host, and he was willing to lay those five hundred lire of credit at the feet of the crucified Jesus but, holy devil! Master 'Ntoni would go to jail for that! There was a law at Trezza, too!

Meanwhile Don Giammaria hastily sprinkled the holy water over the coffin, and Mastro Cirino began going around snuffing out the candles with his pole. The brethren of the Confraternity hurried out, jumping over the benches, their arms waving in the air as they pulled off their hoods, and Uncle Crocifisso went to give a pinch of snuff to Master 'Ntoni to cheer him up, because after all an honest man leaves a good name behind him and earns his eternal reward. To those who asked him about his lupins he had said: "I'm not worried about the Malavoglia, they are honest folk and won't let Compare Bastianazzo stay in the house of the devil." Master 'Ntoni could see with his own eyes that everything had been done without pinching pennies, to honor the dead man; so much for the Mass, so much for the candles and so much for the burial —and Uncle Crocifisso counted it off on his thick fingers bulging in their cotton gloves, and the children gazed with open mouths at all those things that cost so much and were there for their papa: the coffin, the candles, the paper flowers; and the baby girl, seeing that display of lights and hearing the organ play, began crowing with delight.

The house by the medlar tree was full of people. The proverb says: "Sad is that house where there's a wake for the husband!" All those who walked past, seeing the little Malavoglia standing at the doorway with grimy faces and hands in their pockets, shook their heads and said: "Poor Comare Maruzza! Now trouble has come to her house!"

The neighbors brought something, as is the custom, pasta, eggs, wine, and all God's good things, and only someone with a happy heart could have eaten it all. Even Compare Alfio Mosca had come, holding a chicken in each hand. "Take them, Comare Mena," he said, "because I wish I'd been in your father's place, I swear it! At least I wouldn't have been a loss to anyone, and nobody would have cried."

Mena, leaning against the kitchen door, her face hidden in her apron, felt her heart flutter wildly, trying to escape from her breast, like those poor chickens she was holding in her hand. Saint Agatha's dowry had gone down with the *Provvidenza,* and the people who had come to the wake in the house by the medlar tree were thinking that Uncle Crocifisso would soon get his claws into the house, too.

Some of them perched on the chairs for a while and then left without having said a word, like the clods they were; but anyone who knew how to put one word after another tried to get a scrap of conversation going, to chase away the melancholy and divert those poor Malavoglia who'd been weeping like fountains for two days. Compare Cipolla told how the price of anchovies had increased two tarì a keg, which might interest Master 'Ntoni, if he still had some anchovies to sell; he himself, just to be on the safe side, had put money down on a hundred kegs. And they also talked about Compare Bastianazzo, may he rest in peace—who would have thought it, a man in the prime of his life and bursting with health, the poor fellow!

Also the mayor, Mastro Croce Callà, called Silkworm and also Giufà the Puppet, was there, together with the town clerk, Don Silvestro. Silkworm kept his nose in the air, so people said he was sniffing the wind to find out which way to turn, and he watched now this one, now that one as they spoke, as if he were really searching for that mulberry leaf and wanted to eat their words, and whenever he saw the town clerk laugh he laughed too.

Don Silvestro, to cheer them up, led the conversation onto the inheritance tax for Compare Bastianazzo, and slipped in a joke he'd picked up from his lawyer, which, after they'd explained it to him, amused him so much that he never failed to drop it into the conversation when he went on a condolence visit.

"At least you'll have the pleasure," he said, "of becoming Victor Emmanuel's relations, since you have to give him his share."

And everybody laughed long and hard, because the proverb says: "No wake without laughter, no wedding without tears."

The pharmacist's wife looked down her nose at all that brawling and sat with her gloved hands resting on her belly and a long face, as is the custom in the city on such occasions, and if they just looked at her people fell silent, as if the corpse were right there in front of them; and that's why they called her the Signora.

Don Silvestro was strutting for the women, and kept on the move with the excuse of offering chairs to the newcomers, just so he could make his polished shoes squeak. "All those tax collectors should be burnt alive!" grumbled Comare Zuppidda, as yellow as if she'd been eating lemons, and she said it straight at Don Silvestro as though he were the tax collector. She knew very well what certain ink-slingers, who didn't have any socks under their polished shoes, were up to, trying to worm their way into people's houses to gobble up dowry and daughter. "My dear, I don't want you, I want your money." That's why she had left her daughter Barbara at home. "I don't like those types, no, sir."

"You're telling me!" exclaimed Master Cipolla. "Why they skin me alive like Saint Bartholomew!"

"By God!" cried Mastro Zuppiddo, shaking his fist, which looked like his caulker's mallet. "It'll all come to a bad end, it will, with these Italians!"

"You keep quiet!" Comare Venera Zuppidda shouted him down. "You don't know what you're talking about!"

"I'm saying what you said, that they're taking the shirts off our backs, they are!" Compare Turi Zuppiddo muttered dejectedly.

Then Piedipapera, to settle matters, said under his breath to Compare Cipolla: "You ought to take Zuppidda's daughter for Brasi and that'll end your worries; and then both mother and daughter will calm down."

"It's a real scandal!" cried Donna Rosolina, the priest's sister, red as a turkey and fanning herself with her handkerchief; and she went after Garibaldi for levying the taxes, and said that nowadays life had become impossible and nobody got married anymore. "And why should that trouble Donna Rosolina at this late date?" Piedipapera whispered. Meanwhile Donna Rosolina was telling Don Silvestro about all the big chores she had on her hands: ten bobbins of warp on the loom, beans to be dried for the winter, tomato paste to be made, for she had her own little secret and so had fresh tomato paste all through the winter. A house was no good without a woman; but the woman must know how to use her hands—"the way *I* mean, use her hands!" Not one of those giddy flirts who think of preening themselves and nothing else, "with long hair and short brains," because then the poor husband sinks to the bottom, like Compare Bastianazzo, may he rest in peace.

"Wasn't he lucky!" sighed La Santuzza. "He died on a very holy day, the eve of the Sorrows of the Virgin Mary, and he's praying up there for us sinners, among the angels and saints of Paradise. You know the saying: 'God tries most those he loves best.' He was a fine man, the kind who minds his own business instead of speaking evil of this person and that, and sinning against his neighbor, as so many do."

Then Maruzza, sitting at the foot of the bed, as white and worn-out as an old rag, looking like Our Lady of the Sorrows, began crying louder, burying her face in the pillow, and Master 'Ntoni, almost broken in two, a hundred years older, kept staring at her, shaking his head, not knowing what to say because of that great sorrow— the dead Bastianazzo—he had in his heart, gnawing away at it like a shark.

"La Santuzza's mouth spills honey!" observed Comare Grazia Piedipapera.

"That's how you've got to behave if you keep a tavern," replied La Zuppidda. "If you don't know your trade you'll have to shut down, and if you can't swim you'll just have to drown."

La Zuppidda had her belly full of Santuzza's honeyed ways, because even the Signora, with her pursed little mouth, had turned to chat with her, without paying attention to anyone else, wearing her gloves as though she were afraid to dirty her hands and sitting there with her nose wrinkled up, as if all the others stank worse than anchovies, when the person who really stank was Santuzza, stank of wine and all sorts of other filth, despite that flea-colored dress she was wearing and that medal of the Daughters of Mary which wouldn't stay put on her huge, heaving bosom. Sure, they understood each other, because all shopkeepers are kin, and they all made money in the same way, deceiving their neighbors and selling dirty water for its weight in gold, and never giving a hang about taxes.

"They're also going to put a tax on salt!" Compare Mangiacarrube said. "The pharmacist says it was printed in the newspaper. That'll be the end of salting anchovies, and then we might as well break up the boats for firewood."

Mastro Turi, the caulker, was just about to shake his fist and start saying "By God," but he looked at his wife and shut up, swallowing whatever he was going to say.

"With the bad harvest that's ahead of us," Master Cipolla added, for it hadn't rained since Saint Claire's day, "the hunger this winter would have been thick enough to cut with a knife, if it hadn't been for the last storm in which the *Provvidenza* was lost, which was a real godsend."

Each of them recited his troubles, also to console the Malavoglia who, after all, weren't the only ones to have them. This world is packed with trouble, some get half, some get double, and the people who were outside in the yard kept looking at the sky, for another bit of rain would have been as welcome as bread. Master Cipolla knew why it no longer rained as it had in the old days. "It doesn't rain," he explained, "because they've put up that accursed telegraph line, which draws all the rain and carries it away." Compare Mangiacarrube and Tino Piedipapera were stunned by this, for there were telegraph poles right on the Trezza road; but Don Silvestro began to laugh, cackling like a hen, and Master Cipolla, infuriated, got up from the stone wall and began to rant, calling them all dunces and donkeys. Didn't they know that the telegraph carries news from one place to another? And that this is possible because inside the wire there's a kind of sap, as in the vine shoots, which, in just the same fashion, draws rain from the clouds and carries it far away, wherever it's needed most; they could go and ask the pharmacist, who'd said so himself! And that's why they had made a law that anyone who breaks the telegraph wire goes to jail. Then Don Silvestro, too, no longer knew what to say, and put his tongue in his pocket.

"Saints of paradise! All those telegraph poles ought to be cut down and thrown in the fire!" Compare Zuppiddo began, but nobody listened to him and, to change the subject, they all looked into the garden.

"A fine piece of land," Compare Mangiacarrube was saying. "When it's well cultivated, it can give you soup for the whole year."

The house of the Malavoglia had always been one of the first in Trezza; but now, with Bastianazzo's death and 'Ntoni in the navy and Mena still to be married off, and all those little bread-eaters underfoot, it was a house that was leaking on all sides.

Well, how much could the house be worth? They all craned their necks over the garden wall and took a look, to estimate it there and then, offhand. Don Silvestro knew better than anyone else how matters stood, because he had the documents in the town clerk's office at Aci Castello.

"Do you want to bet twelve tarì that it's not all gold that glitters?" he began to say, and he showed everyone a new five lire coin.

He knew that there was a tax of five tarì a year on the house. Then they started to reckon on their fingers how much the house, the garden, and everything could sell for.

"Neither the house nor the boat can be sold because they're part of Maruzza's dowry," somebody said, and at this they all got so excited you could hear them in the room where they were mourning the dead man. "That's right!" Don Silvestro finally exploded, like a bomb. "They're under dotal mortgage!" *

Master Cipolla, who had exchanged a few words with Master 'Ntoni about marrying Mena to his son Brasi, shook his head and didn't say another word.

"Then the real victim is Uncle Crocifisso, who loses the credit on his lupins," added Compare Cola.

All of them turned to look at Dumbbell, who had also come, for appearance's sake, and sat silently in a corner, listening to what was being said, with his mouth open and his nose in the air, so it seemed that he was counting how

---

* The conveyance of property in the marriage contract on the part of the husband (Bastianazzo) as security for his wife's (Maruzza's) dowry. [Translator's note.]

many tiles and beams were on the roof and was trying to estimate what the house was worth. The most curious craned their necks to look at him from the doorway, winking and pointing to him. "He looks like a bailiff making an attachment!" they snickered.

The women, who knew about the talks between Master 'Ntoni and Compare Cipolla, said that it was necessary to help Comare Maruzza forget her sorrow by settling Mena's marriage right away. But La Longa had other things on her mind just then, poor woman.

Master Cipolla went away very coldly, without saying anything; and after everyone had gone, the Malavoglia remained alone in the yard. "Now we are ruined," said Master 'Ntoni, "we are ruined, and Bastianazzo, who isn't here, is better off."

At these words, first Maruzza and then all the others began crying again, and the children, seeing the grown-ups cry, began to cry too, although their papa had been dead for three days. The old man kept walking back and forth, not knowing what he was doing; but Maruzza did not budge from the foot of the bed, as though there was nothing more for her to do. Whenever she spoke, she repeated this over and over, her eyes staring, and it seemed she had nothing else in her head—"Now I have nothing more to do!"

"No!" replied Master 'Ntoni. "Not at all! Because we have to pay the lupin debt to Uncle Crocifisso, and nobody must say to us: 'When the honest man gets poor he becomes a scoundrel.' "

The thought of the lupins drove the sorrow over Bastianazzo even deeper into his heart. Withered leaves fell from the medlar tree, and the wind pushed them here and there in the yard.

"He went because I sent him," Master 'Ntoni repeated. "Just as the wind carries those leaves here and there. And if I'd told him to jump off the Fariglioni rocks with a stone around his neck, he would have done it without a word. At least he died when the house and the medlar tree down to its last leaf were still his. And I, an old man, am still here. A poor man has long, long days."

Maruzza kept quiet, but she had a fixed idea which hammered away in her head and gnawed at her heart—she wanted to know what had happened that night, which she always had before her eyes. If she closed them she thought she could still see the *Provvidenza,* out towards Capo dei Mulini, where the sea was smooth and dark blue and all strewn with boats, which looked like so many seagulls in the sun, and she could count them one by one—Uncle Crocifisso's boat, Compare Barabba's boat, Uncle Cola's *Concetta,* and Master Fortunato's big trawler, and it made her heart ache; and she heard Mastro Turi Zuppiddo singing at the top of his voice with those ox lungs of his, as he banged away with his mallet, and the smell of tar came from the beach, and the thud of the linen that Cousin Anna was beating against the slabs in the wash shed; and she also heard Mena weeping quietly in the kitchen.

"Poor girl," her grandfather said softly. "The house has fallen on your head too, and Compare Fortunato went away very coldly, without saying a word."

And he touched all the gear heaped in a corner, piece by piece, with trembling hands, as old men do; and seeing Luca in front of him, wearing his father's jacket which reached to his heels, he said to him: "This jacket will keep you warm when you come to work. For now we must all help each other to pay the lupin debt."

Maruzza put her hands over her ears so she wouldn't hear La Locca, who was perched on the landing, outside the door, and had been shrieking since morning in that cracked, crazy voice of hers, demanding that they give her back her son and refusing to listen to reason.

"She's acting like that because she's hungry," Cousin Anna finally said. "Uncle Crocifisso has it in for all of them now, because of that lupin deal, and he no longer gives her anything. I'll bring her some food, and then she'll go away."

Cousin Anna, poor woman, had left her wash and her girls to come and give a hand to Maruzza, who was as helpless as if she were sick. If they'd left her alone she wouldn't have even thought to light the fire and put on the pot and they'd all have died of hunger. Neighbors must act like the tiles on the roof, one sending water to the next. But meanwhile those children's lips were pale with hunger. Nunziata helped too, and Alessi, his face besmeared from all the crying he had done at seeing his mother cry, made sure the little ones weren't always in her way, like a brood of chicks, because Nunziata wanted to have her hands free.

"You're a clever girl," Cousin Anna said to her. "When you grow up, your dowry will be in your hands."

CHAPTER FIVE

Mena did not know that they wanted to marry her to Master Cipolla's Brasi to help her mother forget her sorrows, and the first person to tell her, some time afterward, was Compare Alfio Mosca. He told her outside the gate, just after he came back from Aci Castello with his donkey cart. "It's not true! It's not true!" Mena cried; but she became confused, and while he was explaining how and when he'd heard it from La Vespa, at Uncle Crocifisso's house, she suddenly blushed bright red.

Compare Mosca looked distraught, too, and seeing the girl like that, with that black kerchief she wore round her neck, he began twisting the buttons of his jacket, swaying on one foot, then the other, and he would have paid to get away from there.—"Listen, it's not my fault, I heard it in Dumbbell's yard, while I was splitting up the carob tree which was knocked down by the storm on Saint Claire's day, do you remember? Now Uncle Crocifisso has me do the chores around the house, because he won't have anything more to do with Locca's son, after his brother played him that trick you know about with the cargo of lupins." Mena held the latch of the gate in her hand, but she couldn't make up her mind to open it. "And besides, if it isn't true why do you blush so?" She didn't know about it, really and truly, and she kept on twisting and turning the latch. She only knew Brasi by sight, and she didn't know anything else. Now Alfio was reeling off the litany of all of Brasi Cipolla's wealth. After Compare Naso the butcher, he was considered the best match in the village, and the girls couldn't take their eyes off him. As Mena listened to him, her eyes grew large too, and suddenly she said goodbye and ran into the garden. Furious, Alfio ran to reproach La Vespa, because she had told him all those lies and made him quarrel with people.

"I was told by Uncle Crocifisso," La Vespa replied. "I don't go around telling lies!"

"Lies! Lies!" grumbled Uncle Crocifisso. "I don't want to damn my soul for the Malavoglia! I heard it with these very ears. I also heard that the *Provvidenza* is dotal property, and that there's a tax of five tarì a year on the house."

"We'll see, we'll see! Sooner or later we'll see whether you tell lies or not," La Vespa continued, swaying back and forth, leaning against the doorjamb with her hands behind her back, looking at him all the while with melting eyes. "You men are all made of the same stuff, and there's no trusting any of you."

Sometimes Uncle Crocifisso didn't seem to hear well, and instead of swallowing the bait, he went on hopping from one subject to another. Now he was talking about the Malavoglia, who were so concerned about getting married but didn't give a thought to that matter of the forty onze.

"Eh!" La Vespa finally retorted, losing her patience. "If they listened to you, nobody would think of marrying anymore!"

"I don't care if they get married. I want my money. As for the rest, I don't care."

"If you don't care, there's somebody who does. Do you hear me? Because not everybody thinks the way you do, putting things off forever!"

"And why are you in such a hurry?"

"I am, unfortunately. You have plenty of time; but if you think other people want to wait until they're as old as Saint Joseph before they marry! . . ."

"It's a lean year," said Dumbbell, "and this is not the time to think of such things."

Then La Vespa put her hands on her hips and unsheathed a tongue as sharp as a stinger.

"Now listen to what I have to say! When all's said
and done, I have my property and, thank God, I don't
have to go begging for a husband. Or maybe you think
I do? If it weren't for that flea you put in my ear with all
your promises, I would have found a hundred husbands—
Vanni Pizzuto and Alfio Mosca and Cousin Cola, who was
sewed to my shirt before he went away to the army, and
wouldn't let me alone for a minute. They were all seeth-
ing with impatience, and wouldn't have led me around by
the nose for so long, from Easter to Christmas, as you've
done!"

This time Uncle Crocifisso cupped his hand at his ear
to listen, and then he began to flatter her. "Yes, I know
you're a sensible girl, that's why I care for you. I'm not
like those men who run after you to grab your plot of
land, which afterwards they'd drink up at Santuzza's tavern."

"It's not true that you care for me," La Vespa said,
still pushing him away with her elbows. "If it were, you'd
know what you must do, and you'd realize that that's all
I ever think about."

Vexed, she turned her back to him, and as she did,
jabbed him with her shoulder as if by chance. "I know
you don't care for me!" she repeated. Uncle Crocifisso was
insulted by such a vile accusation. "You're saying this
to make me sin!" he began to wail. What, he didn't care
for his own flesh and blood? Because after all she was his
own flesh and blood, just like the plot of land, which had
always been in the family and would have remained in it
if his brother, may he rest in peace, hadn't decided to get
married and bring La Vespa into the world; and so he had
always prized her as the apple of his eye, and had always
worried about her well-being. "Listen," he said, "I thought
of giving you the Malavoglia debt in exchange for the plot.
It's worth forty onze, and with the expenses and interest
could reach fifty, and you might even be able to get the
house by the medlar tree, which would be better for you
than the plot."

"You can keep the house by the medlar tree!" Vespa
answered sharply. "I'll keep my plot, and I know very
well what to do with it!"

At that Uncle Crocifisso flew into a rage too, and told

her that he knew what she wanted to do with it. She wanted to let it be gobbled up by that beggar Alfio Mosca, who was making sheep's eyes at her for the sake of the plot, and he no longer wanted to see him around the house or the courtyard, because when all's said and done he had blood in his veins, too!

"Don't tell me that you're acting jealous now!" exclaimed La Vespa.

"Certainly I'm jealous!" cried Uncle Crocifisso. "I'm jealous as a beast!"—and he wanted to pay five lire to get somebody to beat up Alfio Mosca.

But he wouldn't do it because he was a God-fearing Christian, and nowadays all honest men are cheated and deceived, for good faith lives on fool's lane, where they sell you the rope to hang yourself with, and the proof of it was that all his walking up and down past the Malavoglia house hadn't gotten him anywhere. The people had even started to say that he went on a pilgrimage to the house by the medlar tree like someone who's made a vow to the Madonna of Ognina. And the Malavoglia paid him off by doffing their caps, while the children, as soon as they saw him show up at the end of the road, scurried away as if they'd seen the bogeyman; but until now none of them had even so much as mentioned the money for the lupins, and the Feast of the Dead was coming, while all Master 'Ntoni worried about was marrying off his granddaughter.

But Uncle Crocifisso said he was just going past their house on his way to complain to Piedipapera, who had gotten him into that mess—that's what he told everybody. But people said that he went that way to take a peek at the house by the medlar. And then there was La Locca, who was always roving about those parts, ever since they'd told her that her son Menico had gone out in the Malavoglia boat and she'd gotten it into her head that she might still find him there. She put him off his feed too, because as soon as she saw her brother Crocifisso, she would start cawing and shrieking like a bird of ill omen.

"That woman is going to drive me to sin!" Dumbbell would mutter.

"The Feast of the Dead isn't here yet," Piedipapera re-

plied, waving his hands. "Be patient. Do you want to suck
Master 'Ntoni's blood? Anyway, you haven't lost anything, because the lupins were all rotten, you know it!"

Uncle Crocifisso didn't know anything. All he knew
was that, as things stood, his blood was in the hands of
God. And that the Malavoglia children didn't dare play
on the landing when he walked past Piedipapera's door.

And if he met Alfio Mosca with his donkey cart, who
also doffed his cap to him with that brazen manner of his,
he felt his blood boil, filled with jealousy at the thought of
La Vespa's plot of land. "He's trying to snare my niece
to take the plot away from me!" he grumbled to Piedipapera. "An idler! All he knows how to do is traipse
around with that donkey cart, and that's all he owns. A
beggar! A scoundrel who tells that ugly witch of a niece
of mine that he's in love with her pig's snout, and all
for the sake of her property."

And when he had nothing else to do, Uncle Crocifisso
planted himself in front of Santuzza's tavern, alongside
Uncle Santoro, as though he were begging for alms, too.
And he'd say to him: "Listen, Compare Santoro, if you
notice my niece La Vespa around here when Alfio Mosca
comes to bring the cartload of wine to your daughter
Santuzza, watch and see what's going on between them."
And Uncle Santoro, with his rosary beads in his hand and
his sightless eyes, said yes, he could count on him, for
that's why he was there, and not a fly flew by without his
knowing it. But afterwards his daughter La Santuzza said
to him: "What do you care about all this? Why are you
meddling in Dumbbell's affairs? He doesn't even spend a
cent in the tavern, and he just stands in front of the doorway free of charge."

But Alfio Mosca didn't even think of La Vespa. If
there was anyone he had on his mind, it was Master
'Ntoni's Mena, whom he saw every day in the yard or on
the landing, or when she went to feed the chickens in
the chicken coop. And when he heard the clucking of the
two hens he'd given her, he felt something move inside
him and it seemed that he himself was in the yard with
the medlar tree and if he hadn't been just a poor carter,
he would have asked to marry Saint Agatha and would
have carried her away in his donkey cart. When he thought

of all this, he had so many things in his head he wanted
to say to her, but then, when he met her, he couldn't get
his tongue to say them and talked about the weather and
the load of wine he had brought for Santuzza, and the
donkey which pulled four *quintali* better than a mule,
poor beast.

Mena stroked the donkey with her hand, and Alfio
smiled as though she were stroking him. "Ah! if my
donkey were only yours, Comare Mena!" And Mena
shook her head and her heart swelled with tenderness,
and she thought how much better it would have been if
the Malavoglia were carters, for then her father wouldn't
have drowned.

"The sea is bitter," she said, "and the sailor dies in the
sea."

Alfio was in a hurry to unload Santuzza's wine, but he
couldn't make up his mind to leave, and stayed there talking about what a fine thing it was to be a tavern keeper.
A business which always brings in money, and if the price
of the wine goes up, all you have to do is pour more water
into the barrels. "That's how Uncle Santoro became rich,
and now he begs for alms just to pass the time."

"Do you earn a good living, carting wine?" asked
Mena.

"Yes, in the summer, when you can also travel at night.
Then I make a good day's pay. This poor beast certainly
earns his oats. As soon as I've put aside some money I'll
buy a mule, then I'll pull myself up a notch and become a
real carter, like Compare Cinghialenta."

The girl listened intently to what Compare Alfio was
saying, and meanwhile the grey olive tree rustled as if it
were raining, and strewed the street with dry, curled-up
leaves. "Look, now winter is coming, and it won't be possible to do all that before the summer," said Alfio Mosca.
Mena watched the shadow of a cloud running over the
fields and it looked pale and silvery, as though the grey
olive tree itself were running away. And in the same way
the thoughts ran in her head, and she said to him: "You
know, Compare Alfio, there's nothing to that story about
Master Cipolla's son, because first we must pay the lupin
debt."

"I'm glad to hear that," replied Mosca, "because then you won't be leaving here."

"And now that 'Ntoni is coming back from the navy, together with my grandfather and all the others, we'll try to work and pay off the debt. My mother is weaving cloth for the Signora."

"Pharmacist, that's also a fine trade!" Mosca said.

Just then Comare Venera Zuppidda appeared in the lane, with her spindle in her hand. "Oh, my God, somebody's coming!" Mena cried and ran inside.

Alfio whipped up the donkey and was just going to leave, too.

"Oh, Compare Alfio, what's the hurry?" La Zuppidda called. "I wanted to ask you if the wine you're taking to Santuzza is from the same cask as last week's."

"I don't know. They give me the wine in barrels."

"That last stuff was salad vinegar, real poison!" La Zuppidda said. "That's how Santuzza's gotten rich, and to deceive the world she's put that scapular of the Daughters of Mary on her chest. Fine things that scapular covers! To get ahead nowadays you've got to ply that sort of trade. If you don't, you go backwards like a crab, just like the Malavoglia. Did you know? They've fished up the *Provvidenza*."

"No, I wasn't here; but Comare Mena didn't know about it."

"They just brought the news, and Master 'Ntoni has run to the Rotolo to see them tow the *Provvidenza* to the village, and you'd say he had a pair of new legs, the old man. Now that they've got the *Provvidenza*, the Malavoglia can pull themselves up again and Mena will once more be a good match."

Alfio didn't answer, for La Zuppidda was staring straight at him with her little yellow eyes, and he told her that he was in a hurry to deliver the wine to Santuzza. "He doesn't want to talk to me!" La Zuppidda grumbled. "As if I hadn't seen them with my own eyes. They want to hide the sun behind a net."

The *Provvidenza* had been towed to shore, completely battered, just as they'd found her beyond Capo dei Mulini, with her nose stuck in the rocks and her stern high in the air. In a flash the whole village, both men and women, had gathered on the beach, and Master 'Ntoni, jostled in the crowd, was looking on like everybody else. Some of them even kicked the *Provvidenza*'s belly to show how cracked she sounded, and the poor man could feel each kick in the pit of his stomach. "A finc providence you've got!" said Don Franco, who'd come in his shirt sleeves to take a look too, smoking his pipe and with his big hat on his head.

"Now you can use her for firewood," declared Master Fortunato Cipolla. And Compare Mangiacarrube, who knew his trade, said that the boat must have sunk all of a sudden, without any of the men even having the time to cry "God help me," because the sea had swept away sails, boom, oars and everything, and hadn't left a wooden peg in place.

"This was Papa's place, where there's the new oar-lock," said Luca, who had climbed up on the side of the boat. "And the lupins were stowed under here."

But not a single lupin was left, for the sea had washed and swept the boat clean. That's why Maruzza hadn't left the house. As long as she lived, she never wanted to lay eyes on the *Provvidenza* again.

"The hull's in good shape, and you can still do something with it," Mastro Zuppiddo, the caulker, pronounced at last, and then he too kicked the *Provvidenza* with his big ugly foot. "With a few wedges between the boards, I'll put her to sea again. She'll no longer be a boat that can stand up to a heavy sea, because if a wave hit her broadside she'd stave in like a rotten cask. But for fishing off the rocks near shore and for fine weather, she'll still do." Master Cipolla, Compare Mangiacarrube, and Compare Cola listened in silence.

"Yes," Master Fortunato Cipolla concluded gravely, "instead of throwing her into the fire . . ."

"I'm very glad about it," said Uncle Crocifisso, who'd also come to watch, his hands clasped behind his back. "We're Christians, and one must be happy over other people's good fortune. The proverb says: 'Wish your neighbor well, because you too will profit.' "

The Malavoglia boys were on top of the *Provvidenza,* along with some other kids who'd climbed on her, too.

"When we've patched her up right," Alessi said, "the *Provvidenza* will be just like Uncle Cola's *Concetta*." And then they got busy, panting and straining to help push and drag the boat to the caulker's door, where there were big stones to keep the boats upright, and the tub for the tar, and a heap of ribs and hull planks propped against the wall.

Alessi kept on fighting with the boys who tried to climb into the boat, and wanted to help blow up the fire under the cauldron for the tar, and when they hurt him he whined and threatened them: "Just you wait, my brother 'Ntoni's coming back from the navy!"

The fact is, 'Ntoni had gotten them to send his father's death certificate and had obtained his discharge, although Don Silvestro, the town clerk, had assured them that if he'd stayed in the navy for six more months, he'd have freed his brother Luca from conscription. But, now that his father had died, 'Ntoni didn't want to stay there for six more days. Luca would have done the same. Just imagine, having to mourn his loss down there so far away! If it hadn't been for his damned officers, he wouldn't have done a lick of work after he got the news about his father.

"I don't mind going into the navy instead of 'Ntoni," Luca said. "Because now, when he comes back, you can put the *Provvidenza* to sea and you won't have to hire anybody."

"Now there's a real Malavoglia, born and bred," said Master 'Ntoni, chuckling. "He's the spitting image of his father Bastianazzo, who had a heart as big as the sea and as good as the mercy of God."

One evening, after the boats returned from the sea, Master 'Ntoni came home out of breath and said: "Here's the letter. I just got it from Compare Cirino, when I was taking the lobster pots to Piedipapera's house." La Longa went white as a sheet from happiness, and they all rushed into the kitchen to see the letter.

'Ntoni arrived with his cap cocked over his ear, and his shirt with the stars on the collar, which his mother couldn't stop touching, and then she trailed behind him among all the relations and friends as they walked back from the station. In a moment the house and yard were crowded, just as when Bastianazzo had died some time back, though nobody thought of that anymore. Only old people never stop thinking about certain things, as though they'd happened yesterday. La Locca, for instance, was always there in front of the Malavoglia house, sitting at the base of the wall, waiting for Menico, turning her head to look this way and that down the road every time she heard a footstep.

CHAPTER SIX

'Ntoni had arrived on a holiday, so everybody was
there to watch him as he went from door to door greet-
ing neighbors and friends. His friends trooped after him,
and the girls leaned out of their windows; but the only girl
who wasn't there was Comare Tudda's Sara.

"She's gone to Ognina with her husband," La Santuzza
told him. "She married Domenico Trinca, who is a widower with six children, but he's rich as a pig. They got
married not even a month after his wife died, and the bed
was still warm from her, God forgive them!"

"A widower is like a man who goes off to serve in the
army," La Zuppidda added. "A soldier's love doesn't last,
at the beat of the drum it's farewell, my lass. Besides, the
Provvidenza had been lost!"

Comare Venera, who had gone to the station when
Master 'Ntoni's 'Ntoni had left, just to see if Comare
Tudda's Sara had come to bid him goodbye, since she'd
seen them courting over the vineyard wall, didn't want
to miss 'Ntoni's face when he heard that. But time had
passed for 'Ntoni too, and as they say: out of sight, out
of mind. 'Ntoni had come back with his cap cocked over
his ear. "Compare Menico Trinca wants to die a cuckold!"
he said, to console himself, and this pleased the Mangiacarrube girl, who had called him a cucumber and now
could see that he was a handsome one, and would have
gladly exchanged him for that good-for-nothing loafer

Rocco Spatu, whom she had taken simply because there was nobody else around.

"I don't like these flirts who go courting with two or three at the same time," said the Mangiacarrube girl, tightening the ends of the kerchief under her chin and acting just like a little saint. "If I loved a man, I wouldn't change him even for Victor Emmanuel or Garibaldi, now there!"

"I know who you like!" said 'Ntoni Malavoglia, with his fist on his hip.

"No you don't, Compare 'Ntoni, and what they've told you is just gossip. If you'll come to my door some day, I'll tell you the whole story."

"Now that the Mangiacarrube girl has set her eyes on Master 'Ntoni's 'Ntoni, it'll be a godsend for Cousin Anna," Comare Zuppidda said.

'Ntoni swaggered away, full of conceit and with a bunch of friends at his heels, and he wished that every day was a holiday, so he could stroll around showing off his shirt with the stars on the collar. That afternoon he had fun trading punches in front of the tavern with Compare Pizzuto, who wasn't afraid of God himself, even if he hadn't been in the navy, though finally Pizzuto was knocked down, his nose bleeding. But Rocco Spatu turned out to be stronger and put 'Ntoni on the ground.

"By God!" cried the people who were watching. "That Rocco is as strong as Mastro Turi Zuppiddo. If he'd only decide to work, he'd make a fine living!"

"I say my prayers with this!" said Pizzuto, and he showed his razor, unwilling to admit defeat.

'Ntoni had a good time all day. But that evening, while they were sitting and talking around the dinner table, and his mother was asking him all sorts of questions, and the children, half asleep, were staring at him with eyes full of wonder, and Mena kept fingering his cap and his shirt with the stars to see how they were made, his grandfather told him that he had gotten work for him on Compare Cipolla's trawler, and at a good wage.

"I took them out of the goodness of my heart," Master Fortunato, seated before the barbershop, said to anyone who would listen. "I took them on just not to say 'no' to Master 'Ntoni, when he came to ask under the elm tree whether I needed any men for the trawler. I never need any men, but when prison, illness, and need appear, you know the friends that are dear. Besides, Master 'Ntoni's so old, the wages you give him are practically thrown away! . . ."

"He's old, but he knows his trade," Piedipapera answered. "You won't be throwing your money away. And besides, his grandson is the sort of lad they'd all be happy to take away from you."

"As soon as Mastro Turi fixes the *Provvidenza,* we'll fit out our own boat and we won't have to hire out anymore," Master 'Ntoni said.

In the morning when he went to wake his grandson, it was still two hours before dawn and 'Ntoni would have liked to stay a while longer under the covers. When he came out yawning into the yard, the Three Kings, with their feet upside down, were still high over Ognina, the Pleiades were shining on the other side, and the sky swarmed with stars which looked like sparks running along the bottom of a black frying pan. "It's just like the navy, when they sounded reveille 'tween decks," 'Ntoni grumbled. "So what was the use of coming home!"

"Keep quiet, Grandfather's right there, getting the gear ready, and he got up two hours before we did," Alessi answered. But Alessi was just like his father, God rest his soul. Their grandfather, holding his lantern, was moving around the yard. Outside you could hear the men walk by on their way to the sea, and as they passed from door to door, they knocked to call their fellows. But when the Malavoglia reached the shore and saw the black sea, softly snoring over the pebbly beach and reflecting the stars, and the lanterns of the other boats which glimmered here and there, even 'Ntoni felt his heart expand.

"Ah! it's fine to come home," he exclaimed, stretching his arms. "This beach knows me!" Yes, Master 'Ntoni always said that a fish can't live out of water, and if you're born a fish you've got to get back to the sea.

While they were pulling in the sails and the *Carmela* was moving in a circle, very slowly, dropping her nets behind her like the tail of a serpent, they made fun of

'Ntoni because Sara had jilted him. "Pig's meat and warriors don't last. That's why Sara jilted you."

"When women are faithful to one man, then the Turks will become Christians," Uncle Cola remarked.

"I have all the sweethearts I want," 'Ntoni replied. "In Naples they chased after me like puppy dogs."

"In Naples you had a uniform of good wool cloth, and a cap with an insignia, and shoes on your feet," Barabba said.

"Are there pretty girls in Naples, like here?"

"The pretty girls here can't hold a candle to the girls in Naples. Why, I had a girl who wore a silk dress and red ribbons in her hair, and an embroidered bodice with golden shoulder straps, like the captain's. A big, beautiful girl, who took her master's children out for strolls, and that's all she ever did."

"It must be a fine life in those parts!" said Barabba.

"You, on the left! Hold your oar!" Master 'Ntoni shouted.

"'Blood of Judas! What are you doing? You're putting the trawler through the nets!" Uncle Cola started screaming from his place at the tiller. "Stop all that talk! Are we here to scratch our bellies or to do our job?"

"It's the swell that's pushing us back," 'Ntoni answered.

"Ease off on that side, you son of a bitch," Barabba yelled at him. "With all those queens you've got in your head, you'll make us lose our day's pay."

"Goddamn you! Say that again and I'll split your head," 'Ntoni yelled back, lifting his oar.

"What's this?" Uncle Cola cried from the tiller, "Is that what you learned in the navy? To jump at a word?"

"If that's the way it is, I'm leaving," 'Ntoni said.

"Go ahead and leave. With all his money, Master Fortunato won't have any trouble finding somebody else."

"The servant must be patient and the master must be prudent," Master 'Ntoni said.

Grumbling, 'Ntoni went on rowing, since he couldn't leave out there, and Compare Mangiacarrube, to make peace, said that it was time to eat.

Just then the sun came up and a swig of wine was welcome, because of the chill wind which had lifted.

The boys started working their jaws, the wine bottles gripped between their legs, while the trawler rocked slowly inside the wide circle of the nets.

"The first one who talks gets a kick in the behind!" Uncle Cola declared.

To avoid getting that kick they all began chewing away like oxen, watching the waves which came rolling in from the open sea without foam, like heavy green wineskins, and which even on a sunny day remind you of a black sky and a slate-colored sea.

"Master Cipolla will do some cursing this evening," Uncle Cola suddenly said. "But it's not our fault. When the sea is cold, you can't catch fish."

First Compare Mangiacarrube gave him a kick, because Uncle Cola, who'd made the rules, had been the first to talk; and then he replied: "Since we're here, let's wait a while before we pull up the nets."

"The swell is coming in from the open, and that's to our good," added Master 'Ntoni, and as they waited, Uncle Cola groaned, rubbing his behind.

Now that the silence was broken, Barabba turned to 'Ntoni Malavoglia and asked: "Do you have a cigar butt?"

"No, I don't," 'Ntoni answered, forgetting the argument they'd had just before. "But I'll give you half of mine."

The crew of the trawler, sitting on the bottom of the boat with their backs against the thwarts and their hands laced behind their heads, were singing softly, each to himself, to keep from falling asleep, because their eyes were closing under the bright sun; and Barabba snapped his fingers each time a mullet flashed out of the water.

"They've got nothing to do," 'Ntoni said, "and they play by jumping out of the water."

"This cigar is good!" said Barabba. "Did you smoke cigars like this in Naples?"

"Yes, I smoked a lot of them."

"Look, the corks are starting to sink," said Compare Mangiacarrube.

"Do you see where the *Provvidenza* went down with your father?" said Barabba. "Over there at the Cape, where the sun hits those white houses, and the sea looks all golden."

"The sea is bitter, and the sailor dies at sea," 'Ntoni said.

Barabba handed him his wine bottle, and after that they started grousing together under their breath against Uncle Cola, who behaved like a dog to the crew of the trawler, as if Master Cipolla were right there with them, watching every move they made.

"It's all to make Master Cippola think that the trawler couldn't run without him," added Barabba. "The spy!"

"Now he'll tell Master Cipolla that he's the one who caught the fish, because of his great skill, and in spite of the sea's being cold. Look how the nets are sinking. The corks have disappeared."

"Come on, boys!" yelled Uncle Cola, "Let's pull up the nets! If the swell catches up with us, it'll tear them out of your hands."

"Oohee! Ooohee!" the crew began to chant, pulling the ropes in hand over hand.

"Blessed Saint Francis!" cried Uncle Cola. "With a swell like this, I almost can't believe we caught so much of God's bounty."

The nets seethed and glittered in the sun as they came out of the water, and soon the entire bottom of the trawler seemed to be filled with quicksilver. "Now Master Fortunato will be satisfied!" murmured Barabba, red and sweating. "And he won't begrudge us those three carlini he pays us for the day."

"This is how it works!" said 'Ntoni. "We break our backs for other people. And then when we've put together a bit of money, the devil comes and eats it up."

"What are you complaining about?" his grandfather said. "Doesn't Master Fortunato pay you a day's wage?"

The Malavoglia did everything they could to make money. La Longa took orders to weave some bolts of cloth and also did other people's wash, and Master 'Ntoni and his grandson hired out by the day. They all did what they could, and when his rheumatism bent the old man like a fishhook, he stayed in the yard to mend the nets, or repair lobster pots, and put the gear in order, for he was skillful at everything in his trade. Luca went to work at the railroad bridge for fifty centesimi a day, though his brother 'Ntoni said that the money didn't even pay for the shirts he wore out carrying rocks in his basket. But Luca wouldn't mind even if he wore out his shoulders. And Alessi went to catch shrimp along the rocks, or worms for bait, which he sold at five centesimi a pound, and sometimes he went as far as Ognina and Capo dei Mulini and would come back with his feet torn and bloody. But every Saturday Compare Zuppiddo took a lot of money for patching up the *Provvidenza,* and it required plenty of fixed lobster pots, stones from the railroad, bait at five cents a pound, and linen bleached standing knee-deep in the water under the blazing sun, to scrape together forty onze. The Feast of the Dead had come and gone, and Uncle Crocifisso did nothing but walk up and down the lane, his hands clasped behind his back, looking like a basilisk.

"This is a story that will end up with bailiff!" Uncle Crocifisso kept telling Don Silvestro and Don Giammaria, the parish priest.

"There'll be no need for the bailiff, Uncle Crocifisso!" Master 'Ntoni told him, when he heard what Dumbbell went around saying. "The Malavoglia have always been honest folk, and they've never needed a bailiff."

"It's all the same to me," answered Uncle Crocifisso, leaning against the wall under the courtyard shed, while they were piling up his vine branches. "All I know is that I've got to be paid."

At last, through the good offices of the parish priest, Dumbbell agreed to wait until Christmas to be paid, taking as his interest the seventy-five lire which Maruzza had gathered, cent by cent, in a stocking hidden under the mattress.

"That's how it is!" grumbled Master 'Ntoni's 'Ntoni. "We work night and day for Uncle Crocifisso. And when we manage to scrape together a few lire, Dumbbell takes them away from us."

Master 'Ntoni and Maruzza comforted themselves by building castles in the air about the coming summer, when there would be anchovies to salt down, and prickly pears at ten a grano, and they made great plans to go fishing for tuna and swordfish, where they paid you well for a day's work, and in the meantime Mastro Turi would have finished repairing the *Provvidenza*. These conversations took place on the landing, or after dinner, and the children listened attentively, their chins in their hands. But 'Ntoni, who had been far away and knew the world better than the others, was bored by this talk and preferred to go and hang around near the tavern, where so many people stood about doing nothing. Uncle Santoro was there too, the worst loafer of all, with that easy work of his, holding out his hand to the passer-by and mouthing Hail Marys. Or 'Ntoni went to Compare Zuppiddo's with the excuse of seeing how the *Provvidenza* was coming along, but really to have a chat with Barbara, who came to put twigs under the tar cauldron whenever 'Ntoni was there.

"You're always busy, Comare Barbara," 'Ntoni said. "You're the mainstay of your house. That's why your father doesn't want to give you away."

"He doesn't want to give me to people who are not right for me," Barbara replied. "Like with like, and stay with your own."

"I wouldn't mind staying with your own, by God! If you'd let me, Comare Barbara!"

"What kind of talk is this, Compare 'Ntoni? My mother is spinning in the courtyard and she's listening to us."

"I meant those twigs, which are too green and won't catch fire. Let me do it."

"Is it true that you come here to see the Mangiacarrube girl, when she looks out the window?"

"I come here for something much different, Comare Barbara. I come to see how far along the *Provvidenza* is."

"She's coming along, and my papa has said that you'll put her to sea by Christmas Eve."

Since the nine days before Christmas were approaching, the Malavoglia never stopped going to Mastro Turi Zuppiddo's yard. Meanwhile the whole village was preparing for the holiday. In every house the images of the saints were decorated with green boughs and oranges, and the children trooped in swarms after the bagpiper who went to play before the small shrines festooned with lights which stood next to the doorways. Only in the Malavoglia house the statue of the Good Shepherd remained dark, while Master 'Ntoni's 'Ntoni ran about playing the ladies' man all over the place, and Barbara Zuppidda said to him:

"When you're out at sea, will you at least remember that I melted the pitch for the *Provvidenza?*"

Piedipapera proclaimed that all girls were out to rob him.

"I'm the one who's being robbed!" whined Uncle Crocifisso. "I'd like to see where they'll get the money for the lupins, if 'Ntoni marries, and they also have to give Mena a dowry, with that tax they have on the house, and all that underhanded business about the dotal mortgage which suddenly turned up. Christmas is here, but I've yet to see the Malavoglia."

Each time Master 'Ntoni went to talk to him in the piazza or under the shed, and said: "What do you expect me to do if I have no money? You can't squeeze blood out of a stone! Give me until June, if you can do me this favor, or take the *Provvidenza* and the house by the medlar. I have nothing else."

"I want my money!" Dumbbell replied doggedly, leaning against the wall. "You said that you're honest folk, and that you don't pay with a lot of talk, such as the *Provvidenza* and the house by the medlar tree."

He was wasting away in soul and body, he lost his sleep and his appetite, and he couldn't even let off steam by saying that the whole story would end up with the bailiff, because immediately Master 'Ntoni would send Don Giammaria or the town clerk to ask for pity, and they didn't even let him come into the piazza for his own business without getting after him, so that the whole village was saying that that money was the devil's money. He couldn't complain to Piedipapera because immediately Piedipapera replied that the lupins had been rotten, and that he himself was just a middleman in this business. "But at least there's something he can do for me!" Uncle Crocifisso suddenly said to himself—and he couldn't sleep for the rest of the night, he was so pleased with his brainstorm.

At the crack of dawn he went to see Piedipapera, who

was still stretching and yawning in his doorway. "You must pretend you've bought the lupin credit from me," he told him. "In that way, we can send the bailiff to the Malavoglia, and nobody will say that you're an usurer if you want your money back, nor that it's the devil's money." "Did you get this wonderful idea last night?" Piedipapera jeered. "Is that why you woke me at dawn?" "I've also come about the vine branches. If you want them, you can come and take them." "Then send for the bailiff," answered Piedipapera, "but you'll pay the expenses." Comare Grazia, that good woman, had come to the door in her nightgown to ask her husband: "What did Uncle Crocifisso come here to cook up? Now let those poor Malavoglia alone. They have enough troubles!" "You mind your spinning!" growled Compare Tino. "Women are long on hair and short on brains." And he limped away to drink an anise at Compare Pizzuto's.

"They want to give those poor creatures a sad Christmas," murmured Comare Grazia, her hands folded over her belly.

Before every house stood a small shrine adorned with foliage and oranges, and when the bagpiper came and played in the evening, they lit the candles and sang the litany and the whole village was festive. The children played Peach Stones in the street, and if Alessi stopped to watch, his legs astraddle, they said to him: "Get out of here, if you don't have any peach stones to play with. . . . Now they're going to take your house away."

And so it was. The day before Christmas, the bailiff came in his carriage especially for the Malavoglia, and the whole village buzzed with excitement, and he left a paper with the official seal on the chest of drawers, next to the statue of the Good Shepherd.

"Did you see the bailiff who's come for the Malavoglia?" Comare Venera Zuppidda said to everyone. "Now they're in for it!"

Her husband, who was only too happy to be right for once, started to shout and bellow: "I told you, saints in paradise! I told you that I didn't like that 'Ntoni hanging around the house."

"You keep quiet. You don't know what you're talking

about!" La Zuppidda answered. "This is our business. That's how you marry off a girl. Otherwise you're stuck with her, like an old pot."

"What do you mean, marry off! Now that the bailiff's come?"

Then La Zuppidda waved her hands in his face: "Did you know that the bailiff was coming? You always bark when it's too late, but when it comes to doing anything, you can't even move a finger. Anyway, the bailiff doesn't eat people."

The bailiff, true enough, doesn't eat people, but the Malavoglia looked as if they'd all had a stroke and remained in the yard, sitting in a circle and staring at each other, and the day the bailiff came to the Malavoglia house, they didn't even sit down at the table to eat.

"Goddamn it!" cried 'Ntoni. "We're always scrabbling around like lost chicks, and now they send the bailiff to wring our necks."

"What will we do now?" said La Longa.

Master 'Ntoni didn't know, but finally he picked up the paper with the official seal and went to see Uncle Crocifisso, together with his eldest grandsons, to tell him to take the *Provvidenza,* for Mastro Turi had just finished patching her up. The poor man's voice trembled as it did when his son Bastianazzo had died. "It's not up to me anymore," Dumbbell answered. "I've sold my credit to Piedipapera and you'll have to settle things with him."

As soon as Piedipapera saw the procession heave into sight, he began to scratch his head. "What can I do about it?" he answered. "I'm a poor devil and I need that money, and I can't use the *Provvidenza,* because that's not my trade, but if Uncle Crocifisso wants her, I can help you sell her. I'll be right back."

Those poor souls sat down on the low stone wall to wait, and didn't even have the courage to look at each other, but kept looking down the street, to see if Piedipapera was coming back. At last he appeared, walking very slowly, though when he wanted to he could hobble very quickly on his twisted leg. "He says that the *Provvidenza*'s all broken up, like an old shoe, and he can't use her," he shouted from a distance. "I'm sorry, but I haven't been able to do anything." So the Malavoglia went back, still holding their paper with the official seal.

Yet something had to be done, people told them, because that paper there with the seal, lying on the chest of drawers, would eat up the chest of drawers, the house, and all of them put together.

"What we need is some advice from Don Silvestro, the town clerk," suggested Maruzza. "Take these two hens to him, and then he'll tell you something."

Don Silvestro said that there was no time to be lost, and sent them to a good lawyer, Dr. Scipioni, who lived on Via Ammalati, opposite Uncle Crispino's stables. He was young, but when it came to talk, he had enough to put in his pocket all those old lawyers who demanded five onze just to open their mouths, while he was satisfied with twenty-five lire.

Lawyer Scipioni was busy rolling cigarettes, and he made them come and go two or three times before listening to their case. Besides, the worst of it was that they all went in a procession, one behind the other, and at the start even La Longa went too, holding her baby in her arms, to help them present their arguments, and so they lost the whole day. At last, after he'd read the papers and managed to understand something from the muddled answers which he had to pull out of Master 'Ntoni with a pair of tongs while the others sat on the edge of their chairs, not daring to open their mouths, the lawyer began laughing heartily, and they all laughed with him, without knowing why, just to ease their anguish. "Nothing," the lawyer replied. "Nothing, that's what you must do." And since Master 'Ntoni repeated that the bailiff had come, the lawyer said: "Let the bailiff come even once a day. If he does, the creditor will soon tire of paying for the expenses. They won't be able to take anything away from you, because the house is dotal, and for your boat we'll present a claim in Mastro Turi Zuppiddo's name. Your daughter-in-law has nothing to do with the purchase of the lupins."

The lawyer went on talking for more than twenty-five lire's worth, without even stopping to spit or scratch his head, so that Master 'Ntoni and his grandsons suddenly itched to speak too, to blurt out their whole beautiful defense which they could feel swelling in their heads; and they left dazed, overwhelmed by all those arguments which they now possessed, and all the way home they went over and over the lawyer's speech, gestures and all. This time Maruzza hadn't come and when she saw them appear with flushed faces and gleaming eyes, she felt a great weight lifted from her, too. Her face became serene as she waited for them to tell her what the lawyer had said. But none of them talked, they just looked at each other.

"Well?" Maruzza finally asked. She was dying of impatience.

"Nothing, there's nothing to be afraid of!" Master 'Ntoni answered calmly.

"And the lawyer?"

"Yes, the lawyer said so. There's nothing to be afraid of."

"But what did he say?" Maruzza insisted.

"Ah, he knows how to talk. A man with mustaches. Bless those twenty-five lire!"

"But what did he tell you to do?"

Master 'Ntoni looked at his grandson and 'Ntoni looked at his grandfather.

"Nothing," Master 'Ntoni replied, after a pause. "He told us to do nothing."

"We won't pay Uncle Crocifisso anything," added 'Ntoni recklessly. "Because he can't take the house or the *Provvidenza*. . . . We don't owe him anything."

"And the lupins?"

"That's true. What about the lupins?" repeated Master 'Ntoni.

"The lupins? . . . We didn't eat his lupins, we don't have them in our pockets, and so Uncle Crocifisso can't take a thing from us, the lawyer said so, he'll just lose the money for the expenses."

At this there was a long moment of silence; but Maruzza didn't seem convinced.

"So he said not to pay?"

'Ntoni scratched his head, and his grandfather said: "That's true, he did give us the lupins, and we must pay for them."

There was nothing to say to that. Now that the lawyer

was no longer there, they had to pay for the lupins. Shaking his head Master 'Ntoni muttered: "No, not this. The Malavoglia have never done anything like this. Uncle Crocifisso can take the house, the boat, everything, but we can't do this."

The poor old man was confused, and his daughter-in-law wept silently into her apron.

"There's nothing else to do, we must go to Don Silvestro," Master 'Ntoni decided.

And all together, grandfather, grandsons, and daughter-in-law, even the little baby girl, went again in procession to the town clerk to ask him how they should go about paying the debt, without Uncle Crocifisso's sending them any more of those official papers, which would eat up house, boat and all of them put together. Don Silvestro, who knew the law, was whiling away the time building a cage which he wanted to present to the Signora's children. He didn't act like the lawyer, but let them talk and talk, just continuing to insert thin reed bars into the cage. Then, at last, he told them what they had to do: "Well now, everything will be straightened out if Comare Maruzza takes it in hand." The poor woman couldn't imagine what she had to take in hand. "It's the sale you must take in hand," Don Silvestro told her. "You must give up your dotal mortgage, although you weren't the one who took the lupins." "All of us took the lupins," La Longa murmured, "and the Lord has punished us all by taking my husband."

Those poor ignorant Malavoglia sat stiffly on their chairs and looked at each other, and in the meantime Don Silvestro laughed to himself. Then he sent for Uncle Crocifisso, who came sucking a dry chestnut, for he'd just finished his dinner, and his tiny eyes were shinier than usual. At first he didn't want to hear a word of it, and said that it was no longer up to him and was none of his business. "I'm like a low wall, on which everybody leans and does as he pleases, because I don't know how to talk like a lawyer, and I can't present my arguments; and they all act as if I'd stolen what I own, but what they do to me they're doing to the crucified Jesus who's hanging on the cross," and he went on muttering and grumbling, his back against the wall and his hands pushed into his pockets. You couldn't even understand all that he was saying because of that chestnut he had in his mouth. Don Silvestro sweated like a trooper to drive it into his head that after all the Malavoglia couldn't be considered swindlers since they wanted to pay off the debt, and Bastianazzo's widow was willing to give up her mortgage. "To avoid quarreling, the Malavoglia are satisfied to be left with only the shirts on their backs; but if you push them into a corner, they'll begin sending sealed papers, too, and then you can whistle for your money. After all, you've got to have some charity, holy devil! You want to bet that if you go on digging your heels in the ground like a mule, you won't get anything?"

"When you put it this way," Uncle Crocifisso replied, "I've nothing more to say," and he promised to talk to Piedipapera about it. "I'd make any sacrifice for the sake of friendship." Master 'Ntoni could tell them whether or not he'd do this and more for a friend, and Dumbbell offered the old man his open snuffbox, patted the baby, and gave her a chestnut. "Don Silvestro knows my weak spot; I can't say no. I'll talk to Piedipapera this evening and I'll tell him to wait till Easter, provided Comare Maruzza takes it in hand." Maruzza hadn't understood what she was supposed to take in hand, but she answered that she was ready to do it right away. Before he left, Uncle Crocifisso said to Don Silvestro: "You can send for those broad beans you wanted to sow."

"Fine, fine," said Don Silvestro. "I know that for friends you have a heart as big as the ocean."

When other people were around, Piedipapera wouldn't hear of a postponement; and he screamed and tore his hair, saying that they wanted to leave him with just his shirt on his back, leave him and his wife Grazia without bread for the whole winter, and all this after having convinced him to buy the Malavoglia's debt. Those five hundred lire he had paid out were precious, one more precious than the next, and he'd taken them right out of his mouth to give to Uncle Crocifisso. His wife Grazia, poor thing, opened her eyes wide with astonishment, because she couldn't imagine where he had gotten all that money, and she kept on putting in a good word for the Malavoglia, who were fine people and everybody in the village had always known them for honest folk. And now even Uncle Crocifisso sided with the Malavoglia: "They said they'll pay, and if they won't be able to pay, they'll let you have the house. Maruzza has also promised to take it in hand. Don't you know that these days you've got to do what you can to get back your money?" At this Piedipapera threw on his jacket and left shouting that Uncle Crocifisso and his wife should do as they pleased, since he didn't count for anything in his own house.

CHAPTER SEVEN

That was a bad Christmas for the Malavoglia. Just at that time Luca had also drawn his number in the draft —and a low, poor devil's number it was. When he left for the king's navy there wasn't much weeping and wailing, because by now they'd all become used to it. 'Ntoni went to the station with his brother, wearing his cap cocked over his ear, so you'd have thought he was the one who was leaving, and he told Luca that he had been in the navy too and that there was nothing to it. It rained that day, and the road was one big puddle.

"I don't want you to come," Luca kept saying to his mother. "It's a long way to the station." And he stood in the doorway, his bundle under his arm, watching the rain fall on the medlar tree. Then he kissed his grandfather's and his mother's hand, and he embraced Mena and his brothers.

So La Longa saw him leave under the umbrella, accompanied by all his kin, hopping on the cobblestones of the road, which was one big puddle. The boy, who was as levelheaded as his grandfather, had even thought to turn up his pants on the landing, though he wouldn't be wearing them now that they were going to put a uniform on him.

"This one won't write for money while he's away," the old man thought to himself, "and if God gives him a long life, he'll pull the house by the medlar tree up again." But

God did not give him a long life, just because Luca was made like that—and later, when the news came that he was dead, La Longa always had the regret that she had let him leave in the rain and hadn't gone with him to the station.

"Mama!" Luca had said, coming back, because his heart wept to leave her there so silent on the landing, like Our Lady of the Sorrows. "When I come back, I'll send you word before so you can all come and meet me at the station." And Maruzza remembered those words until her dying day; and till that day she carried in her heart another regret, that her boy did not see the joy when they put the *Provvidenza* to sea again, though the whole village was there and Barbara Zuppidda had come out with her broom to sweep away the shavings. "It's for you I'm doing this," she said to Master 'Ntoni's 'Ntoni, "because it's your *Provvidenza.*"

"With that broom in your hand you look like a queen," 'Ntoni said. "In all of Trezza there's not a finer housewife than you!"

"Now that you're taking away the *Provvidenza* you won't come around here anymore, Compare 'Ntoni."

"Of course I'll come. Besides, this is the shortest way to get to the lava field."

"You'll come to see the Mangiacarrube girl, who always stands at the window when you walk by."

"I leave the Mangiacarrube girl to Rocco Spatu, because I have other things on my mind."

"Who knows how many girls you have on your mind, all those pretty girls outside Sicily, isn't that so?"

"There are pretty girls here too, and I know that very well."

"Really?"

"On my soul!"

"Oh, but why should you care?"

"I care, I care. But they don't care about me. Because they have handsome fellows who stroll under their windows, with their polished shoes."

"I don't even look at their polished shoes, I swear it by the Madonna of Ognina! Mama says that polished shoes are made to devour a girl's dowry and all the rest. And some fine day, she says, she'll come out on the street with her distaff in her hand and give that Don Silvestro something to remember if he doesn't leave me alone."

"Do you really mean that, Comare Barbara?"

"Yes, honest and truly."

"That's what I like to hear!" 'Ntoni cried.

"Listen, go to the lava field on Monday, when my mother is away at the market."

"On Monday my grandfather won't let me breathe, now that we're putting the *Provvidenza* to sea."

As soon as Mastro Turi said that the boat was ready, Master 'Ntoni came to get her with his boys and all of his friends, and the *Provvidenza* went down to sea, that crowd all around her, staggering over the stones as though she were seasick.

"Let go!" Compare Zuppiddo was yelling, louder than all of them, while the others sweated and shouted, pushing her onto the slip-blocks when she bumped and stumbled against the stones. "Leave her to me, or I'll pick her up in my arms like a baby and put her into the water all by myself."

"Compare Turi could even do it, with those arms of his!" some said. And others said: "Now the Malavoglia are in the saddle again."

"That devil Zuppiddo has magic in his hands!" they exclaimed. "Just look how he's fixed her up, and before this she looked like an old shoe!"

And it was true, the *Provvidenza* looked altogether different, shining with her new pitch and with a lovely red stripe painted all along her sides, and on her stern the image of Saint Francis with a beard that looked like cotton. Even La Longa was reconciled to the *Provvidenza,* for the first time since the boat had come back without her husband; but she made peace out of fear, now that the bailiff had come.

"Long live Saint Francis!" they all shouted as they saw the *Provvidenza* slip by, and La Locca's son shouted louder than any of them, hoping that now Master 'Ntoni would hire him too. Mena had come out on the landing and was crying again, but from happiness, and even La Locca got up and went with the crowd to follow the Malavoglia.

"Oh, Comare Mena, this must be a wonderful day for you people," said Alfio Mosca from his window across the way. "That's the way it'll be for me when I can buy a mule."

"Are you going to sell the donkey?"

"What can I do? I'm not rich like Vanni Pizzuto; if I were, I swear that I wouldn't sell him."

"Poor beast!"

"If I could feed another mouth I'd take a wife, and I wouldn't live alone like a dog!" Alfio said, laughing.

Mena didn't know what to say, and then Alfio added: "Now that you have the *Provvidenza* in the water, they'll marry you off to Brasi Cipolla."

"My grandfather hasn't told me anything."

"He'll tell you later. There's still time. Who knows how many things will happen from now until you get married, and what roads I'll travel with my cart? They say that on the plain, behind the city, there's work for everybody on the railroad. Now that Santuzza's made a deal with Massaro Filippo for the wine, there's nothing more for me to do here."

Master Cipolla, though, despite the fact that the Malavoglia were back in the saddle again, went on shaking his head and proclaiming that they were riding a horse without legs; he knew where all that boat's rotten spots were hidden under the new pitch.

"A patched-up Providence!" the pharmacist sneered. "Stuck together with syrup and mucilage, like our constitutional monarchy. Just wait, they'll make Master 'Ntoni pay a property tax on her."

"They'll even make us pay for the water we drink. Now they say that they're going to put a tax on pitch. That's why Master 'Ntoni hurried to get his boat ready, although Mastro Turi Zuppiddo still has fifty lire coming to him."

"Uncle Crocifisso is the one who knows what he's doing, selling the lupin credit to Piedipapera."

"Now, if the Malavoglia aren't lucky, Piedipapera will take the house by the medlar tree, and Compare Turi will get the *Provvidenza*."

Meanwhile the *Provvidenza* had slid into the sea like a duck, her beak in the air. She wallowed in it, enjoying the cool breeze, swaying softly in the green water, which lapped lightly at her sides, while the sun danced on her new paint. Master 'Ntoni reveled in it, too, standing with his hands behind his back and his legs spread apart, frowning a little, as sailors do when they want to see something in the sun. It was a bright winter sun, the fields were green and the sea was gleaming and the sky was a deep, bottomless blue. So the bright sun and the mild winter mornings return even for eyes which have wept and have seen them as black as tar, and all is reborn, like the *Provvidenza,* which had needed only a little pitch and paint and four boards to return to what she'd been; and only eyes which are closed by death can no longer cry or see.

"Bastianazzo was denied this happiness," Maruzza thought to herself, walking to and fro in front of the loom, filling in the weft. Her husband had made those bars and crossbars for her with his own hands, and he himself had fixed them to the wall. Every object in the house still spoke of him. His umbrella stood in the corner and his shoes, almost brand-new, under the bed. Mena, as she sized the warp, had a heavy heart too, thinking of Compare Alfio, who was leaving for Bicocca and was going to sell his donkey, poor beast!—because the young have short memories and eyes only for the rising sun, while only the old, who've seen the sun go down so many times, look to where it sets.

"Now that they've put the *Provvidenza* to sea," Maruzza finally said, seeing her daughter so downcast, "your grandfather is talking with Master Cipolla again. This morning too I saw them together, from the landing. They were in front of Peppi Naso's shed."

"Master Fortunato is rich and doesn't have to work, so he can hang around the piazza all day," Mena answered.

"Yes, and his son Brasi has God's own plenty. Now that we have our boat, and our men don't have to hire out, we'll also get on our feet; and if the souls in purgatory help us get rid of the lupin debt, we can begin to take care of other things. Your grandfather isn't asleep, you can be sure, and when it comes to such things you won't even know you've lost your father, because he's a second father to you."

Soon after Master 'Ntoni came home so loaded down with nets that he was completely covered and you couldn't even see his face. "I went to get them back from Master Cipolla's trawler," he said. "I've got to look them over, for tomorrow we'll fit out the *Provvidenza*."

"Why didn't you get 'Ntoni to help you?" Maruzza asked, pulling at one end while the old man spun around like a reel in the middle of the courtyard to unwind the nets, which never seemed to end. He looked like a snake with a long tail.

"I left him at Mastro Pizzuto's. Poor boy, he has to work all week! And even in January you sweat, carrying all this stuff on your back."

Alessi laughed, seeing his grandfather so flushed and bent like a fishhook. "Listen," his grandfather said to him, "that poor La Locca's right outside. Her son is knocking around the piazza and they have nothing to eat." Maruzza sent Alessio to La Locca with some broad beans, and the old man, mopping his sweat with his shirt sleeve, said: "Now that we have our boat, if nothing happens before the summer, with the help of the Lord that debt will be paid." That was all he ever talked about, and then he sat down under the medlar tree, gazing at his nets as if he could already see them full of fish.

"Now we've got to lay in a stock of salt, before they put a tax on it, if it's true what they say," he went on, his hands under his armpits. "We'll pay Compare Zuppiddo with the first money we make, and he promised me that then he'll give us a stock of kegs on credit."

"There are five onze from Mena's weaving in the chest of drawers," Maruzza said.

"Good! I don't want to run up any more debts with Uncle Crocifisso, because my heart warns me not to, after the lupin deal. But he'll surely give us thirty lire the first time we go to sea in the *Provvidenza*."

"Don't go near him!" cried La Longa. "Uncle Crocifisso's money brings bad luck. Last night again I heard the black hen crow."

"Poor creature!" the old man said, smiling as he watched the black hen strut around the courtyard with her tail in the air and her comb flopping over her ear, as though they weren't talking about her. "She even lays an egg every day."

Mena then came to the door and said: "There's a basketful of eggs, and Monday, if Compare Alfio goes to Catania, you can send them to be sold at the market."

"Yes, they'll help pay off the debt, too," Master 'Ntoni agreed. "But you ought to eat an egg yourself every now and then, when you want one."

"We don't want any," said Maruzza, and Mena added: "If we eat them, Compare Alfio won't have any to sell at the market. Now we're going to put duck eggs under the hen, and ducklings sell for eight soldi each." Her grandfather looked at her and said: "You're a real Malavoglia, my girl!"

Out in the sunlight the chickens were ruffling their feathers in the dirt of the yard, while the hen, bedraggled, her feathers drooping, sat in a corner and shook her beak. Along the wall, under the green, leafy boughs of the garden, more cloth was bleaching in the sun, hanging from poles and kept in place at the bottom by stones.

"All this stuff makes money," Master 'Ntoni said. "And with the help of God, they won't throw us out of the house. As they say: 'My home is my mother.' "

Meanwhile Piedipapera was saying: "Now the Malavoglia must pray to God and Saint Francis that they catch plenty of fish."

"Especially with the bad years we're having!" Master Cipolla exclaimed. "Because, from the way it looks, they've thrown the cholera into the sea for the fish, too."

Compare Mangiacarrube nodded in agreement, and Uncle Cola went back to talking about the tax on salt that they wanted to levy, and if they did, the anchovies could rest easy and no longer be frightened by the steamboats' paddle wheels, because nobody would go out fishing for them anymore.

"And they've thought up something else!" added Mastro Turi, the caulker. "They're also going to put a tax on pitch." Those who didn't care about pitch kept silent; but Zuppiddo continued to shout that he'd shut down, and that anybody who had to caulk his boat could use his wife's petticoat for tow. Then the shouting and cursing began in earnest. At that very moment they heard the whistle of the engine, and the railroad cars suddenly appeared on the side of the hill, out of the hole they'd dug in it, smoking and snorting as though possessed by the devil. "There you are!" Master Fortunato Cipolla concluded. "The railroad on one side and the steamboats on the other. I swear, you can't live at Trezza anymore!"

When they actually tried to put the tax on pitch, the village went into a fury. La Zuppidda, foaming at the mouth, got up on her landing to proclaim that this was just another one of Don Silvestro's dirty tricks. He was out to ruin the village, because the Zuppiddi hadn't wanted him for a husband: why, they didn't even want to walk in the same procession with that man, neither she nor her daughter! Whenever Comare Venera spoke about the man her daughter was supposed to marry, you'd have thought that she herself was to be the bride. Mastro Turi was going to shut down, she said, and then she wanted to see how people would keep their boats in the water. They'd end up by eating each other, instead of bread. When they heard her, all the women came to their doorways, carrying their distaffs and howling that they wanted to kill them all, all those tax collectors, and set fire to their papers and to the house where they kept them. When the men came back from fishing, they left their nets to dry and stood at the windows, watching the revolution their wives were making.

"It's all because Master 'Ntoni's 'Ntoni returned," Comare Venera went on. "And he's always there, hanging onto my daughter's skirts. It's horns that are bothering Don Silvestro. Anyway, what is he after—we just don't want him! My daughter is my property, and I can give her to whomever I please and choose. I told Mastro Callà 'no' right to his face, when he came in person to ask us, and Uncle Santoro heard me. Don Silvestro can make that puppet of a mayor do whatever he wishes; but I don't give a rap for both the town clerk and the mayor. Now they're trying to make us shut down because I won't let just anybody take my property. You call such people Christians? Why don't they increase their tax on wine? Or on meat, which nobody eats? But this wouldn't suit Massaro Filippo, because of Santuzza. They're both in mortal sin, and she wears the scapular of the Daughters of Mary to hide her filthy deeds, and that cuckold, Uncle Santoro, doesn't see a thing. Everyone brings grist to his own mill, like Compare Naso, who's fatter than his own pigs! We're in the hands of a bunch of stinking fish heads. But now we're going to chop off all those rotten heads!"

Mastro Turi Zuppiddo stamped up and down on his landing, brandishing his mallet, and bellowing that he was out to shed blood and not even chains could hold him back. The anger ran from door to door, swelling like waves in a stormy sea. Don Franco, his large hat on his head, rubbed his hands and declared that the people were rising; and when he saw Don Michele walk by, his pistol hanging on his belly, he laughed right in his face. The men had gradually let themselves be worked up by their women, and went looking for each other to talk and feed their anger. They wasted whole days standing in the piazza with their arms folded and their mouths agape, listening to the pharmacist, who, in a low voice, so that his wife upstairs shouldn't hear, was telling them not to be fools and to go ahead and make a revolution. They shouldn't bother with the tax on salt or the tax on pitch, but should make a clean sweep, for the people must be king. Some of them, however, sneered and turned their backs on him, saying: *"He* wants to be the king. The pharmacist preaches revolution so that he can starve the poor people!" And they preferred to go to Santuzza's tavern, where they could be excited by good wine instead, and Compare Cinghialenta and Rocco Spatu drank more and got angrier than ten men put together. Now that that old story of the taxes was starting again, they would certainly bring up the tax on "hair," as they called the tax on beasts of burden, and also the increase in the wine tax. "Holy devil! this time it's going to end up badly, by God!"

The good wine made them shout, and the shouting made them thirsty, especially since the tax on wine hadn't been increased yet; and those who had been drinking shook their fists, their shirt sleeves rolled back, and even got sore at the flies because they were flying.

"This is like a feast day for Santuzza!" they said. La

Locca's son, who had no money for drink, shouted outside the tavern door that he might as well be dead, now that his Uncle Crocifisso didn't want him even at half pay, because his brother Menico had drowned with the lupins. Vanni Pizzuto had also closed his shop, since nobody came to be shaved anymore, and he carried his razor in his pocket, and from a distance vomited insults and spat at those who shrugged and went about their business, their oars over their shoulders. "They're swine, who don't give a damn for their country!" Don Franco bellowed, pulling at his pipe as if he wanted to eat it. "People who wouldn't lift a finger for their country."

"Let them talk," Master 'Ntoni said to his grandson, who wanted to break his oar over the heads of those who called him a swine. "With all their talk, they won't give us bread, nor take a penny of our debt off our shoulders."

Uncle Crocifisso, who was the sort that minded his own business and, for fear of worse, tried to gulp down his anger in silence when they bled him with taxes, no longer even showed up in the piazza to lean against the base of the bell tower, but stayed holed up in his house, in the dark, reciting Our Fathers and Hail Marys to help him digest his rage against all those people shrieking outside. All they wanted to do was put the village to fire and sword and rob anyone who had a little money in the house. "He's got plenty of reason to hide!" they all said in the village. "Because he must have barrels of money. Now he's even got the five hundred lire for the lupins that Piedipapera gave him."

But La Vespa, who had all her property in land and wasn't afraid they'd steal it from her, went around with her face as black as a smoking coal, her hands waving and hair flying, screaming on his behalf. She said that every six months her uncle was eaten alive by the land tax, and that she was going to scratch out the tax collector's eyes with her own hands, if he ever visited her uncle again. She was always buzzing around Comare Grazia, Cousin Anna, and the Mangiacarrube girl with one excuse or another, to find out what was going on between Compare Alfio and Saint Agatha, and the truth is she would have liked to destroy

Saint Agatha, together with all the Malavoglia. So she went around saying that it wasn't true that Piedipapera had bought the lupin credit, because Piedipapera had never had five hundred lire to his name, and the Malavoglia still had Uncle Crocifisso's foot on their necks. He was so rich that he could crush them like ants, and she'd been wrong to turn him down for the lovely eyes of a man who had nothing but a donkey cart, while Uncle Crocifisso cherished her like the apple of his eye, although, just at that moment, he wouldn't open his door for her because he was afraid that the people would rush into his house and put it to fire and sword.

People who had something to lose, like Master Cipolla and Massaro Filippo, the gardener, stayed shut up in the house, their doors locked and barred, and didn't even dare to stick their noses out. And Brasi Cipolla's father gave Brasi a great clout when he caught him at the courtyard door, staring into the piazza like a blockhead. During the squall, the big fish, even those who weren't too smart, stayed under water and remained in hiding, leaving Silkworm, the mayor, to fend for himself, his nose in the air, searching for that leaf to nibble on.

"Can't you see that they're just using you like a puppet?" his daughter Betta said to him, her hands on her hips. "Now that they've got you into the mess, they turn their backs and leave you alone to thrash in the muck. That's what you get for letting that scoundrel Don Silvestro lead you by the nose."

"I don't let anybody lead me by the nose!" Silkworm retorted. "I'm the mayor, and not Don Silvestro."

But Don Silvestro said that his daughter Betta was the mayor, and that Mastro Croce Callà wore the pants by mistake. So, with the two of them, poor Silkworm was between the hammer and the anvil. And now that the storm had risen, and they'd all left him alone to put the halter on that wild beast of a mob, he didn't know which way to turn.

"What do you care?" Betta yelled at him. "Do as the others do; and if they don't want the tax on pitch, let Don Silvestro think up something."

But Don Silvestro was adamant; he continued to walk

about with that brazen face of his; and whenever they saw him, Rocco Spatu and Cinghialenta rushed back into the tavern to avoid doing something they'd be sorry for, and Vanni Pizzuto swore at the top of his lungs, his hand on the razor in his pocket.

Don Silvestro, ignoring them, went to chat with Uncle Santoro and to put a few cents in his hand.

"Praised be the Lord!" the blind man cried. "This is Don Silvestro, the town clerk, because nobody else of all those who come here to shout and bang their fists on the benches ever offers a cent of alms for the souls in purgatory. They come here and say that they want to kill them all, both the mayor and the town clerk. They've all said it —Vanni Pizzuto, Rocco Spatu, and Compare Cinghialenta. Vanni Pizzuto is walking around without shoes, so I won't recognize him. But I recognize him anyway, because he drags his feet on the ground and kicks up as much dust as when a flock of sheep goes by."

"What do you care?" Santuzza said to Uncle Santoro, as soon as Don Silvestro had left. "It's none of your business. A tavern is like a seaport, people come and people go, and you've got to be friends with everyone and faithful to no one. That's why each person has his own soul and must tend to his own interests, and not pass reckless judgments on his neighbor. Compare Cinghialenta and Rocco Spatu spend a lot of money here. I won't say the same of Pizzuto, who sells anise in his shop and tries to steal our customers."

After this, Don Silvestro went to talk to the pharmacist, who shoved his beard right in his face and told him that it was time to put an end to the whole system, blow up everything, and start from scratch.

"Do you want to bet that this time there'll be hell to pay?" Don Silvestro retorted, slipping two fingers into his vest pocket to pull out a brand-new twelve tarì coin. "All their taxes won't cover this, and one of these days we'll have to put an end to it. The tune has to be changed altogether, what with this Silkworm who lets his daughter put a skirt on him, while she acts the mayor." Besides, Master Cipolla felt he was too good for it and said he wouldn't be mayor, even if they slaughtered him, and Massaro Filippo didn't give a damn. "They're a pack of reactionaries. Idiots who say white today and black tomorrow, and the last person they listen to is right. The people have reason to complain against this government which sucks our blood worse than a leech, but somebody will have to pay, by hook or crook. What we need is a mayor with a head on his shoulders, and a liberal like you."

Then the pharmacist began telling what he'd do if he were mayor, and how he would fix up everything; and Don Silvestro listened, silent and intent, as if he were listening to a sermon in church. First of all, the town council had to be overhauled; Master 'Ntoni shouldn't be put on it because he had weird ideas, and had caused his son Bastianazzo's death—now there was a levelheaded man, if he were only alive!—and besides, in that lupin deal, he had gotten his daughter-in-law to sign for the debt and had left her with only the shirt on her back. Imagine if he took care of the town's interests in the same way! . . .

But if the Signora appeared at the window, Don Franco changed the subject and said: "Fine weather, eh?" winking at Don Silvestro to let him understand what he would have really liked to say to her. And Don Silvestro thought to himself: "How can you trust the talk of a man who's afraid of his wife?"

Master 'Ntoni was one of those who shrugged and left with their oars over their backs; and to his grandson, who would have liked to rush into the piazza with the others and see what was afoot, he kept saying: "Mind your own business, because each one of them is only yelling about his own interest. And our biggest interest is the debt we have to pay."

Compare Mosca also went about his own business and drove his cart quietly through the town, right past the people who were shouting and shaking their fists in the air. "Don't you care if they put the tax on 'hair'?" Mena asked him, when she saw him arrive, with his donkey panting and its ears drooping.

"Of course I care, but I've got to keep going if I want to pay it."

"I've heard that they want to kill them all, God preserve us! My grandfather has warned me to keep the door closed and to open it only when they get back. Are you going away tomorrow too?"

"I'm going to haul a load of wine for Mastro Croce Callà."

"Why do that? Don't you know he's the mayor, and they'll kill you, too?"

"He says that he doesn't care. He's a mason and he has to repair the vineyard wall for Massaro Filippo, and if they don't want the tax on pitch, then Don Silvestro will have to think up something."

"Didn't I tell you? It's all Don Silvestro's doing!" cried La Zuppidda, who was always there to fan the fire, her distaff in her hand. "It's all the doing of thieves and people who have nothing to lose and won't pay a cent for the tax on pitch, because they've never had so much as a piece of rotten plank at sea." After that she went shouting angrily all over the village: "It's Don Silvestro's fault and the fault of that swindler Piedipapera, who has no boats and lives off his neighbor, and holds the sack for others to put the loot in. Do you want to know something? It's not true at all that he bought Uncle Crocifisso's credit. That's all a fake that he and Dumbbell got up between them to rob those poor people. Piedipapera doesn't even know what five hundred lire look like!"

Don Silvestro, to hear what was being said about him, often went to buy cigars at the tavern, and whenever he came in Rocco Spatu and Vanni Pizzuto would go out cursing. Or he would stop to chat with Uncle Santoro, on his way back from his vineyard, and so he got to know the whole story of Piedipapera's fake purchase of the lupin credit. But he was a "Christian," with a stomach as deep as a well, and he stored it all away. He knew what he was about, and when Betta jumped at him, baring her teeth like a mad dog, and Mastro Croce Callà said he didn't care, Don Silvestro replied: "Do you want to bet that I'll leave you in the lurch now?"—and from then on he stayed away from the mayor's house. Now they'd have to get out of the mess by themselves, and Betta wouldn't have the chance to shout in his face that he wanted to ruin her father Callà, and that his advice was the advice of a Judas, who'd sold Christ for thirty pieces of silver, and that he did all this to overthrow the mayor for his own ends and rule the roost in the village.

So on Sunday when the council was supposed to meet, after Holy Mass Don Silvestro settled in the big room which used to be the headquarters of the National Guard, sitting at the fir table and quietly cutting quills to pass the time, while La Zuppidda and the other women gathered outside on the street, spinning in the sun, and screaming that they wanted to scratch all the councilmen's eyes out.

They went to get Silkworm, who was working on Massaro Filippo's vineyard wall. He put on his new jacket, washed his hands, brushed off the lime dust, but wouldn't budge unless they brought Don Silvestro. In vain Betta shouted at him and pushed him out of the house by his shoulders, telling him that those who made the soup had to eat it and that, so long as they let him be mayor, he should leave it to the others. But this time Mastro Callà, who'd seen that mob in front of the council hall, brandishing their distaffs, dug in his heels, as stubborn as a mule. "I won't go unless Don Silvestro comes!" he kept repeating, his eyes starting out of his head. "Don Silvestro will find a way out."

"I'll find the way out," Betta replied. "They don't want the tax on pitch? Well, then, forget about it."

"Fine! And where will we get the money from?"

"Where will you get the money from? Make those who've got it pay—Uncle Crocifisso, for instance, or Master Cipolla, or Peppi Naso."

"Fine! But they're councilmen!"

"Then send them packing and get other councilmen. After all, they won't let you stay on as mayor, when everybody else no longer wants you. You've got to satisfy the majority."

"You see, that's how women reason! As if it were the majority that kept me in office! You don't know a thing. The mayor is made by the councilmen, and the councilmen can only be those and no others. Who do you want them to be? The beggars in the middle of the street?"

"Then forget about the councilmen and discharge that swindler Don Silvestro."

"Fine! And who can be the town clerk? Who can do it?

You or I or Master Cipolla, though he spews out wisdom like a philosopher?"

To that Betta had nothing to say, so she relieved her feelings by heaping all sorts of insults on the shoulders of Don Silvestro, who was the tyrant of the village and kept them all in his pocket.

"Fine!" added Silkworm. "You've just said it, if he isn't there I don't know what to say. I'd like to see you in my shoes!"

At last Don Silvestro arrived, his face looking harder than a stone wall and his hands clasped behind his back, whistling a tune. "Ah, now, Mastro Croce, don't lose heart. The world won't collapse this time!" Mastro Croce let Don Silvestro take him in tow and set him behind the fir table in the council room, the inkwell in front of him. But there weren't any councilmen present except Peppi Naso, the butcher, all greasy and red in the face, who wasn't afraid of anyone in this world, and Compare Tino Piedipapera. "Piedipapera has nothing to lose!" La Zuppidda yelled through the doorway. "He comes here to suck the blood of the poor, worse than a leech, because he lives off his neighbor and holds the sack for others to put the loot in! They're all thieves and murderers!"

Piedipapera, though he tried to look unconcerned to uphold the dignity of his position, finally lost his temper, reared up on his crooked leg and turned to Mastro Cirino, the usher, who had to maintain order and for this purpose, when he wasn't working as sexton, wore a cap with a red band. "See that that viper shuts up!"

"You'd like everybody to shut up, wouldn't you, Compare Tino?" La Zuppidda shouted.

"As if everybody didn't know what you spend your time doing, and then you close your eyes when Master 'Ntoni's 'Ntoni comes to talk with your daughter Barbara."

"You're the one who closes his eyes, you cuckold! when your wife covers up for La Vespa who comes and stands at your door every day to see Compare Alfio, and the two of you hold the candle for them. That's what you do! But Compare Alfio doesn't want any part of her, take my word for it. All he thinks about is Master 'Ntoni's

Mena, and you people are wasting your candle wax if La Vespa promised to pay you for your trouble."

"And now I'll split your head for you!" threatened Piedipapera, and he began scrambling up from behind the fir table.

"There'll be hell to pay today!" Mastro Croce muttered.

"Is this the way to act? Do you think you're out in the piazza!" shouted Don Silvestro. "Do you want to bet that I'll throw the lot of you out of here, with a kick in the behind? Now I'm going to settle this whole matter!"

La Zuppidda wouldn't hear of settling anything, and she struggled with Don Silvestro, who grabbed her by the hair and pushed her outside, shoving her into a corner behind a gate nearby.

"Now tell me, what do you want?" he asked her when they were alone. "What does it matter to you if they put a tax on pitch? Are you and your husband going to pay for it? Or won't those who get their boats repaired have to pay for it? Now listen to me! Your husband is a fool to be angry with the council, and to make all this trouble. Now we've got to appoint new councilmen to replace Master Cipolla and Massaro Mariano, who are good for nothing, and we might put your husband in."

"I don't know anything," replied La Zuppidda, suddenly quieted. "I don't meddle in my husband's affairs. But I know that he's tearing his hair with rage. All I can do is go and tell him, if you're sure about it."

"Go and tell him. I'm sure, as sure as there's a God, believe me. Are we or aren't we honest people, holy devil!"

La Zuppidda ran off to get her husband, who was crouching in a corner of the courtyard carding tow, pale as a corpse, and didn't want to go out for all the gold in the world, shouting that they'd make him do something he'd regret, by God!

To open the Sanhedrin and to see which way the cat would jump they still had to wait for Master Fortunato Cipolla, and Massaro Filippo, the vegetable gardener, who were taking ages to get there, so that people began to get bored and the women had started to spin, standing along the low wall around the church.

At last both of them sent word that they weren't coming because they were busy; and that if the others wished, they could levy the tax without them. "That's just what my daughter Betta told me!" grumbled Mastro Croce Giufà.

"Then get your daughter Betta to help you!" exclaimed Don Silvestro. Silkworm didn't breathe another word and went on grumbling to himself.

"Now," said Don Silvestro, "you'll see if the Zuppiddi don't come of their own accord to say that they'll give me Barbara's hand, but they'll have to beg me."

The session was closed without having settled anything. The town clerk wanted to take a little time to think things over. In the meantime the noonday bell had rung and the women had all scurried home. The few who remained, when they saw Mastro Cirino lock the door and put the keys in his pocket, went about their business too, talking about the insults Piedipapera and Zuppidda had flung at each other.

That evening Master 'Ntoni's 'Ntoni heard the talk, and, God damn it, he was going to show Piedipapera that he hadn't been away in the navy for nothing. He met him near the Zuppiddi house, just as he was coming from the lava field, hobbling on that devil's foot of his, and he began to tell him off, saying that he was a swine and should watch out what he said about the Zuppiddi and their doings, because it was none of his business. But Piedipapera hadn't lost his tongue either. "Do you think you've come back here to be a bully?"

"I've come to beat you up, if you say another word." Hearing the shouts, the people ran out and a big crowd gathered. So then they really started fighting, and Piedipapera, who was cleverer than the devil, let himself fall to the ground in a heap with 'Ntoni Malavoglia, since like that 'Ntoni got no advantage from his stronger legs, and they rolled in the mud hitting and biting each other like Peppi Naso's dogs. In the end Master 'Ntoni's 'Ntoni had to hide in the Zuppiddi's yard, for his shirt was all torn, while Piedipapera was led home, bleeding like Lazarus.

"The next thing we'll see," Comare Venera was still screaming after she'd slammed the door in the neighbors' faces, "the next thing we'll see is that I can no longer do as I please and choose in my own house. I'll give my daughter to anybody I want to give her to."

The girl, blushing, had hidden inside the house, her heart quivering like a scared rabbit's.

"He almost tore your ear off!" said Compare Turi, carefully pouring water over 'Ntoni's head. "He bites worse than a Corsican dog, that Tino!" But 'Ntoni still had his blood up and wanted to wreak havoc and slaughter.

"Listen, Comare Venera," he said after a while, in front of them all. "If I don't get your daughter, I won't marry at all." And the girl in her room could hear him. "Compare 'Ntoni," Venera answered, "this isn't the right time to discuss it; but if your grandfather agrees, I, for my part, wouldn't exchange you for King Victor Emmanuel." Compare Zuppiddo kept silent, handing him a piece of cloth to dry himself with; and that evening 'Ntoni went home quite happy.

But when they heard about the fight with Piedipapera, the poor Malavoglia expected any moment to see the bailiff come and chase them out of their house, for Easter was approaching and after great efforts they'd scraped together only half of the money to pay the debt.

"You see what it means to hang around where there are girls to be married off!" La Longa said to 'Ntoni. "Now all the village is talking about you. And I'm sorry for Barbara."

"But I'll take her!" 'Ntoni cried.

"You'll take her?" his grandfather exclaimed. "And who am I? And doesn't your mother count for anything? When your father took a wife, and she's the woman you see there, he waited for me to say so. Your grandmother was alive and she came to talk to me about it in the garden, under the fig tree. Now these things are no longer the custom, and the old people have no use anymore. Once upon a time they used to say: 'Listen to the old folks and you won't go wrong!' First your sister has to get married. You know that, don't you?"

"Damn my luck!" 'Ntoni began to yell, tearing his hair and stamping his feet. "I work all day! I can't go to the tavern! And I never have a penny in my pocket!

And now that I've found a girl that suits me, I can't take her! So why did I come back from the navy?"

"Listen here!" his grandfather cried, straightening up with an effort, because of those pains that gnawed at his back. "The best thing you can do is go to bed. You should never talk like that in front of your mother!"

"My brother Luca, down there in the navy, is better off!" 'Ntoni grumbled as he went off to bed.

CHAPTER EIGHT

Luca, poor fellow, was neither better off nor worse. He did his duty down there as he'd done it at home, and made the best of it. He didn't write often, that's true—a stamp cost twenty centesimi—nor had he sent his photograph as yet, for when he was a boy they'd all made fun of his big donkey ears. Instead, from time to time he'd put in his letter a five lire note, which he managed to earn doing odd jobs for the officers.

Master 'Ntoni had said: "First Mena has to be married." He didn't talk about it, but he always thought about it, and now that they had some money in the chest of drawers towards paying the debt, he figured that after salting the anchovies they would pay Piedipapera and then the house would be freed for his granddaughter's dowry. So he and Master Fortunato Cipolla had been whispering a few times on the shore, while waiting for the trawler to come in, or sitting in the sun in front of the church, when there were no other people around. Master Fortunato didn't want to go back on his word, if the girl really had a dowry, especially since his son Brasi was always a worry to him, running after girls who had nothing at all, like a regular fool.

"A man is known by his word, and an ox by its horns," he would always say.

Mena often had a heavy heart as she sat at the loom weaving, because girls have a keen nose for such things, and now that her grandfather was always putting his head together with Compare Fortunato, and often mentioned the Cipolla at home, she always had the same sight before her eyes, as if that poor fellow, Compare Alfio, were glued to the frame of the loom together with the pictures of the saints. One evening she waited till late for Compare Alfio to return with his donkey cart. She held her hands under apron because it was cold. All the doors of the houses were shut, and not a soul was to be seen on the road. Then she called to him from her doorway, and after a while she asked: "Are you going to Bicocca at the beginning of the month?"

"Not yet. I still have more than a hundred cartloads of wine for Santuzza. After that, God will provide."

She didn't know what else to say, as Compare Alfio worked in his yard, unharnessing the donkey and hanging his gear on the peg, and going about here and there with his lantern. "If you go to Bicocca, who knows when we'll see each other again!" Mena said at last in a faltering voice.

"Why do you say that? Are you going away too?"

The poor girl hesitated for a while before answering, although it was dark and no one could see her face. From time to time you could hear the neighbors talking behind the closed doors, and the children crying, and the clatter of soup bowls as they ate, so nobody could hear her either. "Now we have half the money we need for Piedipapera, and after the salting of the anchovies we'll also pay the rest."

When he heard this, Alfio left the donkey in the middle of the yard and came out on the road. "Then they'll marry you off after Easter?"

Mena didn't reply. "I told you so!" Compare Alfio said. "I myself saw Master 'Ntoni talking with Master Cipolla."

"It will be as God wishes!" Mena said. "I wasn't anxious to get married, as long as they let me live here."

"What a fine thing it is," Mosca said, "to be rich like Master Cipolla's son, who can take the wife he wants and can live where he pleases!"

"Good night, Compare Alfio," Mena said, after staring for a while at the lantern hanging on the gate and the donkey munching at the nettles along the wall. Compare Alfio also said good night, and went back to put the donkey in the stall.

"That brazen Saint Agatha," muttered La Vespa, who was popping in and out the Piedipapera house at all hours on one pretext or another, pretending that she wanted to borrow a pair of knitting needles or give them some broad beans which she had gathered from her plot of land. "That brazen Saint Agatha never lets Compare Mosca alone. She doesn't even give him a minute to scratch his head! Shame on her!" And she was still grumbling on the street when Piedipapera shut the door, sticking his tongue out after her.

"La Vespa is so infuriated you'd think it was July," Compare Tino sneered.

"Why does she care?" asked Comare Grazia.

"She cares because she's got it in for anyone who gets married, and now she's set her eyes on Alfio Mosca."

"You should tell her that I don't like to hold the candle. As if it weren't clear that she comes here for Compare Alfio, and then La Zuppidda goes around saying that we do it because there's something in it for us."

"Zuppidda would do better to scratch her own head, because she has plenty to scratch! What with that dirty business of dragging Master 'Ntoni's 'Ntoni into her house while the old man and all his family kick up a fuss, because they don't want any part of it. Close the window. Today I spent a half hour enjoying the comedy between 'Ntoni and Barbara, and my back still hurts from crouching behind the wall to overhear what they were saying. 'Ntoni had slipped away from the *Provvidenza* with the excuse of going to fetch the big harpoon for the mullet. And he said to her: 'If my grandfather doesn't agree, what shall we do?' And she answered: 'What shall we do? We'll run away together, and then when it's done, they'll have to worry about marrying us and they'll have to say yes.' And her mother was inside listening, I'll wager these two eyes of mine! A nice part that witch is playing! Now I want the whole village to have a good laugh. When I told him about it, Don Silvestro said that he bet he'd make Barbara fall at his feet, like a ripe pear. Don't bolt the door because I'm waiting for Rocco Spatu, who's supposed to come and see me."

Don Silvestro, to make Barbara fall at his feet, had thought up a trick which the monk who gives the lottery numbers wouldn't have been clever enough to think of. "I'm going to get rid of all those fellows who are trying to take Barbara away from me," he said. "When there'll no longer be anybody she can marry, then they'll have to come and beg me and I'll make a nice bargain, like they do at the fair when buyers are scarce."

Vanni Pizzuto was one of the men who had tried to take Barbara, when he'd gone to shave Mastro Turi at his house because he'd had an attack of rheumatism. Another one was Don Michele who, when he wasn't boring himself strolling up and down with his pistol dangling at his belly, without a thing to do, stood behind Santuzza's counter, winking at the pretty girls, just to kill time. At first Barbara had responded to his wink; but afterwards, when her mother told her that such fellows were nothing but parasites and spies, and that all a foreigner deserved was to be whipped, she had slammed the window in his face, despite his mustaches and his visored cap with the gold braid. And Don Michele had eaten his heart out with frustration, and simply for spite had continued to walk up and down her street, twisting his mustaches and with his cap pulled down grimly over his eyes. On Sundays he would put on his plumed hat and go to Vanni Pizzuto's shop to shoot a glowering, meaningful glance at her as she went to Mass with her mother. Don Silvestro also started going there to get shaved, warm himself at the hot water brazier, and exchange jokes with the men who were waiting for Mass to end.

"That Barbara can't take her eyes off 'Ntoni Malavoglia," Don Silvestro said. "Do you want to bet twelve tarì that he gets her? Can't you see how he's waiting for her over there, with his hands in his pockets?"

At that Vanni Pizzuto left Don Michele with the lather on his face and looked out the door.

"What a beautiful piece that girl is! And look how she walks all wrapped up with her nose in her shawl—she looks like a spindle! And to think that she'll be gobbled up by that lout 'Ntoni Malavoglia!"

"If Piedipapera insists on being paid, 'Ntoni won't get

her, take my word for it. The Malavoglia will have something else to worry about if Piedipapera grabs the house
by the medlar tree."

Vanni Pizzuto came back and seized Don Michele by
the nose again. "Well, what do you say, Don Michele?
You were lovesick for her, too. But she's the kind of girl
who makes a man eat gall."

Don Michele didn't say a word, brushed his uniform,
prinked his mustaches, and adjusted his hat in front of the
mirror. "You need more than a plumed hat for that girl!"
Pizzuto snickered.

At last one day Don Michele replied to these taunts:
"Holy devil! if it weren't for this plumed hat, I would
make that lout Malavoglia hold the candle for me." Don
Silvestro made sure to tell all this to 'Ntoni, saying that
Don Michele wasn't the sort of man to tangle with, and
that he certainly must have it in for him.

"I'll laugh right in Don Michele's face!" 'Ntoni replied.
"I know why he has it in for me; but he can wipe his
mouth now, because this time he isn't going to eat, and
he'd do better not to wear out shoe leather parading up
and down past the Zuppiddi house, wearing his braided
cap as if he had a crown on his head; because people
don't give a damn for him and his cap."

Whenever 'Ntoni met Don Michele he stared straight at
him, narrowing his eyes, as befits a spunky young man
who's been in the navy and won't let anyone jostle him.
But Don Michele continued to walk up and down that
particular street, as a matter of principle, so that 'Ntoni
shouldn't think he'd won, because, if it weren't for that
plumed hat of his, he would have finished him off in one
bite, like a piece of bread.

"They'll finish each other off!" Vanni Pizzuto told all
those who came to be shaved, or buy cigars, or fishing
lines, or hooks, or bone buttons, the kind that sell five for
a grano. "One of these days Don Michele and 'Ntoni
Malavoglia will finish each other off in one bite, like a
piece of bread. It's that blessed plumed hat that ties Don
Michele's hands. He'd be willing to pay Piedipapera to
get that lout 'Ntoni out of his way." And he talked about
it so much that La Locca's son, who roamed about all day

long without work, his arms dangling at his sides, whenever he met them stuck to their heels to see what was
going to happen.

Piedipapera, when he went for a shave and heard that
Don Michele was willing to pay him to get 'Ntoni Malavoglia out of his way, swelled like a turkey cock, because
this showed how important he was in the village.

Vanni Pizzuto kept telling him: "The sergeant would
pay anything to hold the Malavoglia in his fist, like you
do. Why on earth did you let 'Ntoni off so easily after that
beating he gave you?"

Piedipapera shrugged and continued to warm his hands
over the brazier.

Don Silvestro laughed and said: "Mastro Vanni would
like Piedipapera to pull the chestnuts out of the fire for
him. We all know that Comare Venera wants no part of
foreigners or braided caps; so if he got rid of 'Ntoni Malavoglia, Vanni would be the only one left courting the girl."

Vanni Pizzuto said nothing, but he thought about it all
night.

"After all, it wouldn't be a bad idea!" he said to himself. "It's all a matter of grabbing Piedipapera by the
throat at the right moment."

The right moment soon arrived, and it seemed made on
purpose for him. One evening Rocco Spatu hadn't shown
up and when it was quite late Piedipapera, pale and with
his eyes bugging out of his head, came looking for him
two or three times at Pizzuto's shop. The customs guards
had been seen running all over the place, in a flurry, their
noses to the ground like hunting dogs, and Don Michele
was with them, his pistol on his belly and his pants stuffed
into his boots. "You could do Don Michele a great favor
if you got 'Ntoni Malavoglia out of his way," Pizzuto said
again to Compare Tino who, just to buy a cigar, hid in
the darkest corner of the shop. "You'd be doing him a
tremendous favor, and you'd really make a friend of him."

"I wish I could!" sighed Piedipapera, and that's all he
said because that evening he was out of breath.

That night they heard rifle shots from out towards Il
Rotolo and all along the beach, so that it seemed the
quail hunt was on. "Some quail!" the fisherman muttered,

sitting up in bed to listen. "They're quails with shoes on their feet, the kind that smuggle sugar and coffee and silk kerchiefs. Last night Don Michele was roving the streets with his pants stuffed in his boots and his pistol on his belly!"

Before dawn, when the lantern was still burning in front of the door, Piedipapera was already in Pizzuto's shop drinking a glass of anise; but he looked as dejected as the dog that's broken the pot. He didn't crack the usual jokes, and he kept asking everyone what that uproar had been about last night, and whether they'd seen Rocco Spatu and Cinghialenta, and he doffed his hat to Don Michele, who had swollen eyes and dusty boots, and tried to force him to accept a liqueur. But Don Michele had already been at the tavern, where Santuzza had said to him as she poured out a glass of good wine:

"Where have you been risking your neck, my dear man? Don't you know that if they kill you, you'll take other people with you into the grave?"

"And where does that leave my duty? If I'd caught them red-handed last night, we'd have made a nice bit of money, by God!"

"If they're telling you that it was Massaro Filippo, trying to smuggle in his wine, don't believe it, by this holy scapular of the Daughters of Mary, which I wear on my breast so unworthily! They're all lies, told by people without conscience, who damn their souls wishing their neighbors evil."

"No, I know what it was! It was all silk kerchiefs and sugar and coffee, more than a thousand lire worth of stuff, by God! and it slipped through my fingers like an eel. But I have my eye on that whole crew, and next time they won't get away with it!"

But Piedipapera kept insisting: "Come, Don Michele, have a glass. It will do your stomach good, after all the sleep you've lost."

Don Michele was in a bad temper and just huffed angrily.

"Since he asks you to take it, take it," Vanni Pizzuto chimed in. "If Compare Tino pays, it means he has money to spend. He's got plenty of money, the fox. Why, he even bought the Malavoglia debt. And all he gets in payment is a beating."

Don Michele unbent a bit and laughed.

"Blood of Judas!" cried Piedipapera, banging his fist on the counter and pretending to become really angry. "I don't want to send that lout 'Ntoni to Rome to do his penance."

"Bravo!" Pizzuto agreed. "I certainly wouldn't have let him off so easy. Am I right, Don Michele?"

Don Michele approved with a grunt.

"Leave it to me! I'll put 'Ntoni and all his family in their place," Piedipapera said threateningly. "I don't want the whole village laughing in my face. You can be sure of that, Don Michele!"

And he left limping wildly and cursing as though in a rage, all the while telling himself that it was best to keep on the good side of these dirty spies. And still wondering what he could do to keep on their good side, he went to the tavern, where Uncle Santoro told him that neither Rocco Spatu nor Cinghialenta had been there, and then to see Cousin Anna, who, poor woman, hadn't slept all night and stood in her doorway, her face white, looking worriedly up and down the street. In front of her house he also met La Vespa who'd come to ask Comare Grazia if she happened to have a bit of yeast.

"I've just seen Compare Mosca," he said to her, with the air of just making conversation. "He didn't have his cart, and I bet that he was going to buzz around the lava field, behind Saint Agatha's garden. To love one's neighbor is a fine thing, you see her often without traveling."

"A perfect little saint, that Mena, fit to stick up on the wall!" Vespa burst out. "They want to marry her to Brasi Cipolla, and she goes right on flirting with everybody! Pooh! It makes you sick to think of it!"

"Don't bother about it! Don't bother about it! This way everybody will find out what she's really like and their eyes will be opened. But doesn't Compare Mosca know that they want to marry her to Brasi Cipolla?"

"You know what men are like—whenever a bit of trash looks at them they all run after her to have a good time. But when they want to be serious, they look for the kind of woman I'm talking about."

"Compare Mosca ought to marry a woman like you."

"I'm not thinking of marrying just now; but a man would certainly find in me what he needs. Anyway, I have my plot of land, and nobody has his claws on it, like the house by the medlar tree. Some day the north wind will sweep it away, if it starts to blow. That will be something to see, when that north wind blows!"

"Just wait! Just wait! The weather isn't always good, and sooner or later the wind will blow all that trash away. Today I have to talk with your Uncle Dumbbell, about that certain business."

Dumbbell was in just the right mood to discuss that business, which never seemed to end, because, as they say, "long things turn into snakes." Master 'Ntoni was always chanting the same tune in his ear—that the Malavoglia were honest folk and would pay him—but what he'd like to know was where they were going to dig up the money. In the village everybody knew what everybody else owned, down to the last cent, and those honest folk, the Malavoglia, even if they sold their souls to the Turks, wouldn't be able to pay even half of their debt between now and Easter. And as for taking the house by the medlar tree, he knew only too well that it required all sorts of legal papers and expenses, and Don Giammaria and the druggist were right when they called the government a thief. He, as true as his name was Uncle Crocifisso, blamed not only the people who levied the taxes but also those who didn't want them and threw the village into such uproar that an honest man was no longer safe living in his own house with his own property; and when they had come to ask him if he wanted to be the mayor, he had told them: "Fine! and who'll take care of my business for me? I mind my own business, thank you." And meanwhile all Master 'Ntoni did was think of marrying off his granddaughter, he'd been seen talking with Compare Cipolla—Uncle Santoro had seen him, and he'd also seen Piedipapera himself, playing the go-between for La Vespa and fending for that beggar Alfio Mosca who was out to snatch her plot of land away from him. "I'm the one who's been telling you that he'll snatch it from you!" Piedipapera shouted into his ear, to convince him. "You can scream all you want and kick up a fuss at home, but your niece is head over heels in love with him and she's always after him. I can't slam the door in her face when she comes to chat with my wife, out of courtesy to you, for after all she is your niece and your kin."

"A fine courtesy you're doing me. With this courtesy of yours, you'll make me lose the plot of land!"

"Sure, you'll lose it! If the Malavoglia girl marries Brasi Cipolla, Compare Alfio Mosca will have to give up, and then, to console himself, he'll take both La Vespa and the plot of land."

"Let the devil take her!" exclaimed Uncle Crocifisso in the end, dazed by Compare Tino's flood of arguments. "I don't care one bit. That unholy woman has done nothing but make me sin! I want my property, which I earned with my own blood, like the blood of Christ in the chalice of the Mass, and they all act as if I'd stolen it and try to grab what they can—Alfio Mosca, La Vespa, and the Malavoglia. But now I'll go to the law and take the house."

"You give the orders. If you say go to the law, I'll do it right away."

"Not yet. We'll wait until Easter. A man is known by his word and an ox by its horns. But I want to be paid down to the last cent, and I'll no longer listen to anyone who begs for a postponement."

Easter was approaching. Once more the hills were covered with green and the cactus was in bloom. The girls kept basil plants on their windowsills, and white butterflies came and lighted on them. Even the puny broom on the lava field put forth a small, pale flower. In the mornings, the green and yellow roof tiles steamed in the rising sun, and the sparrows on them chattered away until sunset.

Even the house by the medlar tree seemed festive; the yard was swept, the fishing gear was neatly lined up along the wall or hung from poles, the garden was all green with cabbages and lettuce, and the room, open and full of sunlight, seemed happy, too. Everything announced that Easter was coming. Towards noon the old people came out to sit in front of the doorways, and the girls sang as they washed the clothes at the wash shed. Carts began to pass again during the night, and in the evening the lane was filled with the buzz of people talking.

"Comare Mena is going to be married," they said.

"Her mother has taken all her trousseau linens out of the chest."

Time had passed, and time carries away the bad as well as the good. Now Comare Maruzza was always busy cutting and sewing things, and Mena didn't even ask for whom they were; and one evening they brought Brasi Cipolla to the house to see her, together with his father, Master Fortunato, and all his kinfolk.

"Here is Compare Cipolla, who has come to pay you a visit," said Master 'Ntoni, letting them in as though it were all by chance, while in the kitchen wine and roasted chick-peas were ready to be brought out, and the women and children were dressed in their Sunday clothes. In her new dress and with that black kerchief on her head, Mena looked so much like Saint Agatha that Brasi kept staring at her, like a basilisk. He perched on his chair, holding his hands between his knees and rubbing them together happily, now and then, whenever he thought nobody was looking.

"He's come with his son Brasi, who has grown up now," Master 'Ntoni went on.

"That's right, the children grow up and push us into the grave," answered Master Fortunato.

"Now have a glass of this good wine," added La Longa, "and some of these chick-peas, which my daughter roasted. I'm sorry I didn't know about this visit, and haven't prepared the sort of food you deserve."

"We were just going past," replied Master Cipolla, "and we said to ourselves: 'Let's go and see Comare Maruzza.'"

Never taking his eyes off Mena, Brasi filled his pockets with chick-peas, and afterwards the children swooped down and cleaned off the platter, while Nunziata, the baby in her arms, tried to stop them, scolding them in a low voice as if she were in church. Meanwhile the old men had gone to talk under the medlar tree, as the women stood around them singing the girl's praises—what a good housewife she was, how she kept that house spick and span and as shiny as a mirror. "The girl is as she is brought up, the tow as it is spun."

"Your granddaughter has grown, too," remarked Master Fortunato, "and it's about time to marry her."

"If the Lord sends her a good match, that's all we ask for," replied Master 'Ntoni.

"Marriages and bishops are made in heaven," said Comare Longa.

"A fine horse never lacks for a saddle," concluded Master Fortunato. "For a girl like your granddaughter a good match can't fail to turn up."

Mena was sitting next to the young man, as is the custom, but she never lifted her eyes from her apron and when they left, Brasi complained to his father that she hadn't even offered him the platter of chick-peas.

"You wanted more of them!" Master Fortunato shouted at him, when they were far enough away. "You were chewing so loud that you couldn't hear anybody else! It sounded like a mule in a bag of barley! Just look, you spilled wine on your pants, you blockhead, and you've ruined a new suit!"

Master 'Ntoni was very happy; he rubbed his hands and said to his daughter-in-law: "I can't believe we've reached port, with God's help! Mena will have everything she wants, and now we'll take care of all our other little worries, and you'll be able to say: 'Poor grandfather told us to remember that laughter follows tears like the day follows the night.' "

That Saturday, towards evening, Nunziata came to the house to get some broad beans for her children and said: "Compare Alfio is leaving tomorrow. He's taking away all his things."

Mena turned pale and stopped weaving.

The light was on in Alfio's house, and everything was out of place. Soon after he came to knock at the door, and looked drawn and troubled too, and kept knotting the whip he held in his hands.

"I've come to say goodbye to all of you, Comare Maruzza. To Master 'Ntoni, the boys, and you too, Comare Mena. The wine at Aci Catena is ended. Now Santuzza has taken Massaro Filippo's wine. I'm going to Bicocca, where there's work for my donkey cart."

Mena didn't speak; and only her mother replied: "Do you want to wait for Master 'Ntoni? He'd like to say goodbye to you."

So then Compare Alfio sat down on the edge of the

chair, still holding his whip, and looked around the room, looked at everything but Comare Mena.

"When will you come back?" La Longa asked.

"Who knows when I'll come back. I go where my donkey leads me. As long as the work lasts, I'll stay there. But I'd like to come back here soon, if I can earn my bread."

"Take care of your health, Compare Alfio. In Bicocca they tell me the people die like flies from malaria."

Alfio shrugged his shoulders and said that he couldn't do anything about that. "I wouldn't go, if I could help it," he said, staring at the candle. "And you have nothing to say to me, Comare Mena?"

The girl opened her mouth two or three times to say something, but her heart failed her.

"You're leaving the neighborhood, too, now that they're marrying you," said Alfio, after a pause. "The world is like a stable, some come and some go, and little by little everyone changes place and all no longer seems the same." As he said this he rubbed his hands and laughed, but with his lips, not his heart.

"Girls go where God wills," said La Longa. "Now they're always happy and without worries, but when they go into the world they start having hardships and sorrows."

Compare Alfio, after Master 'Ntoni had come home and had said goodbye to him, still couldn't make up his mind to leave. He stood on the threshold, with his whip under his arm, shaking hands over and over, even with Comare Maruzza. He kept repeating, as you do when you're going far away and don't know whether you'll meet again: "Forgive me if I've ever done anything wrong." The only one who didn't shake his hand was Saint Agatha, who stayed there crouched at her loom. But everybody knows that this is the way girls are supposed to behave.

It was a beautiful spring evening, the moonlight filling the streets and the yard. People were sitting in front of their doorways, and the girls were strolling about singing with their arms linked. Mena also went out arm in arm with Nunziata, because she felt stifled in the house.

"Now we won't see Compare Alfio's lantern in the

evening," said Nunziata. "And his house will be closed up."

Compare Alfio had loaded a good part of his belongings on the cart, and was putting the little hay left in the rack into a bag, while his pot of broad beans was cooking for the evening meal.

"Are you leaving before dawn, Compare Alfio?" asked Nunziata from the door of the yard.

"Yes, it's a long trip, and that poor beast must rest a little during the day."

Mena still didn't speak and leaned against the doorpost, staring at the loaded cart, the empty house, the unmade bed, and the pot which was boiling for the last time on the hearth.

"Oh, you're here too, Comare Mena!" exclaimed Alfio, as soon as he saw her, and he dropped what he was doing.

She nodded her head, and meanwhile Nunziata had rushed to skim off the pot which was boiling over, like the good housewife she was.

"I'm glad you're here, because now I can say goodbye to you too!" Alfio said.

"I've come to say goodbye," she said, and there were tears in her voice. "Why do you go to Bicocca when they have malaria there?"

Alfio laughed, and also this time it was a forced laugh, just as when he'd gone to bid them goodbye. "Oh, that's good! Why am I going? And why are you getting married to Brasi Cipolla? We all do what we can, Comare Mena. If I could have done what I wanted, you know what I would have done! . . ." She looked at him for a long time, her eyes glistening. "I would have stayed here, because even the walls know me, and I know where to lay my hands, and I can even groom the donkey in the dark. And I would have been the one to marry you, Comare Mena, because I've had you in my heart a long time, and I'm taking you with me to Bicocca, and everywhere I go. But now this is all useless talk, and we must do what we can. My donkey, too, goes where I make him go."

"Now goodbye," Mena said. "I, too, have a thorn in here . . . and now that I'll always see that window closed, I'll feel that my heart's been closed too, closed like that window, which is as heavy as the door of a wine cellar. But that's what God wills. Now I say goodbye and I'm going."

The poor girl was crying quietly, her hands covering her eyes, and she went together with Nunziata to cry under the medlar tree in the moonlight.

CHAPTER NINE

Neither the Malavoglia nor anyone else in the village knew what Piedipapera and Uncle Crocifisso were cooking up. On Easter Day Master 'Ntoni took the hundred lire he had in the chest of drawers and put on his new jacket to carry them to Uncle Crocifisso.

"Is it all here?" Uncle Crocifisso asked.

"It can't be all, Uncle Crocifisso—you know well enough what it takes to earn a hundred lire. But 'little is better than nothing' and 'the man who pays something on account is not a bad debtor.' Now the summer's coming, and with the Lord's help we'll pay it all."

"Why do you tell this to me? You know I have nothing to do with it. This is Piedipapera's deal."

"It's all one to me, because when I see you I still feel that I have the debt with you. And Compare Tino won't say no to you, if you ask him to wait till the feast day of the Madonna of Ognina."

"This money here won't even cover the expenses!" Dumbbell kept saying, bouncing the coins on the palm of his hand. "You go and ask him if he wants to wait. It's not my business anymore."

As usual, Piedipapera began cursing and flinging his cap on the ground, saying that he hadn't the bread to eat and that he couldn't wait even till the Day of the Ascension.

"Listen, Compare Tino," Master 'Ntoni begged him, his hands joined, as though Piedipapera were the Lord God himself. "If you don't want to wait until Saint John's Day, just when I'm going to marry my granddaughter, you might as well finish me off here and now."

"Holy Devil!" shouted Compare Tino. "You're making me do something I can't do, cursed be the day and the minute that I got into this mess!"—and he left, tearing at his old cap.

Master 'Ntoni went home, still pale, and said to his daughter-in-law: "I've convinced him, but I had to beg him like the Lord God," and the poor old man was still trembling. But he was glad that Master Cipolla didn't know about it and that his granddaughter's marriage hadn't gone up in smoke.

On the evening of the Ascension, while the boys were leaping around the bonfires, the women once again gathered before the Malavoglia's landing, and Comare Venera Zuppidda also came to hear what was being said and to speak her piece too. Now that Master 'Ntoni was marrying off his granddaughter and the *Provvidenza* was afloat again, they were all friendly to the Malavoglia—for they didn't know what Piedipapera was plotting, not even his wife Comare Grazia, who was chatting with Maruzza as though her husband wasn't brewing something bad. Every evening 'Ntoni had gone to talk a while with Barbara and he'd told her that his grandfather had said: "First Mena has to get married." "And I come next!" 'Ntoni had concluded. So Barbara had sent Mena the pot of basil,* all decorated with carnations and a lovely red ribbon, which was the invitation to become her kin; and everyone was congratulating Saint Agatha, and even her mother had taken off her black kerchief, because it's bad luck to wear mourning when a marriage is in sight; and they had also written to Luca, to tell him that Mena was getting married.

Only Mena, poor thing, didn't look as gay as the others, and it seemed that everything her heart said to her and

* In Sicily there are the so-called "kin of the basil," and this kinship is sealed by giving a pot of basil to the person with whom one wants to establish a special bond, which afterwards is always respected in daily intercourse. [Translator's note.]

showed her was black and gloomy, though the fields were dotted with small gold and silver stars, and the children were wreathing garlands for the feast day of the Ascension, and she herself had climbed on a ladder to help her mother hang festoons of flowers over the doorways and the windows.

Though all the doors in the village were adorned with flowers, Alfio's door, black and crooked, was forever shut, and there was no one to festoon it with flowers for the Ascension.

"That flirt, Saint Agatha!" La Vespa went around saying, her mouth foaming. "She has talked and intrigued until finally she forced Compare Alfio to leave town!"

In the meantime they'd given Saint Agatha her new dress, and they were waiting for Saint John's Day to take the small silver dagger out of her braids and part her hair over her forehead before she went to church, and when they saw her go by, everybody said: "What a lucky girl!"

Yet her mother, all unawares, was brimming with happiness because her daughter was going to live in a house where she'd never lack for a thing, and she was busy all the time cutting and sewing. When he came home in the the evening, Master 'Ntoni wanted to see everything, and he held the cloth and the skein of cotton for them, and every time he went to Catania he brought back some small purchase. With the good weather they felt hopeful again; the boys were all earning money, some more, some less, and the *Provvidenza* was earning its keep too, and they figured that with God's help, they'd be clear of trouble by Saint John's Day. During that time Master Cipolla sat for entire evenings on the church steps with Master 'Ntoni, talking about what the *Provvidenza* had done that day. Brasi was always roaming around the Malavoglia's lane, dressed in his new suit; and soon after the whole village knew that next Sunday Comare Grazia Piedipapera herself would go to part the bride's hair and take out the silver dagger, because Brasi Cipolla had lost his mother, and the Malavoglia had purposely invited Comare Piedipapera in order to ingratiate her husband; and they'd also invited Uncle Crocifisso and the whole neighborhood and all the friends and relatives, without stint.

"I won't go!" grumbled Uncle Crocifisso to Compare

Tino, as he leaned against the elm in the piazza. "I've swallowed too much bile, and I don't want to poison my soul. Why don't you go, since you don't care and it's not your property. There's still time to send the bailiff! The lawyer said so."

"You're the boss, and I'll do as you say. Now you don't care about it anymore, because Compare Alfio Mosca has gone away. But you'll see—as soon as Mena gets married, he'll come back and take your niece."

Comare Venera Zuppidda made an awful fuss because they had asked Comare Grazia to comb the bride's hair, whereas she should have done it, since she was about to become a relative of the Malavoglia, and her daughter had become Mena's basil kin. Indeed, she'd had Barbara make a new dress as fast as she could, for she had never expected such an insult. In vain 'Ntoni had begged and pleaded with her to forget about it, and not to make a mountain out of a molehill. With her hair all prinked and set—but with her hands coated with flour, for she'd started to prepare the dough for the bread just to show that she no longer cared about going to the Malavoglia party— Comare Venera snapped: "You wanted Comare Piedipapera? Well, keep her! it's either she or I. There isn't room for both of us in this world!"

The Malavoglia knew very well that they'd chosen Comare Grazia for the sake of that money they owed her husband. Now they were all hand in glove with Compare Tino, ever since Master Cipolla, one evening in Santuzza's tavern, had gotten him to make peace with Master 'Ntoni's 'Ntoni over that fist fight.

"They lick his boots because they owe him that money for the house!" La Zuppidda muttered. "They owe more than fifty lire to my husband too, for the *Provvidenza*. Tomorrow I'll see that they give it to me."

"Let it go, Mama, let it go!" Barbara begged. But she too had a sour face, because she hadn't been able to wear her new dress, and she nearly regretted the money she'd spent for the basil pot she'd sent to Comare Mena; and when 'Ntoni came to get them, they sent him away, downcast, his new jacket drooping from his shoulders. Then from the courtyard, while they were putting the bread in the oven, mother and daughter kept an eye on the hullabaloo at the Malavoglia house, which was so loud that even over there they could hear the shouting and laughter, and this made them angrier yet. The house by the medlar tree was packed with people, just like that time Compare Bastianazzo had died; and Mena, without her small silver dagger and with her hair parted over her forehead, looked completely different, so that all the women clustered around her, and the babble and the merrymaking would have drowned out a cannon blast. Piedipapera clowned so much that the women shrieked as though he were tickling them, yet all along the lawyer was preparing the papers, since, as Uncle Crocifisso had said, there was still plenty of time to send the bailiff. Even Master Cipolla was carried away and told a few jokes, which only his son Brasi laughed at. And they all talked at once, while the children scrabbled among the people's legs, fighting for broad beans and chestnuts. La Longa herself, poor woman, was so happy that she'd forgotten her sorrows. And Master 'Ntoni, sitting on the stone wall, nodded his head and laughed to himself.

"Be careful you don't give your pants another drink, like the last time, because they're not thirsty," Compare Cipolla told his son Brasi. Then he announced that he felt merrier than the bride and wanted to dance the *fasola* with her.

"Then I might as well go home, because I have nothing more to do here!" replied Brasi, who wanted to tell his jokes too and was sore because they'd left him in a corner like a fool, and not even Comare Mena paid any attention to him.

"The party's for Mena," Nunziata said, "but she isn't as happy as everybody else."

Then Cousin Anna pretended that the pitcher, which still contained more than a pint of wine, had slipped out of her hands, and she began to shout: "Good luck! Good luck! Where there's broken crockery, there's merrymaking! Spilled wine spells good luck!"

"She almost spilled it on my pants this time, too!" grumbled Brasi, who was on his guard ever since that accident with his suit.

Piedipapera had settled astride the wall, with his glass between his legs, looking as though he owned the house

because of that bailiff he could send, and he said: "Even
Rocco Spatu's not at the tavern today. All the festivities
are going on here. You'd think it was Santuzza's."

"It's much better here," said La Locca's son, who had
come at the tail-end of the crowd and had been invited in
for a glass. "At Santuzza's, if you haven't any money they
don't give you a thing."

From his place on the wall, Piedipapera was watching
a small group of people talking near the fountain, with
faces so grave it seemed that the end of the world was at
hand. The usual idlers stood in front of the pharmacy
haranguing each other, newspaper in hand, or arguing
loudly and waving their hands in each other's faces, as
though they were about to come to blows; and Don Giammaria was laughing and took a pinch of snuff. Even from
there you could see the pleasure it gave him.

"Why didn't the priest and Don Silvestro come?" Piedipapera asked.

"I told them to come, but maybe they're busy," Master
'Ntoni replied.

"There they are, at the pharmacy, and you'd think they
were drawing the lottery numbers. What the devil's happened?"

An old woman went screaming across the piazza, tearing her hair, as if they'd just brought her bad news; and
in front of Pizzuto's store there was the kind of crowd that
gathers when a donkey collapses under a heavy load and
everybody runs to see what's happened; and even the
women were watching from a distance, their mouths agape,
not daring to come any closer.

"Well, I'm going to see what's happened," Piedipapera
said. And he climbed slowly and carefully down from the
wall.

At the center of that group, instead of a fallen donkey,
stood two sailors who'd been discharged, with their sacks
on their backs and their heads bandaged. They'd stopped
for a moment at the barber's to have a glass of anise. They
said that they had been in a great naval battle, and that
ships as large as Aci Trezza had been sunk loaded to the
gunwales with sailors. In short, so many things that they
sounded like the storytellers down at the waterfront in
Catania who narrate the adventures of Roland and the

paladins of France; and the people stood there, thick as flies, straining their ears to hear what they said.

"Maruzza's son is on the *Re d'Italia,* too," remarked Don Silvestro, who had come closer to hear.

"I'll go and tell my wife right away," said Mastro Turi Zuppidda quickly. "So maybe she'll decide to go to Comare Maruzza's, because I don't like grudges between friends and neighbors."

Meanwhile La Longa knew nothing about it, poor woman, and was laughing and having a good time with her family and friends.

One sailor, waving his arms like a preacher, went on talking to all who would listen to him. "Yes, there were Sicilians, too. Sicilians from every town. Besides, believe me, when the bugle calls you to the battle stations, all differences end—the carbines all speak the same language. They were all brave boys, and with plenty of guts under their shirts. Listen, when you've seen what I've seen, and the way those boys stood their ground and did their duty, you really have the right to wear this cap over your ear, by God!"

The young man's eyes were glistening, but he said that he was all right, and that it was because he'd been drinking. "Her name was the *Re d'Italia,* there wasn't another ship like her. She was armored, which is the same as saying that you women are wearing a corselet, and this corselet is made of iron, and they could fire a cannon shot at you without hurting you. She sank in a second, and we never saw her again with all that smoke, like the smoke of twenty brick kilns going full blast."

"There was a hell of an uproar at Catania!" added the pharmacist. "There were such crowds around the people reading from the newspapers that it looked like a fair!"

"Newspapers are all printed lies!" Don Giammaria declared.

"They say it's been a serious blow. We lost a great battle," said Don Silvestro.

Master Cipolla had also rushed over to find out why the crowd had gathered. "You believe that?" he finally sneered. "It's all a lot of talk, just to sell newspapers."

"But everybody says we've lost!"

"Lost what?" said Uncle Crocifisso, cupping his hand behind his ear.

"A battle."

"Who lost it?"

"I, you, in short, everybody, Italy," the pharmacist said.

"I haven't lost a thing!" Dumbbell answered, shrugging. "It's Piedipapera's business now, and he'll have to take care of it." And he looked at the house by the medlar tree, where they were celebrating so noisily.

"You want to know how it is?" Master Cipolla concluded. "It's like when the Commune of Aci Trezza and the Commune of Aci Castello quarreled over the boundaries. Did we put anything into our pockets, you or I? What did it mean to us?"

"It means plenty!" cried the pharmacist, red in the face. "It means that you're a pack of animals!"

"The real trouble is for all those poor mothers!" someone ventured timidly. Uncle Crocifisso, who wasn't a mother, shrugged his shoulders.

"I'll tell you what it's like, in two words," the other sailor was saying meanwhile. "It's like at the tavern, when people get excited and angry, and plates and glasses start flying amid the smoke and the yelling. Have you ever seen that? It's just the same! At first, when you're leaning against the sacks of stuffed straw at the bulwarks, holding your carbine, you don't hear anything in the great silence but the noise of the engines, and you think that *punf!* *punf!* comes from inside your stomach: nothing else. Then, after the first cannon shot and as soon as the things start hopping, you want to dance too, and chains wouldn't hold you, just like when the violins start playing at the tavern after you've eaten and drunk, and you aim your carbine wherever you think you see a man in the smoke. On land it's all different. A *bersagliere* who came back with us to Messina told us that as soon as you hear the zing of the bullets, your legs start itching and you want to charge in head first. But *bersaglieri* aren't sailors, and they don't know how to hang on to the rigging with a firm foot on the rope and a steady hand on the trigger, in spite of the ship's rolling, while your comrades are dropping down around you like rotten pears."

"By the Holy Virgin!" cried Rocco Spatu. "I wish I'd been there myself, to get a smack at them."

The rest of them kept quiet and listened, with their eyes popping. Then the other young man told them how the *Palestro* had blown up. "When she passed alongside us she was burning like a stack of firewood, and the flames leaped as high as the foremast. But all the boys were at their posts, at the batteries or in the rigging. Our captain asked if they needed anything. 'No, thanks a lot,' they replied. Then she passed on the port side, and we never saw her again."

"I certainly wouldn't like to be roasted alive," Rocco Spatu said, "though I'm all for a good fist fight." And when he went back to the tavern, Santuzza said to him: "Call them over here, those poor boys. They must be thirsty after the long road they've walked, and they need a glass of good wine. That Pizzuto poisons people with his anise, and he doesn't even go to confession. Some people carry their conscience on their backs, so they can't see it. I pity them!"

"In my opinion, sailors are all crazy," said Master Cipolla, blowing his nose with great care. "Would you let yourself be killed if the King told you: 'Go and get yourself killed for my sake'?"

"Poor fellows, it's not their fault!" said Don Silvestro. "They've got to do it, because a corporal with a loaded gun stands behind each soldier, and all he's got to do is make sure the soldier doesn't run away. And if he does try to run away, he shoots him down like a quail."

"Ah, that's just fine! That's a dirty trick, if there ever was one!"

In the Malavoglia yard they laughed and drank all evening under the bright moon. And only much later, when they were all tired and slowly munched at their broad beans, and some sitting against the wall sang in low voices, somebody came and told them the story the two sailors had brought to the village.

Master Fortunato had gone away early, taking along Brasi in his new suit. "Those poor Malavoglia!" he said, when he met Dumbbell in the piazza. "God have mercy on them! They have a curse on them!"

Uncle Crocifisso kept silent and scratched his head. He

wasn't involved anymore, he'd washed his hands of it. Now it was Piedipapera's affair; but, in all conscience, he felt sorry for them.

The next day the rumor spread that there had been a battle in the sea near Trieste between our ships and those of the enemy—and nobody even knew who that enemy was—and that a great many people had been killed. Some told the story one way, some another, but all in bits and pieces, mumbling their words. The neighbors came holding their hands under their aprons to ask Comare Maruzza if Luca was up there, and stopped to gape at her before turning to leave. The poor woman began to stand at the door all day, as she did each time something terrible happened, turning her head this way and that, looking from one end of the road to the other, as if she expected Master 'Ntoni and the boys to come back from fishing sooner than usual. The neighbors also asked her if Luca had written, and how long it was since she'd gotten a letter from him. In fact she hadn't thought of a letter; and all night she couldn't sleep a wink, and her mind was always up there, on the sea near Trieste, where that catastrophe had occurred; and she kept seeing her son, pale and motionless, staring at her with wide, frightened, glistening eyes and saying yes, yes, as he did when they'd sent him off to be a sailor. And then she felt thirsty too, a terrible, burning dryness in her throat. For out of all those stories which were running around the village and which they had come to tell her, one detail had stuck in her mind—about a sailor whom they'd fished out of the water after twelve hours, just when the sharks were going to eat him, and in the midst of all that water he was dying of thirst; and then she had to go and drink from the water pitcher, as though she herself had that burning thirst inside her, and she opened her eyes wide in the darkness, and all she could see was that poor sailor.

As the days passed, however, nobody talked again about what had happened. But since La Longa didn't get a letter, she no longer felt like working or staying in the house. She was always going about, talking to everyone from door to door, as if in that way she could find out what she wanted to know. "Did you ever see a cat that's lost her kittens?" her neighbors said. But the letter didn't come. Even Master

'Ntoni stopped going out on the boat and was always cling-ing to his daughter-in-law's skirts, like a puppy. Some people told him: "Go to Catania, it's a big city, and they'll certainly tell you something."

In the big city the poor old man felt more lost than on the sea at night, and he didn't know which way to steer. At last they took pity on him and told him to go to the captain of the port, because he ought to know the latest news. Down there, after sending him back and forth for a while, from pillar to post, some clerks finally decided to leaf through certain big books they had, and ran their fingers down a list of the dead. When they reached his name, La Longa, who was listening with a face as white as those pages and hadn't even heard well because her ears were roaring, slumped slowly to the floor, half dead.

"It's been more than forty days," the clerk concluded, closing the register. "It happened at Lissa. Didn't you know yet?"

La Longa was carried home in a cart, and she was ill for several days. From then on she was seized by a great devotion for Our Lady of the Sorrows, who is on the altar of the small church. It seemed to her that that long body stretched out over the Mother's knees, with a black wound in its ribs and its knees red with blood, was the picture of her Luca, and she felt all those silver swords, which are around the Holy Virgin, sticking in her heart. Every eve-ning, when they went to benediction and Compare Cirino jangled his keys before locking up, the women saw her, always there, at the same spot, down on her knees, and they called her Our Lady of the Sorrows, too.

"She's right," they said in the village. "Luca was going to come back soon, and he would have earned his thirty soldi a day. For a leaking ship, every wind blows the wrong way."

"Did you see Master 'Ntoni?" Piedipapera added. "After his misfortune with his grandson, he looks just like an owl. Now the house by the medlar tree is really shipping water on all sides, like a torn shoe, and every honest man must look after his own interests."

La Zuppidda always had a long face and grumbled that now 'Ntoni had to take care of the whole family. A girl would have to think twice before taking him for a husband.

"What have you got against that poor fellow?" asked Mastro Turi.

"You keep quiet, because you don't know what you're talking about!" his wife yelled at him. "I don't like messes! Go back to work, because this is none of your business." And she pushed him out of the door, his arms dangling at his sides and that huge mallet in his hand.

Barbara, sitting on the wall of the landing, plucking dry leaves off the carnations, also looked sour and slipped into her conversation such remarks as "married people and mules must live by themselves" and "mother-in-law and bride together always make bad weather."

"After Mena is married," 'Ntoni replied, "my grandfather will give us the room upstairs."

"I'm not used to staying in a room upstairs, like the pigeons!" Barbara said, shutting him up. She spoke so sharply that even her father, glancing around cautiously as they walked down the road, said to 'Ntoni: "She'll become like her mother, that Barbara. Just be careful she doesn't put the halter on you from the start, otherwise you'll end up like me."

But Comare Venera had declared: "Before my daughter goes to sleep in that pigeon loft, I want to know who keeps the house. And I want to wait and see how this business of the lupins is going to end."

This time it ended in Piedipapera insisting on being paid, by the Holy Devil! The feast of Saint John had come, and the Malavoglia were once again talking about paying something on account, because they didn't have all the money, and they hoped to scrape it together when they harvested their olives. Piedipapera had taken that money right out of his mouth, and he didn't have a crust of bread to eat, as true as there's a God above! He couldn't live on air till it was time to gather in the olives.

"I, for my part, am sorry, Master 'Ntoni," he'd told him, "but what can I do? I have to look after my own interests. Saint Joseph shaved himself first and then the others."

"It'll soon be a year!" said Uncle Crocifisso, when he was alone with Compare Tino and could complain, "and not a penny of interest have I seen. Those two hundred lire will be just about enough for the expenses. You'll see, when the olive harvest comes they'll tell you to give them time till Christmas, and then till Easter. That's how a family goes to its ruin. But I earned my property by the sweat of my brow. Now one son's in heaven and the other wants the Zuppidda girl; they can't even keep that leaking boat afloat and yet they're trying to marry the girl. Those people don't think about anything else but getting married. They're in a frenzy, like my niece, La Vespa. Now that Mena is marrying, you'll see, Compare Mosca will come back to grab La Vespa's plot of land."

In the end they both started blaming the lawyer, who never finished drawing up the papers to send the bailiff.

"Most likely Master 'Ntoni went to see him and told him to go slow," Piedipapera said. "Two pounds of fish are enough to buy ten lawyers."

This time he really was through with the Malavoglia, because La Zuppidda had taken Comare Grazia's laundry off the edge of the washtub and had put her own in its place: the kind of insolence nobody can tolerate. La Zuppidda dared to behave that way because she was egged on by that lout 'Ntoni Malavoglia, who was a regular bully. A pack of curs, those Malavoglia, and Piedipapera swore that he wanted nothing more to do with them—may he no longer be called by that name which that filthy Don Giammaria had stuck on his brow with his filthy christening.

Then the sealed papers began raining down, and Piedipapera said that the lawyer probably hadn't been satisfied enough with Master 'Ntoni's present to let himself be bought, which just showed the kind of skinflints they were, and how much you could trust them when they promised to pay. Master 'Ntoni again ran to the town clerk and Lawyer Scipioni; but the lawyer laughed in his face and told him that the best place for fools was at home, and that he should never have let his daughter-in-law sign that paper. He'd made the mess and he had to eat it. Woe to the man who waits till he falls before he calls for help!

"Listen to me," Don Silvestro advised. "You might as well give him the house, otherwise even the *Provvidenza* along with the hair on your head will go to cover the costs. And besides, you'll lose many days of work, going back and forth to the lawyer."

"If you give us the house quietly, without making a fuss," Piedipapera said to him, "we'll let you keep the *Provvidenza,* with which you'll always be able to earn your bread, and you'll still be your own masters and the bailiff won't have to come with the sealed papers."

Compare Tino didn't bear a grudge and went to talk to Master 'Ntoni as though he weren't involved, putting his arm around his neck and saying: "Forgive me, my friend, but what can I do? I'm a poor devil! I took those five hundred lire right out of my mouth and, as you know, Saint Joseph shaved himself first. If I were as rich as Uncle Crocifisso, I wouldn't even talk to you about it, upon my soul!"

The poor old man didn't have the courage to tell his daughter-in-law that they had to leave the house by the medlar tree quietly, after having lived there so long. And it was like leaving the village to go abroad, or like those who'd left with the idea of returning but had never come back. For Luca's bed was still there, and so was the nail on which Bastianazzo used to hang his coat. But finally they had to move out with all those poor household goods, taking them from their places, and each left a mark where it had been, and without them the house no longer seemed the same. They moved their things at night into the small house they'd rented from the butcher, as if the whole village didn't know that the house by the medlar tree now belonged to Piedipapera and that they had to leave it. But at least nobody could see them carrying their goods on their backs.

When the old man pulled out a nail or took a stool from its corner where it had lived, he shook his head. Then they sat down on the mattresses which were piled in the center of the room to rest for a while, and looked about to see if they'd forgotten anything. But soon after the old man got up and went out into the yard, into the open air.

In the yard, too, there was straw scattered everywhere and pieces of broken crockery and wrecked lobster pots, and in one corner stood the medlar tree, and over the doorway the vine's tendrils were sprouting. "Let's leave!" Master 'Ntoni said. "Let's leave, children. Today or tomorrow, what's the difference!" But he didn't move.

Maruzza looked at the yard gate through which Luca

and Bastianazzo had gone away, and the road down which her son had walked with his pants rolled up in the rain and his oilskin umbrella hiding him from her. Compare Alfio Mosca's window was shut too, and the vines grew over the wall of his yard, and everybody who passed gave them a tug. Each of them had something to look at in that house and, as he left, the old man rested his hand stealthily on the broken door, which Uncle Crocifisso had said needed a few nails and a stout piece of wood.

Uncle Crocifisso had come together with Piedipapera to take a look at the house, and they talked loudly in the empty rooms, and their words echoed as if they were in church. Compare Tino hadn't been able to hold out until then living on air, and, to get his money, he had been forced to sell it all back to Uncle Crocifisso.

"What could I do, Compare Malavoglia?" said Piedipapera, putting his arm around his neck. "You know I'm a poor devil, and five hundred lire mean a lot to me! If you'd been rich, I'd have sold it to you." But Master 'Ntoni couldn't bear walking through his house like that, with Piedipapera's arm around his neck. And now Uncle Crocifisso had come with the carpenter and the mason, and all sorts of people were trooping through the empty rooms as though they were in the piazza, and they were saying: "Here you need some bricks. Here you need a new beam. Here the shutter has to be repaired," as if they were the owners; and they also said that it should be whitewashed, and then it would look like another house entirely.

Uncle Crocifisso was pushing the straw and the broken crockery to the side with his feet, and from the floor he picked up a torn hat which had belonged to Bastianazzo and threw it into the garden where it would fatten the soil. The medlar tree was still rustling softly, and the garlands of daisies, now withered, still hung over the door and windows, just as they'd been put up for the Ascension.

Also La Vespa, with her knitting hanging from her neck, was there to take a look around and rummaged everywhere, now that it was her uncle's property. "Blood is thicker than water," she said in a loud voice, so that even the deaf old man could hear her. "My uncle's property is close to my heart, just as my plot of land should be close to his."

Uncle Crocifisso let her talk and didn't hear a word, now that he saw Alfio Mosca's door across the way bolted tightly. "Now that Compare Alfio's door is bolted, I hope you'll set your heart at rest and you'll believe that I'm not thinking about him!" La Vespa whispered in Uncle Crocifisso's ear.

"My heart is at rest!" he replied. "Don't you worry."

From then on the Malavoglia didn't dare show their faces on the streets or in the church on Sundays, and they went all the way to Aci Castello for Mass, and nobody greeted them anymore, not even Master Cipolla, who went around saying: "Master 'Ntoni should never have played that dirty trick on me. This is what you'd call deceiving your neighbor, getting his daughter-in-law to sign for the lupin debt."

"That's just what my wife says!" chimed in Mastro Zuppiddo. "She says that even the dogs won't have anything to do with the Malavoglia now."

But Brasi, that oaf, stamped his feet and wanted Mena, because they'd promised her to him, and he behaved just like a little boy in front of a toy stall at the fair.

"Do you think that I stole your property, you oaf," his father said, "so you can throw it away on a girl who owns nothing?"

Even his new suit had been taken away from him, and Brasi got back at his father by spending his time snaring lizards on the lava field, or sitting astride the low wall of the wash shed, and he swore that he was through working, even if they killed him, since they didn't want to give him a wife and had taken back his new wedding suit. Luckily Mena didn't see him in his old clothes, because the Malavoglia, poor people, always kept their door shut and stayed inside the butcher's house, which they'd rented on Black Lane, near the Zuppiddi, and if Brasi chanced to see them in the distance, he ran and hid behind the wall or among the cactus plants.

Cousin Anna, who could see everything from the riverbed, where she was laying out the laundry, told Comare Grazia: "Now poor Saint Agatha will have to stay on the shelf, worse than an old pot. Just like my daughters who don't have a dowry."

"Poor girl," said Comare Grazia. "And they even parted her hair!"

But Mena wasn't upset and had put the small silver dagger back in her braids all by herself, without saying a word. Now she was very busy in the new house, where everything had to be rearranged, and there was no medlar tree, or Cousin Anna's and Nunziata's doorways to look at. As they worked side by side, her mother never took her eyes off her and spoke to her in a caressing voice when she said: "Hand me the scissors," or "Hold this skein for me," because now that everyone had turned their backs on Mena, her bowels ached for this daughter of hers.

But the girl sang like a starling, for she was eighteen and at that age if the sky is blue it laughs in your eyes, and the birds sing in your heart. Besides, she told her mother in a whisper while they were laying out the woof, she had never felt any affection for that Brasi. Her mother was the only one who had read her heart and had spoken kindly to her in her misfortune. "If Compare Alfio were here, he wouldn't turn his back on us," she said. "But when the new wine is ready, he'll be back."

The neighbors, poor things, hadn't really turned their backs on the Malavoglia. But Cousin Anna was always busy, what with all the work she had to do to make ends meet for her daughters, who'd remained on the shelf like old pots, and Comare Piedipapera was ashamed to show her face, after that dirty trick Compare Tino had played on them. She had a good heart, Comare Grazia, and she didn't say, like her husband: "Forget them, because now they have neither king nor kingdom. After all, what do you care about them?" The only person who came around now and then was Nunziata, with her baby brother in her arms and all the other children trailing after her; but she too had her own business to tend to.

That's how the world goes. "Everyone must tend to his own business," Comare Venera told Master 'Ntoni's 'Ntoni. "Everyone must shave his own beard before shaving the other fellow's. Your grandfather doesn't give you anything; so what obligation do you have to them? If you marry, it'll mean that you set up your own house, and what you earn, you'll earn for your own house. God blesses a hundred hands, but not all in the same plate!"

"Sure," 'Ntoni replied. "Now that my relatives are out in the street, you expect me to leave them in the lurch, too! How can my grandfather run the *Provvidenza* and feed so many, if I leave him?"

"Well, handle it yourself but leave me out of it!" cried La Zuppidda, turning her back on him and starting to rummage through the drawers or in the kitchen, pushing things around just to keep busy, so she wouldn't have to look at him. "I didn't steal my daughter. We could shut our eyes to the fact you don't have anything, since you're young and still have your health and can work. Besides, you do have a trade, especially nowadays when husbands are scarce, with this accursed military service that sweeps all our young men out of the village. But if somebody's got to give you a dowry so that you can eat it up together with your whole family, that's something else again. I only want to give my daughter one husband, not five or six, and I don't want to put two families on her neck."

In the next room Barbara pretended she couldn't hear and went on turning the wool winder faster and faster. But as soon as 'Ntoni poked his head in, she lowered her eyes to the spools and pulled a long face too. So the poor fellow went yellow and green and a hundred other colors, and didn't know what to do, because with those great black eyes of hers, Barbara kept him ensnared like a sparrow, and on top of everything else she said to him: "It means that you don't love me as much as your family!" and when her mother wasn't there, she began crying into her apron.

"Damn it!" shouted 'Ntoni, "I wish I were back in the navy!" and he tore at his hair and banged his head with his fists, but he couldn't bring himself to make the right decision, like the helpless lout he was. At that La Zuppidda said: "Bone, bone, bone, stick with your own." And her husband repeated her words: "I told you that I don't like messes," and then she yelled: "Go back to work, because you don't know what you're talking about."

Every time 'Ntoni went to the Zuppiddi house they all looked sore and sulky, and Comare Venera always threw into his face that the Malavoglia had asked Comare Piedipapera to part Mena's hair—and a fine parting she'd made for her!—just to lick Compare Tino's boots because of those few pennies for the house; and afterwards he'd taken the house anyway and left them with only their shifts, like the Infant Jesus.

"Do you think I don't know what your mother Maruzza was saying in those days when she went around looking down her nose? She said that Barbara wasn't the right kind of girl for her son 'Ntoni, because she'd been brought up like a little lady and didn't know what's needed to be a good fisherman's wife. Comare Mangiacarrube and Comare Francesca told me all about it at the wash shed."

"Comare Mangiacarrube and Comare Francesca are two sluts," 'Ntoni replied, "and they talk that way out of envy because I didn't marry the Mangiacarrube girl."

"As far as I'm concerned, you can take her! A fine catch that Mangiacarrube girl will be getting!"

"Well then, Comare Venera, if that's how you talk, it's just like telling me: 'Don't set foot in my house again.' "

'Ntoni tried to be a man and didn't come around for two or three days. But little Lia, who didn't know about all these arguments, continued to go to Comare Venera's yard to play, as she used to when Barbara gave her prickly pears and chestnuts because she liked her brother 'Ntoni. But now they didn't give her anything, and La Zuppidda said to her: "Are you looking for your brother? Your mother must be afraid that somebody wants to steal him!"

Comare La Vespa also came to the Zuppiddi yard, with her knitting around her neck, to say fierce things about men who, she said, are worse than dogs. And Barbara said to the little girl Lia: "I know that I'm not a fine housekeeper like your sister!" And Comare Venera concluded: "Your mother, since she's washing clothes for everybody, should wash that rag of a dress you're wearing, instead of talking about other people's business at the wash shed."

The child didn't understand most of this, but the few times she answered back, she drove Barbara's mother into a fury; Comare Venera said that Lia's mother Maruzza had put those words into Lia's mouth and sent her over just to poison her existence. At last the little girl quit going there, and Comare Venera said that it was just as well, for this way they no longer came into the house to spy because they were still afraid that the Zuppiddi wanted to steal that precious oaf from them.

Things reached the point where Comare Venera and La Longa no longer spoke to each other and turned their backs when they met in church.

"You'll see, they'll soon be putting the brooms in front of their doors!" said the Mangiacarrube girl, chuckling with delight. "If they don't, my name isn't Mangiacarrube! A fine catch La Zuppidda landed when she got that oaf!"

Usually the men don't get involved in these women's quarrels, for if they did, they would grow bigger and bigger and end up in a knifing. But the women, after they've put out the brooms and turned their backs on each other and worked off their anger by insulting each other and pulling at each other's hair, make up right away, embrace and kiss and stand at the doorways chattering as before.

'Ntoni, bewitched by Barbara's eyes, came back on the sly to stand under her window, to make peace, and sometimes Comare Venera wanted to throw the bean soup on his head, and even her daughter shrugged her shoulders, now that the Malavoglia had neither king nor kingdom.

And at last, to rid herself of the nuisance, Barbara said it right to his face, for the fellow was always hanging around her door like a dog, and if anyone else had wanted to walk down the lane to see her, he would have ruined her chances.

"Well, Compare 'Ntoni," she said, "the fish in the sea are for those who'll eat them. Let's set our hearts at rest, you and I, and let's forget about it."

"You can set your heart at rest, Comare Barbara, but for my part 'falling in and out of love is decided up above.' "

"Just try, and you'll manage too. You won't lose anything by trying. I wish you all good luck and good fortune, but let me see to my own affairs, because I'm already twenty-two."

"I knew that you were going to say this to me when they took our house, now that they all turn their backs on us."

"Listen, Compare 'Ntoni, my mother might come any minute, and it's not right for her to find me here with you."

"Yes, that's true. Now that they've taken the house by the medlar tree, it's not right." Poor 'Ntoni had a heavy heart, and he didn't want to leave her like that. But Barbara had to go and fill the pitcher at the fountain and she said goodbye, tripping off quickly and moving her hips gracefully—she was called Zuppidda or "lame," because her father's grandfather had broken a leg in a collision between two carts during the fair at Trecastagni, but Barbara had both her legs and they were in excellent shape.

"Goodbye, Comare Barbara!" the wretched fellow said, and so he set a stone on what had been and went back to rowing like a galley slave, for that's what it amounted to, from Monday to Saturday, and he was sick and tired of breaking his back for nothing, because when you're poor what's the point of sweating from morning till night, and in the end you can't find a dog who'll marry you. He was fed up with his life and he'd rather do nothing at all, and lie in bed pretending he was sick, as he'd done when he was fed up in the navy. Besides, his grandfather didn't examine him as carefully as the doctor on the frigate.

"What's wrong?" Master 'Ntoni asked him.

"Nothing. Just that I'm a poor devil."

"And what do you want to do about it? We must live as we are born."

He let himself be loaded with the gear, slackly, like a donkey, and all through the day he never opened his mouth except to curse and complain: "He who falls in the water must surely get wet." If his brother sang while they were setting the sail, he would say: "Sure, go ahead and sing. When you're old, you'll bark like Grandpa."

"And what are you getting by barking now?" the boy replied.

"You're right. Because this is a beautiful life!"

"Beautiful or not, we didn't make it the way it is," his grandfather said, to settle it.

In the evenings he sullenly ate his meal, and on Sundays he buzzed around the tavern, where people had nothing to do but laugh and enjoy themselves, without thinking that the next day they'd have to go back to doing what they had done all week; or he sat on the church steps for hours on end, his chin in his hand, watching the people go by and brooding over all those trades where you didn't have to work hard.

At least on Sundays he could enjoy all those things one can get without money—the sun, sitting with folded arms not doing anything—and then it became too much for him even to think of his condition, or to long for what he had seen when he was a sailor, which at work he would remember to make the time pass quickly. He liked to stretch out like a lizard in the sun and not do a blessed thing. And when he met the carters, riding perched on their shafts, he grumbled: "Now there's a great trade! They ride around in a carriage all day long!" And if he saw some poor old woman go by, on her way back from the city, bent under her load like a weary donkey and lamenting as she trudged along, as old folks do, to comfort her he'd say: "I'd like to do what you're doing, sister! After all, it's just like taking a stroll."

CHAPTER TEN

'Ntoni took a stroll on the sea every blessed day, and he had to travel on his oars, breaking his back. But when the sea was rough and threatened to gulp all of them down in one big mouthful—them, the *Provvidenza* and all the rest —that boy had a heart greater than the sea.

"It's the Malavoglia blood," his grandfather said. And you had to see him when he set the sail, with his hair whipping in the wind while the boat leaped over the waves like a mullet in love.

Though old and patched up, the *Provvidenza* often ventured far from shore for the sake of that bit of fish, especially now when there were so many boats in the village, sweeping the sea clean, like a broom. Even on the days when the clouds hung low towards Agnone and to the east the horizon bristled with black streaks, the *Provvidenza's* sail was always there, as tiny as a pocket handkerchief, far, far out on the leaden sea, and everybody said that Master 'Ntoni's crew were looking for trouble with a candlestick.

Master 'Ntoni replied that he was looking for his bread, and when the cork floats disappeared one by one in the open sea which was as green as grass, and Trezza's little houses were so far away that they looked like a white blur, and nothing but water spread all around them, he became so happy that he began chattering away to his grandsons. Later, in the evening, as soon as they saw the sail appear between the Faraglioni rocks, La Longa and the children would be waiting for them on the shore, and they'd watch the fish which leaped in the traps and filled the bottom of the boat like silver. And before anyone could say a word, Master 'Ntoni answered: "A hundred kilos," or "A hundred and twenty-five," and he wouldn't be a *rotolo* off in the weight; and then they would talk about it all evening, while the women were pounding salt between the stones and they counted the barrels one by one, and Uncle Crocifisso came to see what they'd caught and threw in an offer with his eyes shut, and Piedipapera shouted and cursed to obtain the right price, and then his shouts were good to hear—which only went to show that in this world one mustn't bear a grudge. And afterwards La Longa would count the money that Piedipapera had brought them in his handkerchief, coin by coin, in front of her father-in-law, saying: "These are for the house, and these are for the food." And Mena also helped pound the salt and prepare the barrels. And she wore her bright blue dress again and the coral necklace which they'd had to give Uncle Crocifisso as a pledge. Now the women could go to Mass again in the village, because they were arranging for Mena's dowry in case some young man should set his eyes on her.

"There's one thing I'd like to see," said 'Ntoni, slowly moving his oar so that the current wouldn't make them drift out of the ring of nets, while his grandfather was thinking of all these things, "I'd like to see that bitch Barbara chew her hands with rage when we also have our property, and be sorry she ever slammed that door in my face!"

"In a storm you can tell the good pilot," the old man answered. "When we'll once more be what we've always been, they'll all be our friends and open their doors to us."

"Nunziata didn't close hers," said Alessi. "And neither did Cousin Anna."

" 'When prison, illness, and want appear, you know what friends are dear.' That's why the Lord helps them, with all those hungry mouths they have to feed."

"When Nunziata goes to gather brush on the lava field, or her bundle of cloth is too heavy for her, I help her too, poor girl," Alessi said.

"Now help us pull up the net on this side, because this time Saint Francis has sent us God's own bounty!" The boy dug in his heels and pulled, panting so loud you'd think he was doing all the work. Meanwhile 'Ntoni was singing, lying on the stretcher with his arms crossed behind his head, watching the white gulls fly through a boundless blue sky, and the *Provvidenza* rocked on the green waves which came rolling in from far out, as far as you could see.

"Why is the sea sometimes green and sometimes dark blue, and then it's white, and then black like the lava field? And why isn't it always the same color, the color of the water?" Alessi asked.

"It's the will of God," his grandfather replied. "This way, the fisherman knows when he can put out to sea without fear, and when it's better not to go out at all."

"Those gulls have a fine life, always flying high up, and when the sea is stormy, they don't have to fear the waves."

"But then they don't eat either, poor creatures."

"So we all need good weather, just like Nunziata, who can't go to the fountain when it rains," Alessi concluded.

"Neither good weather nor bad weather lasts forever!" the old man said.

But when the weather was bad or the nor'wester blew, and all day long the corks danced on the water as though somebody were playing the violin for them, or the sea was as white as milk, or so frothy it seemed to be boiling and the rain pelted down on their backs until evening so that no coat could keep them dry, and all around them the water hissed and sizzled like a fish in a frying pan, then it was another story entirely. With his hood pulled over his nose, 'Ntoni didn't feel like singing and he had to bail the water out of the *Provvidenza,* a job that went on and on and never ended. And his grandfather kept dinning into their ears: " 'When the sea is white, sirocco's in sight,' " and " 'White caps at sea, a fresh wind there'll be,' " as though they were there to learn proverbs; and in the evening while he looked out the window and sniffed the air, he went right on with his blessed proverbs, saying: " 'When the moon is red, the wind rises; when it's white, that means fair weather; and when it's pale, it'll rain.' "

"If you know when it's going to rain, why are we out with the boat today?" 'Ntoni would say. "Wouldn't it have been better to stay in bed a few more hours?"

" 'Water from heaven, sardines in the net!' " the old man would reply.

Then 'Ntoni, standing in the water up to his knees, would curse so much the devil could have snatched him there and then.

"Tonight Maruzza will have a big beautiful fire waiting for us and we'll all get dry," his grandfather said.

And in the evening, at dusk, when the *Provvidenza* came in with her belly full of God's bounty and her sail swelling like Donna Rosolina's skirt, and the lights from the houses winked one by one from behind the black Faraglioni and seemed to be calling to each other, Master 'Ntoni showed his boys the big fire blazing in La Longa's kitchen at the end of their small yard on Black Lane, because the wall was low there and from the water you could see the whole house, with that bit of tile roofing under which the chickens roosted and the bread oven at the other side of the door. "Didn't I tell you that La Longa would have a fire waiting for us!" he cried jubilantly. And on the shore La Longa was waiting for them, with the baskets all ready. When they had to carry the baskets back empty they didn't feel like talking, but if there weren't enough baskets and Alessi had to run home to get more, his grandfather cupped his hands to his mouth and called out from the boat: "Mena! Hey, Mena!" And Mena knew just what he wanted, and all of them came down in a procession: she, Lia, and even Nunziata, with all the children trailing after her. Then everybody was gay and nobody minded the cold or the rain, and they sat before the fire talking till late about God's great bounty that Saint Francis had sent and what they were going to do with the money.

In that desperate gamble, though, they risked their skins for a few *rotoli* of fish, and once, like Bastianazzo, they all came within a hair of losing their lives for the sake of money. Along towards evening they were off Agnone and the sky was so dark you couldn't even see Mount Etna, and the wind was blowing gusts so shrill you'd think it was speaking.

"Nasty weather!" Master 'Ntoni said. "Today the wind is whirling about worse than a giddy girl's head, and the sea looks like Piedipapera when he's about to play you a dirty trick."

The sea was as black as the lava field, although the sun hadn't yet gone down, and from time to time it seethed all around them like a kettle on the stove.

"The gulls must have all gone to sleep now," Alessi said.

"They ought to have lit the Catania light by now, but you can't see a thing," 'Ntoni said.

"Keep the tiller pointing northeast, Alessi," his grandfather ordered. "In half an hour we won't see a thing —it'll be worse than being inside an oven."

"On an ugly night like this, it's better to be sitting in Santuzza's tavern."

"Or lying in bed asleep, is that what you mean?" his grandfather replied. "Then you should have been a clerk, like Don Silvestro."

The poor old man had been groaning all day because of his aches and pains. "It's the changing weather!" he kept saying. "I can feel it in my bones."

All of a sudden it grew so dark you couldn't even see enough to curse. Only the waves rushing past the *Provvidenza* glittered as though they had eyes and wanted to devour her; and in the midst of that sea bellowing on all sides as far as they could see, nobody dared speak.

"If you ask me, tonight we'll have to give our catch to the devil," 'Ntoni suddenly said.

"Quiet!" his grandfather cried, and in that darkness his voice made them shrink and cower on their seats.

The wind was shrieking in the *Provvidenza*'s sail, and the rigging twanged like the string of a guitar. Suddenly the wind began to whistle as loud as the engine on the railroad, when it comes out of the hole in the mountain above Trezza, and a wave which rose up out of nowhere crashed down on the *Provvidenza,* making her grate like a bag of nuts, and then tossed her up in the air.

"Drop the sail! Drop the sail!" Master 'Ntoni yelled. "Cut it! Cut it!"

'Ntoni, with his knife between his teeth, was clinging to the yardarm, standing upright on the gunwale to balance the boat. Then he let himself dangle over the sea which was howling below and wanted to devour him.

"Hold on! Hold on!" his grandfather shouted to him through the crash of the waves which were trying to tear him loose. They battered at the *Provvidenza* which was already filled with water up to their knees, making her heel way over on her side.

"Cut it, cut it," his grandfather kept yelling.

"Damn it!" shouted 'Ntoni. "If I cut it, what will we do when we need it?"

"Don't curse! Now we're in the hands of God!"

Hearing these words, Alessi, who was clutching the tiller, began to scream: "Mama! Mama!"

"Quiet!" his brother yelled at him, his knife between his teeth. "Shut up or I'll kick you!"

"Cross yourself and keep quiet!" his grandfather repeated, and the boy fell silent.

Suddenly the sail came down all at once, because it was stretched so tight, and in a flash 'Ntoni had hauled it in and tied it fast.

"At this trade you're as good as your father," his grandfather said. "You're a Malavoglia, too."

The boat righted itself and bounded forward with a great leap; then it continued to plunge up and down on the waves.

"Give me the tiller. Now it needs a steady hand!" shouted Master 'Ntoni; and although the boy was hanging on to the bar like a cat, such big waves struck the boat that they slammed it against their chests.

The boat creaked and groaned under the powerful tug of 'Ntoni's arms. And Alessi too, upright against the foot brace, put all his strength and will into pulling the oars.

"Hold on!" his grandfather shouted. The wind was howling so loud that he could barely be heard from one end of the boat to the other. "Hold on, Alessi!"

"Yes, Grandpa, yes," the boy answered.

"Are you afraid?" 'Ntoni asked.

"No," his grandfather answered for him, "but we must put ourselves in God's hands."

"Holy devil!" cried 'Ntoni, his chest heaving. "We ought to have iron arms, like the steam engine. The sea is beating us."

His grandfather fell silent, and they listened to the storm.

Alessi said: "Mama must be standing on the shore now, to see if we're coming back."

"Don't talk about Mama now," his grandfather said. "It's better not to think of her."

After another long stretch, 'Ntoni, gasping through his teeth from exhaustion, asked: "And now, where are we?"

"In the hands of God," the old man replied.

"Then let me cry!" cxclaimed Alessi, who was at the end of his rope. And in all that tumult of wind and sea, he began to scream and call for his mother at the top of his lungs; and nobody had the heart to scold him.

"You can sing till doomsday, nobody can hear, so you might as well keep quiet," his brother finally said, but in a changed voice which sounded strange even to him. "Keep quiet, it's no good acting this way now, either for yourself or for us."

"Put up the sail!" Master 'Ntoni ordered. "And keep the boat headed into the wind. The rest is up to God."

The wind fought them as they carried out the order, yet in five minutes the sail was unfurled, and the *Provvidenza* began leaping over the crests of the waves, tilted over like a wounded bird. The Malavoglia all stayed on one side, clinging to the gunwale. None of them even breathed, because when the sea speaks like that you haven't the courage to open your mouth.

Master 'Ntoni simply said: "Right now they're praying for us, back there."

And then they kept mum, swept along by the wind and waves in the night which had suddenly fallen as black as pitch.

"The light on the jetty!" 'Ntoni cried. "Can you see it?"

"To starboard!" Master 'Ntoni shouted. "It's not the light. We're running on the rocks. Pull in the sail! Pull it in!"

"I can't," 'Ntoni answered, his voice stifled by the storm and his struggle with the sail. "The sail's wet. The knife, Alessi, the knife!"

"Cut it! Cut it! Quick!"

At that very moment they heard a crash. The *Provvidenza,* which at first heeled way over on her side, bounced back like a spring and nearly threw them all into the sea. The yardarm snapped like a straw and fell into the boat together with the sail. Then they heard a voice crying: "Ah! Ah!" like the voice of a man about to die.

"Who is it? Who's crying?" asked 'Ntoni, using both his knife and teeth to cut the bolt-ropes of the sail, which had fallen into the boat along with the yardarm and covered everything. Suddenly a gust of wind tore the sail loose and carried it away with a shriek. Then the brothers were able to disentangle the stump of the yardarm and fling it overboard. The boat came upright again, but not Master 'Ntoni, nor did he answer 'Ntoni, who was calling him. Now, when wind and sea howl together, there's nothing more frightening than not getting an answer to your shouting voice. Alessi was also yelling: "Grandpa! Grandpa!" and when they didn't hear anything, the two brothers were stiff with fright. The night was so black that you couldn't see from one end of the *Provvidenza* to the other, and Alessi was so paralyzed by terror that he stopped crying. The old man was stretched out on the bottom of the boat, with a broken head. 'Ntoni, groping in the dark, found him at last and thought he was dead, for he didn't breathe or move at all. The tiller banged from side to side, while the boat leaped and plunged.

"Oh, Saint Francis of Paola! Blessed Saint Francis!" the two boys shrieked, for they no longer knew what to do.

And merciful Saint Francis heard them while traveling through the storm to help his faithful and stretched his mantle under the *Provvidenza,* just as she was going to crack like a nutshell on the Rock of the Doves below the customs lookout. The boat leaped like a colt over the ledge and fell nose down among the rocks. "Courage! Courage!" the customs guards shouted to them from the shore, running back and forth with their lanterns, trying to throw them a rope. "We're here. Don't lose heart!" At last one of the ropes fell athwart the *Provvidenza,* which was trembling like a leaf, and lashed 'Ntoni's face like the blow of a whip, but at that moment it felt sweeter than a caress.

"Here, here," he yelled, grabbing the rope which was sliding quickly away, trying to slip through his hands. And Alessi also grabbed it with all his might, and so they managed to wind it two or three times around the tiller, and the customs guards hauled them to shore.

But Master 'Ntoni gave no sign of life, and when they brought the lantern close they saw that his face was smeared with blood, so everyone thought he was dead, and his grandsons began tearing their hair. But after a couple of hours Don Michele, Rocco Spatu, and Turi Pizzuto, and all the idlers who were at the tavern when the news arrived, came running, and with the help of cold water and massages they got him to open his eyes. And the poor old man, when he found out where they were, at least an hour away from Trezza, asked them to carry him home on a ladder.

So Maruzza, Mena, and all the neighbors, who were shrieking and beating their breasts in the piazza, saw him come back like that, stretched out on the ladder, his face as white as a corpse.

"It's nothing! It's nothing!" said Don Michele, who was at the head of the crowd. "It's nothing to worry about." And he ran to the pharmacist to get the herb vinegar of the "Seven Thieves." Don Franco came in person, holding the small bottle with both hands, and also Piedipapera, Comare Grazia, the Zuppiddi, Master Cipolla and the whole neighborhood rushed to Black Lane, because on such occasions all disputes are forgotten. La Locca had come too. She always went wherever a crowd gathered, whenever she heard a babble of voices in the village, day or night, as though she never closed her eyes and were forever waiting for her Menico. So the people crowded the narrow lane in front of the Malavoglia house as though somebody had died, and Cousin Anna had to shut the door in their faces.

Then Nunziata rushed up, half dressed, and began banging on the door and screaming: "Let me in! Let me in! I want to see what's happened at Maruzza's."

"What's the use of sending us for the ladder, if afterwards they won't let us into the house to see what's happened!" La Locca's son blustered.

Venera Zuppidda and the Mangiacarrube girl had forgotten all the insults they'd hurled at each other and were chattering at the door, their hands under their aprons.

"Yes, that's what it means to be a fisherman. In the end they all leave their skins at sea," La Zuppidda said. "If you marry your daughter to seagoing folk, sooner or later she'll come back home a widow and with orphans into the bargain, because if it hadn't been for Don Michele, tonight there wouldn't have been even the seed of the Malavoglia left." The best thing was to do like the people who do nothing and still earn a day's wage, like Don Michele, for instance, who was as plump and fat as a canon priest and always went about dressed in woolen clothes, and devoured half the town, and everyone flattered him and even the pharmacist, who wanted to eat the King for breakfast, doffed his big black hat to him.

"It's nothing," Don Franco came out to say. "We bandaged him. But if he doesn't get a fever, he'll go."

Piedipapera went to see for himself, because he was a friend of the family, and Master Fortunato too, and whoever else managed to push his way in.

"I don't like the looks of his face at all!" Master Cipolla declared in grave tones, shaking his head. "How do you feel, Master 'Ntoni?"

"That's why Master Cipolla refused to give his son to Saint Agatha," said Venera Zuppidda, whom they'd left behind at the door. "Oh, that man has a sharp nose!"

And La Vespa added: "He who has goods at sea has nothing! You've got to have land in the sun, that's what."

"What a night has come for the Malavoglia!" cried Comare Piedipapera.

"Did you notice that all the misfortunes in this house come at night?" observed Master Cipolla, coming out of the house with Don Franco and Compare Tino.

"Just to get a piece of bread, poor things!" Comare Grazia added.

For two or three days, Master 'Ntoni was closer to the next world than to this one. The fever had come, as the pharmacist had said, but it was so high that it nearly finished him off. The poor man, with his bandaged head and long beard, lay in his corner and didn't even complain. But he had a great thirst, and when Mena or La Longa brought him water he seized the jug with shaking hands, as if they were going to steal it from him.

Don Ciccio, the doctor, came every morning, dressed the wound, felt his pulse, asked him to stick out his tongue, and then left shaking his head.

One night, after Don Ciccio shook his head more than usual, they even kept the candle burning; La Longa hung the image of the Holy Virgin next to it, and she told her rosary beads in front of the bed of the sick man, who didn't say a word anymore and didn't even ask for water. None of them went to sleep, and Lia yawned so much from tiredness she nearly broke her jaw. An ill-omened silence filled the house, and the carts passing along the road made the glasses on the table rattle and startled the group watching the sick man. The whole next day went by in the same way, with the neighbors standing around the door, talking among themselves in low voices and looking through the doorway to see what was going on. Towards evening Master 'Ntoni, with his eyes dim and spent, called to them one by one and wanted to know what the doctor had said. 'Ntoni stood at the head of his bed, crying like a little boy, because the lad had a good heart. "Don't cry like that!" his grandfather said to him. "Don't cry. Now you're the head of the family. Just remember that you have all the others on your shoulders, and do as I have done."

When they heard him talk that way, the women began to scream and tear their hair, even little Lia, because in such circumstances, women don't have any sense and they didn't realize that the old man's face grew more troubled at seeing them so desperate, as if he were about to die. But he continued speaking in a feeble voice: "Don't spend too much money when I'm gone. The Lord knows that we can't spend any money, and He'll be satisfied with the prayers Maruzza and Mena will say for me. And you, Mena, always do as your mother has done, because she has been a saintly woman, and she's seen plenty of trouble, too. And keep a good watch over your sister, like the mother hen protects her chicks. As long as you help each other, your troubles won't seem too heavy. 'Ntoni is a grown man now, and soon Alessi will be able to help, too."

"Don't talk that way!" the women begged him, sobbing as though he himself wanted to die. "For mercy's sake, don't talk like that." He shook his head sadly and said: "Now that I've said what I wanted to say, I don't care. I'm an old man. When the oil is gone, the lamp goes out. Now turn me on the other side, because I'm tired."

Later he called to 'Ntoni again and said to him:

"Don't sell the *Provvidenza,* even though she's so old. If you do, you'll be forced to hire out by the day and you know how hard it is when Master Cipolla and Uncle Cola tell you: 'I don't need anyone for Monday.' And I want to tell you another thing, 'Ntoni. When you've put together some money, you must first marry off Mena, and give her to somebody who does the same work as her father did and is a good man. And I also want to tell you that after you've married off Lia too, if you save some money, put it aside and buy back the house by the medlar tree. Don Crocifisso will sell it to you, if he can make his profit, because it's always belonged to the Malavoglia, and it's from there that your father departed, and Luca too, bless his soul."

"Yes, grandfather, yes!" 'Ntoni promised, crying. Alessi was listening too, as serious as if he were already a grown man.

Hearing him talk and talk, the women thought that the sick man was delirious, and they kept putting wet cloths on his forehead. "No, I'm in my right senses," Master 'Ntoni said. "I want to finish saying everything I have to say before I go."

Meanwhile they began to hear the fishermen calling to each other from door to door, and the carts had again begun to pass along the road. "In two hours it will be day," Master 'Ntoni said, "and you can go and call Don Giammaria."

Those poor people waited for daylight as for the Messiah, and went to the window every other minute to see whether the dawn had come. At last the small room began to grow light, and Master 'Ntoni said again: "Now go and call the priest, because I want to confess."

Don Giammaria came when the sun was already high, and all the neighbor women, when they heard his bell on Black Lane, ran to see the viaticum which was going to the Malavoglia, and they all went in, because where Our Lord goes you can't shut the door in people's faces, and the Malavoglia family, seeing the house full, didn't even dare to cry or give way to despair, while Don Giammaria muttered through his teeth, and Mastro Cirino held the candle under the nose of the sick man, who was as yellow and stiff as a candle himself.

"He looks just like the patriarch Saint Joseph, lying on that bed with that long beard of his! Ah, the lucky man!" exclaimed Santuzza, who always left her wine jugs and everything else to rush to wherever Our Lord had gone. "She's like a raven," the pharmacist said.

Don Ciccio, the doctor, arrived while the priest was still there with his holy oil, and he became so angry that he wanted to turn his donkey around and go right home. "Who told you that you needed a priest? Who went to call for extreme unction? We doctors are supposed to tell you when the time has come. And I'm surprised the priest came without a note from me. You want to know something? There's no need for extreme unction. He's getting better, I tell you, he's getting better!"

"It's the miracle of Our Lady of the Sorrows!" La Longa cried. "Our Lady has given us a miracle, because the Lord has been in this house too many times!"

"Ah! Blessed Virgin!" cried Mena, her hands joined. "Ah, Holy Virgin, you've listened to our prayers!" And they all cried with relief, as if the sick man were already able to set out to sea on the *Provvidenza*.

Don Ciccio left, grumbling: "That's how they thank me! If they live, the Virgin has brought about a miracle! If they die, I'm the one who killed them!"

At the door, the women were still waiting to see the dead man pass, for they thought they'd be coming for him any minute. "Poor man!" they muttered.

"That old man has a tough hide," Venera Zuppidda preached. "If he doesn't fall on his nose like a cat, he won't die. Listen to what I'm telling you right now. We've been here for two days waiting: will he die or won't he? I tell you that he'll bury all of us." The women made the sign to ward off bad luck. "Devil be wary, I'm a Daughter of Mary," they chanted, and La Vespa also kissed the medal on her scapulary and cried: "Shatter and scatter! Thunder in the air, and sulphur in the wine!" Venera Zuppidda said: "You at least don't have children to marry off, as I do, and if I were to be buried, I'd do great harm to everyone." The other women laughed, because La Vespa had only herself to marry and she couldn't even manage that. "When it comes to that, Master 'Ntoni would do even greater harm, because he's the mainstay of his family," Cousin Anna replied.

"What about that oaf 'Ntoni, he's no longer a boy!"

But all of them shrugged and said: "If the old man dies, you'll see how fast that house will fall apart."

Just then Nunziata arrived, walking quickly, her water pitcher on her head. "Let me through, let me through," she cried. "Comare Maruzza's waiting for this water. And if my children start playing, they'll throw everything I've got into the street!"

Lia had come to the door, perky and full of importance, and said to the women: "My grandfather feels better. Don Ciccio said that my grandfather won't die just yet." And she was very pleased to have them all listening to her as if she were a grown woman.

Alessi also came and said to Nunziata: "Now that you're here, I'll run over and take a look at the *Provvidenza*."

"This boy has more good sense than his older brother!" Cousin Anna said.

"They're going to give Don Michele a medal for throwing the rope to the *Provvidenza*," the pharmacist remarked. "And there's a pension with it, too. That's how they spend the people's money!"

To defend Don Michele, Piedipapera kept saying that he deserved the medal and the pension because he'd thrown himself into the water up to his knees, even with his boots on, to save the Malavoglias' lives. Wasn't that enough? Three people! And he'd come close to losing his own skin. And everybody talked about it, so that on Sunday, when Don Michele put on his new uniform, the girls kept staring at him to see if he had the medal.

"Now that Barbara Zuppidda has driven that Malavoglia lout out of her head, she won't turn her back on Don Michele any longer," Piedipapera said. "I've seen her myself, with her nose stuck between the shutters when he walks down her street!"

And hearing this, Don Silvestro said to Vanni Pizzuto: "You made a fine bargain. You got rid of Master 'Ntoni's 'Ntoni and now Barbara has set her eyes on Don Michele!"

"If she has set her eyes on him, she'll have to take them off, because her mother can't stand policemen, loafers, or outsiders."

"You'll see, you'll see! Barbara's twenty-three years old.

And once she gets it into her head that if she waits any longer for a husband she'll start to get mouldy, she'll take him, by hook or crook. You want to bet twelve tarì that they're talking at the window?" And he pulled out a brand-new five lire coin.

"I don't want to bet anything," Pizzuto replied, shrugging his shoulders. "I don't give a damn about it."

Piedipapera and Rocco Spatu, who were listening, laughed so hard they almost wet themselves. "I'll bet you for nothing," said Don Silvestro, whose mood had improved. And he went together with the others to chat with Uncle Santoro in front of the tavern. "Listen, Uncle Santoro, do you want to earn twelve tarì?" he asked, and pulled out the new coin, though Uncle Santoro couldn't see. "Mastro Vanni Pizzuto wants to bet twelve tarì that in the evening Don Michele, the sergeant, goes to talk with Barbara Zuppidda. Do you want to make twelve tarì?"

"Oh blessed souls in purgatory!" cried Uncle Santoro, kissing his rosary beads. He had listened very carefully, his dead eyes raised; but he looked worried and kept twisting his lips, just like a hunting dog twitches his ears when he strikes a scent.

"They're friends, don't be afraid," Don Silvestro added, snickering.

"They are Compare Tino and Rocco Spatu," the blind man said, after having listened a little longer.

He knew all those who went by from the sound of their footsteps, whether they were wearing shoes or went bare-footed, and he would say: "You're Compare Tino," or "You're Compare Cinghialenta." And since he was always there, chattering with one person or another, he knew what was happening all over the village, and so to earn those twelve tarì, when the children came to get wine for the evening meal, he called over Alessi, or Nunziata, or Lia, and asked them: "Where are you going? Where are you coming from? What did you do today?" or "Did you see Don Michele? Has he been walking down Black Lane?"

'Ntoni, poor fellow, as long as he'd had to, had run all over the place, out of breath, and had torn his hair, too. But now that his grandfather was better, he began knocking about the village, his arms folded, waiting for the time when they could take the *Provvidenza* to Mastro Zuppiddo again, to patch her up. And he went to the tavern, just to talk for a while, since he hadn't a cent in his pocket, and he told whoever happened to be there how they'd seen death face to face—and that's how he spent his time, gabbing and spitting. When they treated him to a few glasses of wine, he began to curse Don Michele, who had stolen his girl and went every evening to talk to her. Uncle Santoro had seen them, he'd even asked Nunziata whether Don Michele passed along Black Lane.

"By the blood of Judas! My name's not 'Ntoni Malavoglia if I don't wipe out this insult, by the blood of Judas!"

People enjoyed seeing him eat his heart out, and that's why they paid for his wine. Santuzza, while she was rinsing the glasses, turned away so as not to hear the curses and the dirty words; but when she heard them talk about Don Michele, she forgot everything and listened with her eyes wide open. She'd become curious too and was all ears when they talked about him, and she gave apples or green almonds to Nunziata's little brother or Alessi when they came for wine, to find out whom they'd seen walking on Black Lane. Don Michele swore up and down that it wasn't true, and often at night, when the tavern was already closed, you heard a hell of a row behind the closed doors. "Liar!" Santuzza screamed. "Murderer! Thief! Enemy of God!"

In the end Don Michele stopped going to the tavern and for the sake of peace, he just sent for his wine and drank it in Pizzuto's shop, all alone with his bottle.

Massaro Filippo, instead of being happy that one more dog had been pulled off that bone Santuzza, put in some kind words for him and tried to bring them together, and nobody could figure it out. But he was wasting his time. "Don't you see he's giving me a wide berth and that he doesn't show his face here anymore?" Santuzza cried. "This is the sign that it's true, as true as God! No, I don't want to hear his name again. Even if this means that I've got to close the tavern and start knitting!"

Then Massaro Filippo felt his mouth go bitter with anger and he went to the customs barracks or Pizzuto's shop, to beg Don Michele like a saint to end his quarrel with Santuzza, after they'd been such good friends, because now they were really giving people something to gossip about. And he put his arms around him and pulled him by the sleeve; but Don Michele dug in his heels like a mule and said no. And the people who happened to be there to enjoy the spectacle said that Massaro Filippo was cutting a fine figure indeed, as true as there's a God! "Massaro Filippo needs help," Pizzuto said. "Can't you tell? That Santuzza would devour the crucifix itself!"

Then one fine day Santuzza put on her shawl and went to confession, though it was a Monday and the tavern was packed with customers. Santuzza usually went to confession on Sunday, and she stayed there for an hour with her nose pressed against the grill of the confession booth, rinsing out her conscience, which she liked to keep even cleaner than her glasses. But this time Donna Rosolina, who was jealous of her brother the priest and often confessed too, just to keep her eye on him, was amazed, as she waited there on her knees, that Santuzza should have so much on her stomach, and she noticed that her brother the priest blew his nose more than five times.

"What was wrong with Santuzza today? She took so long?" she asked Don Giammaria, when they sat down at the table.

"Nothing, nothing," her brother replied, reaching out for his plate.

But she, knowing his weak spot, wouldn't uncover the soup bowl and tormented him with so many questions that finally the poor man had to say that after all there was the seal of the confessional. And all the time he sat at the table he kept his nose in his plate, gobbling down his macaroni as if he hadn't seen God's bounty for two whole days, eating so fast that they turned sour on him, and all the while muttering that people never left him in peace. After dinner he took his hat and cloak and went to call on Venera Zuppidda.

"There must be something going on!" Donna Rosolina muttered to herself. "It must be some dirty business between Sister Santuzza Mariangela and Venera Zuppidda, and it's going on right under the seal of the confessional." And she went to the window to see how long her brother stayed in Comare Venera's house.

When she heard the message that Sister Mariangela had sent her through Don Giammaria, Venera Zuppidda was seized by fury and went out on her landing to blare that she didn't want other people's property, let Santuzza open her ears good and wide! And if she so much as saw Don Michele walk down her street, she was going to gouge his eyes out with the distaff she held in her hand, despite that pistol he carried on his belly, for she wasn't afraid of pistols or anyone, and she wasn't going to give her daughter to a man who ate the King's bread and was a spy, and was in mortal sin with Santuzza, besides. Don Giammaria had told her all about it under the seal of the confessional, but when it came to her daughter Barbara, she had no more use for that seal than for her old slippers—and her curses came so thick and fast that La Longa and Cousin Anna had to close their doors so that the girls wouldn't hear them; and her husband, Mastro Turi, not to be outdone, was also bawling: "If they step on my tail, they'll make me do something rash, blessed God! I'm not afraid of Don Michele and Massaro Filippo and Santuzza's whole crew!"

"Keep quiet!" Comare Venera outshouted him. "Didn't you hear that Massaro Filippo has nothing more to do with Santuzza?"

Other people, however, went on saying that Santuzza had Massaro Filippo to help her say her prayers, Piedipapera had seen them. "Sure! Massaro Filippo needs help himself!" Pizzuto repeated. "Didn't you see how he came to beg and implore Don Michele to help him?"

In his pharmacy Don Franco buttonholed people just so he could snicker over the whole affair.

"I told you, didn't I? They're all like that, those saint-huggers! They've got the devil under their skirts! Some business, eh? Two at a time, just to make a pair! Now that they're giving Don Michele that medal, they'll hang it on the wall, together with the Daughter of Mary medal Santuzza's got." And he stuck his head out of the door to see if his wife was at the window upstairs. "Aha! the church and the customs barracks! The throne and the altar! Always the same story, take it from me!"

He wasn't afraid of either the saber or the holy water sprinkler; and he didn't give a damn about Don Michele, in fact he told him off when his wife wasn't at the window and couldn't hear what was being said in the shop, but Donna Rosolina gave her brother a good scolding as soon as she found out that he'd gotten into that mess, because it's always better to keep on friendly terms with those people who carry the saber.

"Friends? Some friends!" Don Giammaria retorted. "Friends with the people who've stolen the bread right out of our mouths? I've done my duty. I don't need them! They need us!"

"At least you should say that Santuzza sent you, under the seal of the confessional," Donna Rosolina insisted. "That way, you won't be the one to make an enemy."

But to all the women who buzzed around her to find out how that nasty mess had come out into the open, she kept repeating with a mysterious air that the whole matter was under the seal of the confessional. Piedipapera, since he had heard Don Silvestro say that he wanted to make Barbara fall with his feet like a ripe pear, went about whispering: "This is all a trick of Don Silvestro's, who wants to make Barbara Zuppidda fall with his feet."

And he said it so many times that it reached the ears of Donna Rosolina, as she was preparing her tomato paste, with her sleeves rolled up. And she began shouting and gesticulating to defend Don Michele in the people's eyes, for everybody ought to know that she had nothing against Don Michele personally, even though he was one of those people in the government. And she said that man is a hunter, and that it was up to Comare Zuppidda to keep an eye on her daughter, and that if Don Michele had some other affairs going, this was a matter for him and his conscience.

"This is all the work of Don Silvestro, who wants Barbara Zuppidda, and has bet twelve tarì that he'll make her fall with his feet," La Vespa told Donna Rosolina, as she helped her make the tomato paste. She kept going there to beg Don Giammaria to drive some scruples into the head of that rascal, Uncle Crocifisso, who had a head harder than a mule's. "Doesn't he realize that he's got both feet in the grave?" she said. "Does he want to have that sin on his conscience, too?"

But when she heard the story about Don Silvestro,

Donna Rosolina immediately changed her tune, got red as
her tomato paste, and began to wave her ladle in the air
and to preach against men who give false hopes to unmarried girls and all those flirts who stand at their windows
just to deceive them. Everybody knew what sort of a flirt
that Barbara was; but she was amazed that a man like
Don Silvestro should be taken in, he looked like a levelheaded person, and nobody would have expected such a
betrayal from him. But instead he went out of his way to
get into trouble with Barbara Zuppidda and Don Michele,
while all the time he had his good fortune right within
reach and didn't seize it. "Nowadays to find out what a
man is really like, one has to eat seven pecks of salt."

Don Silvestro, however, strolled around arm in arm
with Don Michele, and though all that gossip was raging
behind their backs, nobody dared breathe a word of it to
their faces. Now, whenever the town clerk stood in the doorway of the pharmacy and looked up, Donna Rosolina
slammed her window shut in his face and didn't even turn
her head when she was putting tomato paste out to dry in the
sun. Then once she went to confess at Aci Castello, for
she'd committed a sin she couldn't tell her brother, and
somehow she chanced to meet Don Silvestro, just as he
was returning from his vineyard.

"Oh, look who's there!" she said, stopping to catch her
breath, for she was flushed and panting. "You must have
a lot on your mind, because you don't seem to remember
your old friends."

"I've nothing on my mind, Donna Rosolina."

"But they've told me you do, and it's such foolishness
that, if it's true, you really do have something to worry
about."

"Who told you?"

"The whole village is talking about it."

"Let them talk. Besides, you want to know something?
I do as I please. And if I have any worries, I'll take
care of them."

"Well, good health to you then!" Donna Rosolina retorted, her face as red as a beet. "If that's the way you
answer me, this means your worries have started already.
I never thought you'd act like this, and until now I considered you a sensible man. Forgive me if I've made a

mistake. So let's say that it's all water under the bridge, and that neither good weather nor bad weather lasts forever. But just remember what the proverb says: 'He who changes old for new will be disappointed through and through,' and 'he who chooses beauty chooses a pair of horns.' Enjoy your Barbara Zuppidda in peace and quiet, because I don't care. But I wouldn't want people to talk about me the way they talk about your Barbara, not for all the gold in the world!"

"Don't fret about that, Donna Rosolina, because by now it's too late to say anything about you."

"At least they don't say that I'm eating up half the village. I'm sure you know what I mean, Don Silvestro?"

"Let them talk, Donna Rosolina. 'He who has a mouth eats, and he who doesn't eat dies.' "

"And they don't say about me what they say about you —that you're a swindler," Donna Rosolina went on, green as a clove of garlic. "Do you understand me, Don Silvestro? You can't say that about everybody! By the way, when you don't need them anymore, you can give me back those twenty-five onze I loaned you. I don't steal my money, like certain people do."

"Don't worry, Donna Rosolina, I never said that you stole your twenty-five onze, and I won't tell your brother Don Giammaria. I don't care to know whether or not you stole them from the household money. All I know is that I don't owe you anything. You told me to get some interest on the money so you could put together a dowry, in case somebody wanted to marry you, and I put it in the bank for you under my name, so your brother wouldn't find out, because then he would have asked where you'd found it. Now the bank has failed. Is that my fault?"

"Crook!" Donna Rosolina spat at him, foaming at the mouth. "Swindler! I didn't give you that money to put in a bank that was going to fail. I gave it to you so you could watch it, as though it were your own!"

"Yes, that's just what I did!" the town clerk answered brazenly, and Donna Rosolina, afraid that she'd burst from rage, turned her back on him and went back to Trezza, sweating like a sponge in the afternoon sun, her shawl over her shoulders. Don Silvestro stood there sneer-

ing in front of the stone wall around Massaro Filippo's
vegetable garden until she had turned the corner, and then
he shrugged, muttering to himself: "I don't give a damn
about what they say."

And he was right not to bother about what they said.
They said that if Don Silvestro had gotten it into his head
to make Barbara fall with his feet, she would certainly
fall, because he was a scoundrel through and through. But
they still tipped their caps to him, and when he went to
chat at the pharmacy his friends nodded their heads and
winked and snickered. "You're a despot!" Don Franco
said to him, patting him on the back. "A real feudal lord.
You're the man of destiny, sent on this earth to show how
this old society has got to be cleaned up without wasting
another minute." And when 'Ntoni came to get the medicine for his grandfather, Don Franco said: "You are the
people. So long as you're as patient as a donkey, you can
expect a beating." And then, to change the subject, the
Signora, who was knitting behind the counter, asked:
"How is your grandfather now?" But 'Ntoni was afraid
to open his mouth in the Signora's presence and left grumbling to himself, holding the medicine glass in his hand.

His grandfather was feeling better and they sat him in
front of the door in the sun, wrapped in a cloak and with
a handkerchief over his head. And he looked so much like
a dead man who's been resurrected that people came to
see him just out of curiosity. And the poor old man nodded his head to everyone like a parrot and smiled, happy
to be out there beside the door, in his cloak, with Maruzza
spinning next to him, and the thwack of Mena's loom resounding through the house, and the chickens scrabbling
on the road. Now that he had nothing else to do he'd
learned to recognize the neighbors, one by one, and he
watched what they did, and passed the time listening to
their voices. He'd say: "That's Comare Venera, scolding
her husband," or: "That's Cousin Anna, coming back
from the wash shed." Then he watched the shadow cast
by the houses grow longer; and when the sun no longer
struck the door, they set him against the wall across the
way, because he was like Mastro Turi's dog, which always
sought a sunny spot to lie down in.

Finally his legs could carry him; holding him up by his

armpits, they helped him to the shore, because he liked to doze curled up on the pebbles, facing the boats, and he said that the smell of the salt water did his stomach good; and he enjoyed watching the boats and hearing how the day's fishing had gone for this fisherman or that. And as they went about their work, the fishermen every now and then threw him a word; and to cheer him up they'd say: "There's still oil left in the lamp, eh, Master 'Ntoni?"

In the evening, when the whole family was in the house and the door was closed, and La Longa said her prayers, he enjoyed seeing them around him and he would look at all their faces, one by one, and then at the walls of the room and the big chest with the statue of the Good Shepherd, and the little table with the lamp. Then he always said the same thing: "I can't believe that I'm still here with all of you."

La Longa said that her head and all her blood had been put into such a commotion by the fright he'd given her that she no longer had before her eyes those poor dead souls, who till that day had been like two thorns in her breast, and she even went to Don Giammaria to confess this. But the priest had given her absolution, for that's what happens with people who have troubles, one thorn drives out the next, and the Lord doesn't want to stick them into us all at once, because then we'd die of a broken heart. Her husband had died; her son had died; she'd been thrown out of her house; but now she was happy because she'd been able to pay the doctor and the pharmacist and didn't owe a cent to anyone.

Gradually the old man had begun to say: "Give me something to do. I can't live like this, not doing anything." He mended the nets; and he plaited the fish traps; then he began walking with a cane as far as Mastro Turi's yard to see the *Provvidenza* and stayed there to enjoy the sun. At last he went out in the boat with his grandsons.

"Just like the cats!" La Zuppidda said. "If they don't bang their noses on the ground, they never die."

La Longa had set up a small stand in front of her door and was selling oranges, nuts, hard-boiled eggs, and black olives.

"Just wait and see, they'll soon begin selling wine too!" Santuzza said. "And I'm glad, because they're God-fearing people!" And Master Cipolla shrugged his shoulders when he walked down Black Lane past the house of the Malavoglia, who were trying to become shopkeepers.

But the shop fared well because the eggs were always fresh and now that 'Ntoni was hanging around the tavern, Santuzza sent him to Comare Maruzza for olives when she had customers who weren't thirsty. So, penny by penny, they paid Mastro Turi Zuppiddo and once again patched up the *Provvidenza,* which by now really looked like an old shoe; and they even managed to set aside a few lire. They had also bought a good stock of kegs and salt for the anchovies, in case Saint Francis might send them good fortune, and a new sail for the boat, and they had put a little money in the chest of drawers. "We're doing like the ants do," Master 'Ntoni said; and every day he counted the money and went to prowl around the house by the medlar tree, pretending that he was looking up in the air, his hands clasped behind his back. The door was shut, sparrows twittered on the roof, and the vines swayed softly over the window. The old man crawled up on the wall of the kitchen garden, in which they'd planted onions, whose blossoms were like a sea of white plumes, and then he ran after Uncle Crocifisso and said to him for the hundredth time: "Remember, Uncle Crocifisso, if we manage to put together that money for the house, you must sell it to us, because it's always belonged to the Malavoglia. As the saying goes, 'Every bird thinks its nest is beautiful!' I want to die where I was born. Blessed is the man who dies in his own bed." Uncle Crocifisso mumbled "yes, yes," because he didn't want to promise anything, and afterwards, to boost the price, he would put a tile on the roof or a trowelful of plaster on the wall in the yard.

"Don't worry, don't worry," he reassured Master 'Ntoni. "The house is there. It won't run away. All you have to do is keep an eye on it. Everyone keeps his eye on what he cares for." And one time he added: "Aren't you marrying off your Mena anymore?"

"I'll marry her when God wishes it!" replied Master 'Ntoni. "For my part, I'd even marry her tomorrow."

"If I were you, I'd give her to Alfio Mosca, who's a good lad, honest and hard-working. And he's always looking for a wife, that's his only fault. They say he's coming back to town now, and he seems just made for your granddaughter."

"But didn't they say he wants to marry your niece La Vespa?"

"You too! You too!" Dumbbell began shouting. "Who says so? It's all gossip; he wants to get his hands on my niece's plot, that's what he wants! Fine thing, eh? What would you say if I sold your house to somebody else?"

Piedipapera, who was always on hand trying to drum up trade whenever there were two people talking together in the piazza, chimed in: "Now La Vespa has her hands full with Brasi Cipolla, after the marriage with Saint Agatha went up in smoke. I've seen them with my own eyes, walking together down the path to the stream. I'd gone there to look for two smooth stones to mend the leak in the water trough. She was mincing and making all sorts of faces at him, the flirt! holding the ends of her kerchief over her mouth, and she said to him: 'By this blessed medal which I have here, it's not true! Pooh! You make me sick to my stomach when you talk to me about my uncle, that old codger!' She was talking about you, Uncle Crocifisso. And then she let him touch the medal, and you know where she keeps it, don't you?" Dumbbell pretended that he was deaf and his head jerked like Tartaglia's. Piedipapera went on: "And then Brasi said: 'So what are we going to do?' 'I don't know what you want to do,' La Vespa replied, 'but if it's true you like me, you wouldn't leave me in this state, because when I don't see you I feel my heart's split in two, like two halves of an orange, and if you marry someone else I swear by this blessed medal which I wear here, the village will see something, for I'll throw myself into the sea with all my clothes on.' Brasi scratched his head and continued: 'For my part, I'd take you, but what will my father do?' 'Let's run away from the village,' she said, 'as if we were husband and wife, and after the soup is spilled, your father will have to say yes. After all, he doesn't have any other sons, and who else can he leave his property to?' "

"What people, eh!" Uncle Crocifisso began to scream, forgetting that he was supposed to be deaf. "That witch has the devil tickling her under the skirt! And to think that such women wear the Holy Virgin's medal on their breasts! We'll have to tell Master Fortunato, we must! Are we honest people or aren't we? If Master Fortunato isn't careful, that witch of a niece of mine will play him the dirty trick of grabbing his son, poor man."

And he ran down the street like a madman.

"Please, don't tell them that I told you!" Piedipapera shouted, running after him. "I don't want to have that viper of a niece of yours slandering me."

In a minute Uncle Crocifisso had turned the whole village upside down, because he even wanted to send Don Michele with the guards to take La Vespa into custody. After all, she was his niece and he had to watch over her; and that's what Don Michele was paid for, to protect honest men's interests. People laughed at seeing Master Cipolla also running here and there, his tongue hanging out, and they were glad that his son Brasi, that oaf, had fallen into La Vespa's trap, for you'd have thought that even Victor Emmanuel's daughter wasn't good enough for him, and he'd left the Malavoglia girl in the lurch without so much as a goodbye.

But Mena hadn't put on a black kerchief when Brasi left her in the lurch. Just the contrary, she sang again as she worked at the loom, or helped to salt the anchovies on the fine summer evenings. This time Saint Francis had really sent them good fortune. The anchovies were running as never before, a godsend for the whole village. The boats came back loaded to the gunwales, the fishermen singing and waving their caps while still far out, signaling to the women who were waiting for them with their babies in their arms.

Dealers came from Catania in droves, on foot, horseback, and cart, and Piedipapera didn't even have the time to scratch his head. Along about vespers there was a real market fair on the shore, with people yelling and shoving. In the Malavoglia's yard the lamp remained lit until midnight, and it looked just like a holiday. The girls were singing, and the neighbors also came to help, Nunziata and the daughters of Cousin Anna, because there was money to be made for everyone, and four rows of kegs were already filled and prepared, the stones heaped on them, and lined up along the wall.

"I wish Barbara Zuppidda was here now!" cried 'Ntoni, sitting on the stones, like another weight, with his arms folded. "Now she'd see that we've got money too, and that we don't give a damn about either Don Michele or Don Silvestro!"

The dealers ran after Master 'Ntoni, money in hand, and Piedipapera tugged at his sleeve, saying: "This is the time to sell." But Master 'Ntoni held out and said: "We'll talk about it on All Saints' Day; then the anchovies will get a good price. No, I don't want any down payment; I don't want my hands tied. I know how these things go." And then he beat his fists on the kegs and said to his grandchildren: "Here's your house and Mena's dowry. Your own house hugs and welcomes you. Saint Francis has granted me the grace of letting me die content."

At the same time they had laid in all the provisions for the winter, wheat, beans, and oil; and they had given Massaro Filippo a down payment for the bit of wine they drank on Sundays.

Now they were at peace. Old Master 'Ntoni and his daughter-in-law again and again counted the money in the sock, the kegs lined up in the yard, and figured out how much they still needed for the house. Maruzza knew that money coin by coin—the money they'd gotten for the oranges and eggs, the money Alessi had brought home from working on the railroad, the money Mena had earned with her loom, and she said: "There's money from all of us here."

"Didn't I tell you that to pull an oar the five fingers of the hand must help each other?" replied Master 'Ntoni. "By now we've almost got enough." Then he and La Longa went off in a corner to whisper, and they looked at Saint Agatha who, poor girl, deserved to be talked about because "she had neither say nor will" and just kept busy working, singing to herself as the birds do in their nest before the sun comes up, and it was only when she heard the carts go by in the evening that she thought of Alfio Mosca's cart, which was traveling through the world, God knows where, and then she would stop singing.

All over the village you saw nothing but people carrying nets on their backs and women seated on their doorsteps grinding bricks; and before every door stood a row

of kegs, so a man's nose had a feast when he walked down
the street, and a mile from town you could smell that
Saint Francis had sent them his bounty. All they talked
about were anchovies and brine, even at the pharmacy,
where they fixed up the world in their own fashion, and
Don Franco was trying to teach them a new way to salt
anchovies that he had read about in some book. When
they laughed in his face, he shouted: "You're a pack of
idiots! And you want progress! You want the republic!" The people turned their backs on him and left him
blustering there like a madman. Ever since the world
began, anchovies have been packed with salt and crushed
bricks.

"The usual talk! That's how my grandfather did it!"
the pharmacist went on shouting after them. "You're a
pack of donkeys and all you lack is a tail! What can you
do with people like that? They're satisfied with that
dummy of a Mastro Croce Giufà, because he's always
been the mayor; and they'd be quite capable of telling
you that they don't want the republic, because they never
saw one!" Then he repeated all this to Don Silvestro,
apropos a certain discussion they'd had in private, though
Don Silvestro hadn't opened his mouth, it's true, but had
just kept quiet and listened. Besides, everyone knew that
Don Silvestro was on the outs with Mastro Croce's Betta,
because she wanted to be the mayor and her father had
let her put a skirt on him, so that one day he said white
and the next black, just as Betta wished. All he knew
how to say was: "I'm the mayor, by heavens!" as his
daughter had taught him, but when she talked to Don
Silvestro she put her hands on her hips and started to
scream:

"You think that they'll always let you lead my father
by the nose, so you can do your business and eat like a
hog? Why even Donna Rosolina goes about saying that
you're gnawing away the whole village! But you won't eat
me, absolutely not! Because I'm not in a frenzy to get
married, and I protect my father's interests."

Don Franco preached that without new men nothing
could be accomplished, and there was no point in getting
rich men like Master Cipolla, who said that he had his
property, thank God, and didn't have to work as a public

servant for nothing; or like Massaro Filippo, who never thought of anything but his plots of land and his vineyards, and the only time he'd listened was when there'd been talk of putting a tax on the new wine. "Has-beens!" Don Franco concluded, his beard stabbing the air. "They were all right for the time of the camarilla. These days we need new men!"

"So let's send to the kiln and have some made to order," replied Don Giammaria.

"If things went as they should, we'd all be swimming in gold!" Don Silvestro said, and that was his contribution.

"Do you know what we need?" the pharmacist whispered, glancing into the back of his shop. "People like us!"

And after having hissed that secret into their ears, he rushed to the door on tiptoe and stood there, his beard in the air, bouncing up and down on his little legs, his hands clasped behind his back.

"Fine people they'd be!" grumbled Don Giammaria. "You can find as many as you want in Favignana, or the other prisons, without sending to the kiln for them. Go and tell it to Compare Tino Piedipapera or to that drunkard Rocco Spatu, because they'll like your up-to-date ideas! All I know is that someone's robbed twenty-five onze from my house and nobody has gone to the Favignana jail. There's your new times and your new men!"

At that moment the Signora came into the store, holding her knitting, and the pharmacist quickly swallowed what he was about to say, but went on muttering in his beard, pretending to watch the people going to the fountain. Finally Don Silvestro, seeing that nobody was going to breathe another word, said straight out that the only new men were Master 'Ntoni's 'Ntoni and Brasi Cipolla, for the pharmacist's wife didn't scare him.

"Don't you get mixed up in it," the Signora warned her husband. "You have nothing to do with all this." "I'm not saying a word," replied Don Franco, smoothing his beard.

And now that he had the upper hand, since Don Franco's wife was there and he could throw his stones from behind a wall, the priest amused himself goading the pharmacist. "Fine fellows, these new men of yours! You know what Brasi Cipolla's doing, now that his father is looking for him to box his ears on account of La Vespa? He runs to hide here, there, and everywhere, like a brat. Last night he slept in the sacristy; and yesterday my sister had to bring him a plate of spaghetti in the hen-house where he'd hidden, because the big oaf hadn't eaten for twenty-four hours, and was all covered with chicken lice. And 'Ntoni Malavoglia! Another fine new man! His grandfather and all the others in his family sweat and strain to pull themselves up again, but whenever he has an excuse to run off, he goes knocking about the village and stands in front of the tavern, just like Rocco Spatu."

So the high council adjourned as per usual, without settling anything and each person still had the opinion he had before, and besides, this time the Signora was there, so Don Franco couldn't tell them off as he would have liked to.

Don Silvestro cackled like a hen; and as soon as the conversation ended, he left too, with his hands behind his back and his head full of worries. "Don't you see that Don Silvestro has more good sense than you?" the Signora said to her husband as he was closing his shop. "That man has a real stomach and when he has something to say he swallows it down and doesn't say a single word. Everybody in the village knows that he cheated Donna Rosolina out of twenty-five onze, but to a man like that nobody dares say it to his face! But you'll always be a fool and you'll never learn how to mind your own business. A fathead who barks at the moon! A windbag!"

"But, after all, what did I say?" the pharmacist whined, following her up the stairs with the lamp in his hand. Did she know what he'd said? He didn't dare repeat all that garbled nonsense of his to her. All she knew was that Don Giammaria had left, crossing himself as he walked through the piazza and muttering: "A fine bunch of new men, like that 'Ntoni Malavoglia over there, who goes knocking about the village at this time of day!"

CHAPTER ELEVEN

Once 'Ntoni Malavoglia, while knocking about the village, had met two young men who had shipped out from Riposto a few years before to seek their fortunes and had returned from Trieste, or Alexandria in Egypt or, anyway, some far-off place, and were spending money hand over fist in the tavern, even more money than Compare Naso or Master Cipolla. They sat astraddle the bench, told funny stories to the girls, and had silk kerchiefs in every single one of their pockets; and they set the whole village talking.

In the evening, when he returned home, all 'Ntoni found were the women changing the brine in the kegs, sitting on the stones and gossiping with the neighbors. They made the time pass by telling stories and asking riddles, good enough for the children who, already half-asleep, listened with their mouths agape. Master 'Ntoni listened too, meanwhile keeping an eye on the draining of the brine and nodding his head, approving those who told the best stories and the children who showed as much sense as the grown-ups in solving the riddles.

"You want to hear a really good story?" 'Ntoni finally said. "It's about the strangers who came today, with so many silk kerchiefs you wouldn't believe it. And when they pull their money out of their pockets, they don't even look at it. They've been all over the world, and they say that Trezza and Aci Castello put together are nothing in comparison. I've seen this myself; and up there the people spend their time enjoying themselves all day long instead of salting anchovies; and the women, all dressed in silk and covered with more rings than the Madonna of Ognina, do nothing but go out on strolls to catch handsome sailors."

The girls opened their eyes wide, and even Master 'Ntoni listened attentively, just as when the children solved the riddles. Alessi was carefully draining the kegs and handing them to Nunziata. "When I grow up," he said to her, "if I get married, I'll marry you."

"There's still plenty of time for that," Nunziata answered gravely.

"They must come from one of those big cities, like Catania, where you get lost in the streets if you're not used to them. And you can hardly breathe, always walking between two rows of houses, and never seeing the sea or the fields."

"Cipolla's grandfather was up there, too." Master 'Ntoni added. "He got rich in those towns. But he never came back to Trezza and just sent money to his children."

"Poor man!" Maruzza said.

"Let's see if you can guess this one," said Nunziata. "It's got two that shine, two that prick, four hooves and a broom."

"An ox!" Lia answered quickly.

"You knew it! Because you got it right away," her brother exclaimed.

"I'd like to go there too and get rich, like Master Cipolla," 'Ntoni said.

"Forget it, forget it!" said his grandfather, content because of the kegs he saw lined up in the yard. "Now we've got to salt the anchovies." But La Longa looked at her son and felt her heart shrink in her breast and didn't say a word, because every time there was talk of going away, those who had gone and never returned rose before her eyes.

And his grandfather added: "Neither head nor tail is the best choice of all."

The rows of kegs kept growing along the wall, and every time Master 'Ntoni set a new one in place with the stones on top, he said: "Here's another. On All Saints' Day they'll all be good money."

Then 'Ntoni laughed and he sounded like Master Fortunato when he talked about other people's property. "A fat lot of money!" he muttered; and he started thinking again about those two strangers who traveled everywhere and stretched out on the benches in the tavern and jingled their coins in their pockets. His mother watched him as though she could read his thoughts, and she didn't laugh at the stories they were telling in the yard.

"These anchovies," Cousin Anna began, "will be eaten by a king. He'll be as beautiful as the sun and he'll travel on his white horse for a year, a month and a day, until he reaches an enchanted fountain of milk and honey. There he'll get off his horse to drink and find my daughter Mara's thimble, which was carried there by the fairies from the fountain in the piazza, where Mara dropped it when she went to fill her pitcher. And when the king's son drinks from Mara's thimble, he'll fall in love with her and he'll travel another year, a month and a day until he reaches Trezza, and the white horse will take him to the wash shed where my daughter Mara is spreading out the wash to dry; and the king's son will marry her and put a ring on her finger; and then he'll lift her onto his white horse and take her to his kingdom."

Alessi listened with his mouth open as though he could actually see the king's son on his white horse, riding away with Cousin Anna's Mara.

"And where will he take her?" Lia asked, after a pause.

"Far, far away, to his country on the other side of the sea, from which no one ever returns."

"Like Compare Alfio," Nunziata said. "I wouldn't want to go away with the king's son, if I couldn't come back anymore."

"Your daughter doesn't have a cent of dowry, and so the king's son won't come and marry her," 'Ntoni said. "And they'll all turn their backs on her, because that's what happens to people when they've lost everything."

"That's why my daughter is working here now, after having been at the wash shed all day, so she can put together a dowry. Isn't that so, Mara? At least if the king's son doesn't come, somebody else will. I know that that's how the world goes, and we have no right to complain about it. And why didn't you fall in love with my daughter, instead of falling in love with that Barbara, who's as yellow as saffron? Because Barbara had property, isn't that true? And when misfortune made you lose your money, it's only natural that Barbara had to leave you."

"You put up with everything," 'Ntoni said sullenly. "And they're right to call you 'Cheerful Heart.' "

"And if I weren't a 'Cheerful Heart,' would that change things? When a man has nothing, it's best for him to go away, like Alfio Mosca did."

"That's just what I say!" cried 'Ntoni.

"The worst thing," Mena finally said, "is to leave your own town, where even the stones know you, and it must break your heart to leave them behind on the road. 'Blessed is the bird that makes its nest at home.' "

"Right, Saint Agatha!" her grandfather cried. "Now this is what I call talking sense."

"Sure!" 'Ntoni grumbled. "But after we've sweated and slaved to build the nest, we won't have any millet to eat. And when we'll finally manage to buy back the house by the medlar tree, we'll still have to go on breaking our backs from Monday to Saturday. And we'll always be where we started!"

"What? You want to get off without working? What would you like to do? Be a lawyer?"

"I don't want to be a lawyer!" 'Ntoni growled, and he went off to bed in a foul temper.

But from then on he thought of nothing but the life without work and worries that other people had; and in the evening, so he wouldn't have to hear that insipid talk, he stood at the door, leaning against the wall, watching the people pass by and brooding over his sad lot; at least this way he rested up for the next day, when he would go back to doing the same thing all over again, just like Compare Mosca's donkey, which arched its back when it saw Alfio pick up his pack-saddle, and waited to be harnessed. "That's what we are!" he grumbled. "Donkey meat! Beasts of burden!" And it was quite clear that he was fed up with that miserable life, and wanted to leave to seek his fortune, as the others had; so that his mother, poor thing, put her arm around him and spoke to him tenderly, her eyes full of tears, staring at him to read his thoughts and to touch his heart. But he wasn't convinced and said that it would be better both for him and for them; and afterwards, when he came back with his fortune made, they would all be happy. The poor woman didn't close her eyes all night and soaked her pillow with her tears. Finally his grandfather noticed it and called him outside, next to the little shrine, to ask him what was bothering him.

"Come, what's new? Tell your grandfather, tell me!" 'Ntoni shrugged his shoulders; but the old man nodded and spat and scratched his head, searching for the right words.

"Yes, yes, you've got something on your mind, my boy. Something that wasn't there before. 'He who goes with the lame will limp within the year.' "

"I'm just a poor devil! That's what's new!"

"Well, what's new about that? Didn't you know? You are what your father was and what your grandfather was! As the saying is, 'the less you want on earth, the richer you are.' It's better to be content than always lament."

"Some consolation!"

This time the old man found the right words immediately because his heart was on his lips.

"At least don't talk like that in front of your mother."

"My mother? It would have been better if she hadn't given birth to me, my mother!"

"Yes," Master 'Ntoni agreed, "yes! It would have been better for her not to have given birth to you, if you have to talk like this now."

For a moment 'Ntoni didn't know what to say. Then he exclaimed: "Very well, I'm doing it for her, for you, and for everybody. I want to make my mother rich! That's what I want. Now we're struggling with the house and Mena's dowry; then Lia will grow up, and if the fishing is scarce, we'll always be poor. I don't want to live this kind of life anymore. I want to change my lot, mine and that of all of you. I want us to be rich—mother, you, Mena, Alessi, everybody."

Master 'Ntoni stared at him, and turned those words over in his mouth, trying to swallow them. "Rich!" he repeated. "Rich! And what will we do when we're rich?"

'Ntoni scratched his head, and he also tried hard to figure out what they would do. "We'll do what other people do. . . . We'll do nothing, nothing! We'll go and live in Catania, and not do a thing, and eat pasta and meat every day."

"Go, go and live in Catania. As for me, I want to die where I was born." And thinking of the house where he was born, and which was no longer his, Master 'Ntoni let his head sink on his chest. "You're still young, and you don't know! You don't know! . . . You'll see what it means when you can't sleep in your own bed and the sun doesn't shine through your own window! . . . You'll see! I'm an old man and I'm telling you!" The poor old man coughed, bent over and almost choking, and sadly shook his head. "Every bird thinks its own nest is beautiful. Do you see those sparrows? Do you see them? They've always built their nest here, and they come back to it and don't want to leave."

"I'm not a sparrow," 'Ntoni answered. "I'm not an animal like them! I don't want to live like a dog on a chain, like Alfio Mosca's donkey, or like a mule tied to a pump, always turning the wheel. I don't want to die of hunger in some corner, or end up in a shark's mouth."

"You ought to thank God for being born here; and watch out you don't go and die far from the stones that know you. 'He who changes old for new will be disappointed through and through.' You're afraid of work, you're afraid of being poor; and I who no longer have your strong arms or your health, am not afraid, you see! 'In a storm you can tell the good pilot.' You're afraid of having to earn the bread you eat—that's what it is! When my father, may he rest in peace, left me the *Provvidenza* and five mouths to feed, I was younger than you are and I wasn't afraid; and I did my duty without complaining and I still do it. And I pray to God to help me do it so long as my eyes stay open, just as your father did, and your brother Luca, bless him, who wasn't afraid to go and do his duty. Your mother has also done her duty, poor woman, hidden inside those four walls; and you don't know how many tears she's shed, and how many she sheds now that you want to go away. In the morning your sister finds her sheet all soaked! And yet she keeps quiet and doesn't talk about the things you have on your mind; and she's worked and done her best too, like an ant. And she's done nothing else all her life, even before she had so much to cry about, when she fed you at her breast and you didn't know how to button your breeches yet, and in those days the temptation of going away and traveling through the world like a gypsy hadn't come into your head."

In the end 'Ntoni began to cry like a baby, because at bottom the boy had a heart as good as bread; but the next day he started all over again. In the morning he stood there slackly and let them load him with the gear, and walked to the sea muttering and complaining: "Just like Compare Alfio's donkey! When daylight comes I stretch my neck to see if they're coming to put the pack-saddle on me." After the nets were in the water, he let Alessi pull the oar slowly so that the boat wouldn't drift away, crossed his arms and gazed off into the distance, way up there where all people did was have a good time and never work; or he thought about those two sailors who'd returned and had now shipped out again a long time ago, but he had the notion that all they did was wander about the world from one tavern to the next, spending the money they had in their pockets. In the evening, after having put the boat and gear in order, his family let him roam about like a mongrel without a penny in his pocket, so they wouldn't have to see his long face.

"What's the matter, 'Ntoni?" La Longa said to him, looking timidly in his face, her eyes glistening with tears; because the poor woman guessed what the matter was. "I'm your mother, so you can tell me!" He did not reply; or he said that nothing was the matter. But at last he told her what was troubling him—his grandfather and all the others wanted his skin, and he couldn't stand it anymore. He wanted to go away and seek his fortune, like all the others had.

His mother listened with her eyes full of tears and didn't have the courage to open her mouth because she was so hurt by what he'd said, crying and stamping his feet and tearing at his hair. She would have liked to talk to him and throw her arms around his neck and cry too, so that she could stop him from leaving; but when she tried to say something, her lips trembled and she couldn't utter a single word.

"Listen," she finally said, "you can go if you wish, but

you won't find me here anymore; for I feel old and tired now, and I don't think that I could bear this new heartache."

'Ntoni tried to reassure her that he would be back soon, loaded with money, and that then they would all be happy. Maruzza shook her head sadly, still staring into his eyes and saying no, no, he wouldn't find her.

"I feel old!" she repeated. "I feel old! Look at me. Why, I no longer have the strength to cry as I did when they brought me the news about your father and your brother. If I go to the wash shed, I come home so tired in the evening I can't bear it, and before it wasn't like this. No, my son, I'm no longer the same woman! In those days, when it happened to your father and brother, I was younger and strong. You see, the heart gets tired too; and it falls apart bit by bit, like an old cloth wears out in the wash. Now I don't have the courage, and everything makes me afraid; I choke on my heart, like when a wave passes over your head when you're out at sea. You can go, if you want; but first let me close my eyes."

Her face was streaming with tears; but she didn't know she was crying, and she thought that she was again looking at her son Luca and her husband, when they'd gone away and nobody had ever seen them again.

"I'll never see you again!" she said. "Now the house is emptying little by little; and when your grandfather, poor old man, is gone too, who'll take care of those poor orphans? Oh Mary, Mother of Sorrows!"

She held her boy close, his head on her breast, as though he wanted to run away immediately; and she felt his shoulders and his face with trembling hands. Then 'Ntoni couldn't bear it any longer and began to kiss her and talk with his mouth close to hers.

"No, no, I won't go if you don't want me to. Please, don't say such things! All right, I'll go right on working like Compare Mosca's donkey. And when he's no longer able to drag the cart, they'll throw him into a ditch to croak. Does that make you happy? But don't cry like that! You see how Grandfather has slaved all his life? And now that he's old, he's still slaving as if it were the first day, trying to drag himself out of the swamp! That's what we have in store for us!"

"Do you think that other people don't have troubles? 'All the holes have their nails, some old and some new!' Just look how Master Cipolla runs after his Brasi so he won't throw the property he's sweated for into La Vespa's apron, and Massaro Filippo, as rich as he is, always gazing at the sky and saying Hail Marys for his vineyard at every cloud that passes! And Uncle Crocifisso, who takes the bread out of his mouth to save money and is forever quarreling with this person or that! And do you think those two sailors who came here don't have their troubles, too? And who knows whether they'll still find their mothers when they go home? . . . And if we manage to buy back the house by the medlar tree, and we have wheat stored away and broad beans for the winter, and we marry off Mena, what will we lack? After I'm buried, and that poor old man is dead too, and Alessi can earn his bread, then you can go where you wish. But by then you won't go, I tell you, because you'll know the pain we all had in our breasts when we saw you set on leaving home, even though we go on doing our work without saying anything to you. Then you won't have the heart to leave the place where you were born and grew up, and where your dead will be buried beneath that marble slab, in front of the altar of Our Lady of Sorrows, which has been worn smooth by all the knees that have kneeled there every Sunday."

From that day on 'Ntoni stopped talking about getting rich and gave up the idea of leaving, for whenever his mother saw him sitting at the door, looking sad, she watched him with a tender, hungry look in her eyes. And at those moments, when she had nothing to do and sat down next to him, already as bent and bowed as her father-in-law, the poor woman looked so pale, tired, and worn out that it made your heart ache. But she did not know that she herself was about to go, and just when she least expected it, go on a journey to where one rests forever, beneath the church's smooth marble slab; and she would have to leave them all behind, those she loved and who were bound to her heart and were tearing at it, first one, then the other.

In Catania there was a cholera epidemic, and so everyone who could ran away from the city, scattering through the nearby villages and countryside. And it was Providence itself for Trezza and Ognina, with all those outsiders there spending their money. But when it came to selling a dozen barrels of anchovies, the dealers looked glum and said that the money had been frightened away by the cholera. "What? Don't people eat anchovies anymore?" Piedipapera asked them; but to Master 'Ntoni and whoever else had anchovies to sell, in order to close the deal Piedipapera would say that because of the cholera people didn't want to ruin their stomachs with anchovies and such slop; they'd rather eat pasta and meat, so the best thing was to close one's eyes and be satisfied with the going price. The Malavoglia certainly hadn't reckoned with this! So, not to go backward like the crabs, La Longa went to the villas of the city folk selling eggs and fresh bread while the men were out at sea, and she managed to earn a few pennies. But you had to beware of running into danger, or accepting even a pinch of snuff from someone you didn't know! When you walked down the street, you had to stay right in the middle and far from the walls, where you ran the risk of picking up a thousand evil things; and you had to be sure not to sit on the rocks or the stone walls.

One time, as she was coming back from Aci Castello with her basket on her arm, La Longa felt so tired that her legs shook and were as heavy as lead. Then she gave in to temptation and rested for a few moments on those smooth stones set in a row in the shade of a wild fig tree which stands next to the shrine before you come into the village; and she didn't notice—though she remembered it afterwards—that a stranger who seemed tired too, poor fellow, had been sitting there a few minutes before and had left on the stones some drops of a dirty liquid that looked like oil. In short, she was trapped by it too; she caught the cholera and came home half dead, hollow as a wax ex-voto for the Madonna, and with big black circles under her eyes. So Mena, who was alone in the house, began to cry just at seeing her, and Lia rushed off to pick some rosemary and mallow leaves. Mena shivered like a leaf as she prepared the bed; and yet the sick woman, sitting on the chair, mortally tired, with her yellow face and black, sunken eyes, kept saying: "It's nothing. Don't be frightened. As soon as I lie down, it'll go away." And she tried to help Mena too, but her strength kept failing and she had to sit down again.

"Holy Virgin!" Mena stammered. "Holy Virgin! And the men are at sea!" And Lia just cried and cried.

When Master 'Ntoni came home with his grandsons and saw the door pulled half shut and the lamp shining through the shutters, he tore his hair. Maruzza was already in bed, and in the dark at that hour her eyes looked as though death had sucked them dry, and her lips were black as coal. In those days neither the doctor nor the pharmacist went about after sunset; and for fear of the cholera, even the neighbors barred their doors and pasted pictures of saints all over the cracks. So Comare Maruzza had only the help of her family, poor people, who seeing her dying like that in her small bed, rushed around the house, crazed, and didn't know what to do and began to beat their heads against the wall. Then, seeing that there was no more hope, La Longa asked them to put on her chest that round piece of cotton steeped in holy oil she had bought at Easter, and she told them to leave the candle lit, just as they'd done when Master 'Ntoni was going to die, for she wanted to see them all around her bed and fill herself with the sight of them, one by one, staring with those wild eyes which could no longer really see. Lia wept so much it broke your heart; and all the others, white as sheets, looked at each other as though asking for help; and they clasped their chests tightly, to keep from bursting into tears before the dying woman, who, though she couldn't see, knew how they felt, and in dying was most of all distressed at leaving them so miserable. She called to them by name, one by one, in a hoarse voice; and she wanted to lift her hand, which she could no longer move, to bless them, as though she felt she was leaving them a treasure. " 'Ntoni," she said over and over, in a voice that could scarcely be heard. " 'Ntoni! You're the oldest, so I beg you, take care of those poor orphans!" And hearing her talk like this when she was still alive, the whole family could not keep it back any longer and began weeping and sobbing.

So they passed the whole night around the bed in which Maruzza lay motionless, until the candle began to flicker and died out too, and the light of dawn came through the window, pale as the dead woman, whose face was consumed and sharp as a knife and whose lips were black. Yet Mena didn't stop kissing her on the mouth and talking to her, as if she could still hear her. 'Ntoni beat his breast and sobbed: "Oh Mama, Mama! You went away before me, and I wanted to leave you!" And Alessi could never forget the sight of his mother, with her white hair and that yellow face as sharp as a knife, not even when his own hair had turned white too.

In the evening they came and rushed La Longa away and nobody thought of coming to the vigil for the dead, because they were all thinking of their own skins, and even Don Giammaria halted at the threshold when he sprinkled the holy water with his aspersorium, gathering up his Franciscan habit and holding it clear of the ground—like the selfish friar he was, the pharmacist went around saying. *He,* Don Franco, would have opened the pharmacy if they'd brought him the doctor's prescription, and even at night, because he wasn't afraid of the cholera! He also said that it was pure stupidity to believe that somebody was throwing the cholera on the streets and behind the doors. "That's the proof that he's the one who's spreading it!" Don Giammaria went about whispering and that was why the people in the village said they wanted to skin the pharmacist alive; but he just cackled like a hen, exactly like Don Silvestro, and said: "Me? A Republican? If I were a clerk or one of those lickspittles who go around doing the government's dirty work, there'd be some sense to it! . . ." But the Malavoglia were left alone, looking at that small empty bed.

After La Longa had passed through it, they didn't open their door for a long time. Fortunately they had broad beans, firewood, and oil in the house, because Master 'Ntoni had worked like the ants in good weather, otherwise they would have died of hunger, and nobody would have ever come to see whether they were dead or alive. But little by little, their black kerchiefs around their necks, they began to go out on the street, like snails after a rainstorm, pale and still bewildered. From a distance the women asked them how the misfortune had taken place; because Comare Maruzza had been one of the first to catch the plague. But when Don Michele or any of those who ate the King's bread and wore the cap with the gold braid went by, the women stared at them with burning eyes and ran to lock themselves up in their houses. The village was deserted and squalid, and you couldn't even see a chicken in the street; even Mastro Cirino didn't come out anymore and didn't ring for noonday or vespers, for he too ate the Commune's bread, because of those twelve tarì a month he got working as custodian at the Town Hall, and he was afraid that they'd murder him as a government lickspittle.

Now Don Michele was master of the street, since Pizzuto, Don Silvestro, and all the rest had burrowed underground like rabbits, and he was the only person who strolled back and forth before La Zuppidda's closed door. It was a pity that only the Malavoglia saw him, people who had nothing more to lose and so sat at their doorway, motionless, their chins on their hands, watching to see who went by. So his stroll shouldn't be wasted, Don Michele stared at Saint Agatha; and he also did it to show that big lout 'Ntoni Malavoglia that he wasn't afraid of anyone in this world. And besides, Mena was so pale that she really looked like Saint Agatha; and her little sister, with that black kerchief, was also becoming a pretty young girl.

Poor Mena felt as though twenty more years had suddenly crashed down on her. And now she acted with Lia as La Longa had acted with her; she felt that she had to keep her under her wing, just like a mother hen, and that she had the whole house on her shoulders. She had gotten used to staying alone with her sister when the men went out fishing, and that small empty bed was always before her eyes. If she had nothing to do, she sat down with her hands folded in her lap, gazing at that empty bed, and at such times she felt that her Mama had really and truly left; and when people on the street said: "This one died, that one died," Mena thought: "That's how they heard it, 'La Longa died!'"—La Longa, who had left her alone with that poor orphan, who was wearing a black kerchief just like her own.

Nunziata or Cousin Anna came from time to time,

walking silently and with long faces, not saying a word; and they stood by the door, watching the deserted street, their hands under their aprons. Coming back from the sea, the fishermen walked by quickly, their nets on their backs and a wary look on their faces, and the carts didn't even stop at the tavern.

Who knows where Compare Alfio's cart was traveling right now? And maybe at this very moment the poor man, who had nobody in the world, was dying of cholera, abandoned behind some hedge! Sometimes Piedipapera walked past too, glancing all around him with the face of a starving man, or Uncle Crocifisso, who had money loaned out here, there, and everywhere and went to feel the pulse of his debtors, because if they died they'd rob him of what they owed him. The viaticum also rushed past, held by Don Giammaria, his cassock tucked up and a barefoot boy ringing the bell, because Mastro Cirino had disappeared. That bell ringing through the street, where not even a dog went by and even Don Franco kept his door partly closed, made your heart shrivel.

The only person you saw wandering about day and night was La Locca, with her white, disheveled hair. And she sat down in front of the house by the medlar tree or waited for the boats on the shore, and not even the cholera wanted her, poor woman.

The city people had also fled, like birds when the winter comes; and the fish couldn't find a soul who would buy them. So everybody said: "After the cholera comes the famine." Master 'Ntoni had begun to use the money set aside for the house, and he watched it dwindle, coin by coin. But all he could think of was that Maruzza hadn't died in her own house, and he couldn't get this thought out of his head. When he saw the money being spent, 'Ntoni also shook his head.

At last, when the cholera ended and only half of the money they'd so painfully put together was left, 'Ntoni began saying again that he couldn't stand it any longer, this pointless life of doing and undoing; and that it would be better to make one big plunge to get out of trouble once and for all, because he didn't want to stay there, surrounded by all that accursed misery in which his mother had died.

"Don't you remember that your mother left Mena in your hands?" said Master 'Ntoni.

"What help can I give Mena if I stay here? You tell me that!"

Mena looked at him with timid eyes, but in them you could see her whole heart, just like her mother, though she didn't dare to say a word. But one time, huddled against the doorpost, she got up the courage to say to him:

"I don't care about being helped, so long as you don't leave us. Now that Mama's not here anymore, I feel like a fish out of water, and I don't care about anything. But I'm sorry for Lia, for if you go she'll be alone in the world, like Nunziata when her father left."

"No!" 'Ntoni said. "No, I can't help you if I don't have anything. The proverb says 'Help yourself and I'll help you.' When I've earned enough money too, then I'll come back and we'll all live happily."

Lia and Alessi opened their eyes wide, staring at him with dismay; but his grandfather bowed his head. "Now you have neither mother nor father and you can do as you please," he said at last. "As long as I live I'll take care of these children, and when I'm no longer here the Lord will do the rest."

Since 'Ntoni wanted to go at all costs, Mena prepared all his things, as his mother would have done, and she thought that up there far from home her brother would have nobody to look after him, just like Alfio Mosca. And as she was sewing his shirts and patching his clothes, her mind ran far, far away to so many things of the past that her heart grew heavy with them.

"I can no longer walk by the house by the medlar tree," she said, when she sat down next to her grandfather, "because I feel it in my throat and it suffocates me, after all the things that have happened since we left it!"

And as she was preparing her brother's things, she cried as though she would never see him again. At last, when all was ready, the old man called the boy to give him the final talking-to, the last piece of advice for when he'd be alone and would have to rely on his own good sense and wouldn't have his family beside him to tell him what he should do and to share his troubles; and he also gave him some money, in case he'd need it, and his own fur-lined cloak, because he was old now and had no use for it anymore.

The children, seeing their elder brother bustling around preparing to leave, followed him silently through the house, not daring to say a word to him, as though he were already a stranger.

"That's how my father left," Nunziata finally said. She had come to say goodbye and stood at the doorway. After that, not another word was said.

The women came one by one to say goodbye to Compare 'Ntoni, and then waited outside on the street to see him leave. He lingered there with his bundle on his back and his shoes in his hand, as though at the very last minute his heart and legs had suddenly failed him. And he looked about him to stamp the house and the village, everything, on his mind, and his face was just as distraught as theirs. His grandfather took his cane to accompany him to Catania, and Mena sat in a corner, weeping quietly. "Now stop, stop it," 'Ntoni said to her. "I'm leaving, but I'm coming back! Didn't I come back that other time from the navy?" Then, after he had kissed Mena and Lia and said goodbye to the women, he started to leave and Mena ran after him with open arms, wailing, crazed, and crying: "What will Mama say now? What will Mama say now?" as though their mother could see and speak. But she was repeating what had stuck in her mind from the other time when 'Ntoni had said that he wanted to leave, and she'd seen her mother cry every night, and when she'd made her bed in the morning, she had found her sheet soaked with tears.

"Goodbye, 'Ntoni!" Alessi shouted after him, screwing up his courage when his brother was already down the street; and then Lia began to scream. "That's how my father left," said Nunziata, who had remained in the doorway.

Before turning off Black Lane, 'Ntoni looked back, his eyes full of tears too, and waved his hand. Then Mena closed the door and went to sit in a corner with Lia, who was crying loudly. "Now there's one more missing from the house," she said. "And if we were in the house by the medlar tree, it would seem as empty as a church."

As one by one all those who loved her went away, Mena really felt like a fish out of water. And Nunziata, standing there with her little ones in her arms, kept saying: "That's how my father left!"

CHAPTER TWELVE

Now that only Alessi was left to help him run the boat, Master 'Ntoni had to hire someone by the day. He took either Compare Nunzio, who was loaded down with children and had a sick wife, or La Locca's son, who came to their door blubbering that his mother was dying of hunger and that Uncle Crocifisso didn't want to give him anything, because, he said, the cholera had ruined him, what with all the people who had died and cheated him out of his money. And Uncle Crocifisso had caught the cholera himself, but he hadn't died, La Locca's son added, shaking his head sadly. "If he'd only died, now we'd have food to eat, I and my mother and all my family. We took care of him for two days, together with La Vespa, and it looked like he was going any minute, but he didn't die!"

But often what the Malavoglia earned wasn't enough to pay Uncle Nunzio or La Locca's son, and they had to dig into the money for the house by the medlar tree, which they'd put together with so much toil. Each time Mena went to get the stocking under the mattress, she and her grandfather sighed. La Locca's son wasn't to blame; he was ready to do the work of four to earn his day's pay; it was the fish that didn't want to be caught. And when they came back dispiritedly, pulling listlessly at the oars, their sail slack, La Locca's son would say to Master 'Ntoni: "Let me cut some wood or tie up some bundles of vine branches. If you want me to, I can work till midnight, as I did for Uncle Crocifisso. I don't want to steal my day's pay."

At last, after thinking it over for some time, Master 'Ntoni decided with an aching heart to tell Mena what they now had to do. She was as sensible as her mother, and of all those who'd once been in the house she was the only one left to talk to. The best thing was to sell the *Provvidenza,* which did not bring them anything and ate up the pay they gave to Nunzio and La Locca's son. If they didn't, bit by bit all the money for the house would be gone. The *Provvidenza* was old, and they continually had to spend money to patch her up and keep her afloat. Later, when 'Ntoni came back and a fair wind set them sailing again and they'd put together the money for the house, they'd buy a new boat and call her the *Provvidenza* again.

On Sunday, after Mass, Master 'Ntoni went to the piazza to discuss it with Piedipapera. Compare Tino shrugged, shook his head, and said the *Provvidenza* was only fit to be burnt under the pot. And, while saying these things, he dragged Master 'Ntoni down to the shore, where you could see the *Provvidenza's* patches under the new pitch; she was like certain sluts he knew, with wrinkles under their corsets. And he kicked her in the belly with his lame foot, just as he'd done the last time. Besides, he said, fishing was in a bad way; instead of buying, the fishermen would all have liked to sell their boats, and much newer ones than the *Provvidenza.* And then, who would buy her? Master Cipolla had no use for such junk. This was a deal for Uncle Crocifisso, but just at that moment Uncle Crocifisso had other things to worry about, with that fury, La Vespa, who was damning his soul chasing after every unmarried man in the village. Finally, in the holy name of friendship, Piedipapera agreed to go and talk to Uncle Crocifisso when the right moment came, if Master 'Ntoni wanted at all costs to sell the *Provvidenza* for a pittance; because he, Piedipapera, could get Uncle Crocifisso to do anything he wanted.

In fact, when he talked to him, taking him aside near the watering trough, Uncle Crocifisso shrugged, shook his head like a puppet, and tried to slip away from him. Compare Tino, poor fellow, seized his jacket and forced him to stay there and listen. He tugged at him, and embraced him tightly to whisper into his ear. "You hear, you're a fool if you don't grab this opportunity. You'll get it for a pittance! Master 'Ntoni is selling her only because he can't handle her, now that his grandson has gone away. But you could let Compare Nunzio run her, or La Locca's son, who are both dying of hunger and would work for nothing. You'll gobble up everything they catch. You're a fool, I tell you! The boat's in good condition, like new. Master 'Ntoni knew his trade when he had her built. This is a golden opportunity, I tell you, just like the lupin deal!"

But Uncle Crocifisso, his face still yellow from the cholera, was almost in tears and didn't want to hear any of it; and he pulled to get away, quite ready to leave his jacket in Piedipapera's hands. "I'm not interested!" he kept saying. "I'm not interested! You don't know what I have got inside here, Compare Tino! They all want to suck my blood like leeches, and to take my property. Now even Pizzuto is chasing after La Vespa, all of them, like hunting dogs!"

"So take her yourself! After all, isn't she your flesh and blood, and her plot of land too? She wouldn't be another mouth to feed, not her! Because that woman has blessed hands, and you won't be wasting the bread you give her to eat! You'll have a servant in your house without paying her a salary, and you'll also take the plot. Listen to me, Uncle Crocifisso, this deal is as good as the lupin deal!"

Meanwhile Master 'Ntoni was waiting for an answer in front of Pizzuto's shop, gazing like a soul in purgatory at those two who seemed to be fighting, trying to guess whether Uncle Crocifisso was saying yes. Piedipapera came to tell him what he'd been able to obtain from Uncle Crocifisso, and then returned to talk to him again, back and forth across the piazza like a shuttle in a loom, dragging that twisted leg of his after him, until he finally succeeded in getting them to agree. "Excellent!" he said to Master 'Ntoni, and to Uncle Crocifisso he said: "You got it for a pittance!" and he also arranged the sale of all the gear, since now that the Malavoglia no longer had so much as a plank of wood on the water, they had no more use for it. But when they carried off the lobster pots, the nets, the harpoons and poles and everything else, Master 'Ntoni felt as though they were ripping the guts out of his belly. "Don't worry," Piedipapera told him. "I'll make it my business to get work for you and your grandson Alessi. But you know you can't ask for too much—'the strength of the young and the wisdom of the old.' What you'll owe me, I'll leave to your good heart." "In time of famine, barley bread will do," replied Master 'Ntoni. "Nobility gives way to necessity."

"All right, all right, we're agreed on it!" Piedipapera concluded, and he actually talked about it to Master Cipolla at the pharmacy, where Don Silvestro had managed to bring them all together again—him, Massaro Filippo, and a few other big fish, to discuss the Commune's affairs, because after all it was their money, and it's stupid not to have a say in the village when you're rich and pay more taxes than the other people. "You're so rich, you could easily give work to poor Master 'Ntoni," Piedipapera added. "You wouldn't lose anything by hiring him and his grandson Alessi. He knows his trade better than anyone else, and he'd be satisfied with little pay, because they really don't have a crust of bread to eat. It's a golden opportunity, take it from me, Master Fortunato!"

Caught like this, at that particular moment, Master Fortunato had to say yes; but only after haggling over the wages, because times were hard, there was no work for the men, and if he took on Master 'Ntoni, he did so only out of charity.

"Yes, I'll hire him if he comes and asks me himself! Why, would you believe it, he bears me a grudge ever since I called off my son's marriage to Mena? A fine deal I would have made there! And on top of it, the Malavoglia have the nerve to bear me a grudge!"

All of them, Don Silvestro, Massaro Filippo, and even Piedipapera, hastened to say that Master Fortunato was completely right. Ever since they'd put the idea of marriage into his head, Brasi hadn't given him a moment of peace and chased after all the women like a cat in January, so he'd become a continual worry to his poor father. And now even the Mangiacarrube girl had joined in and set her mind on taking him for herself, that Brasi, since he was there for the taking. At least she was a handsome girl, with a fine pair of shoulders, not old and mangy like La Vespa. But La Vespa, people said, had her plot of land, while the Mangiacarrube girl had nothing but her black braids.

Now that Brasi's father had towed him home again because of the cholera, and he no longer went to hide on the lava field, or in the plot, the pharmacy and sacristy, the Mangiacarrube girl knew just what she had to do if she intended to snare him. She grazed right past him, tripping along on her new shoes. In the midst of the crowd coming from Mass, she let him bump into her elbow; or, with her kerchief on her head and her hands clasped over her belly, she waited for him at the door and threw him a killing glance, a real heart-stealer, and then turned and tightened the ends of her kerchief under her chin, just to see if he was following her. When he appeared at the end of the street, she ran into her house and hid behind the basil on the windowsill, furtively devouring him with her eyes. But if Brasi stopped to stare at her like an oaf, she turned her back, bowed her head, blushed and lowered her eyes, chewing at a corner of her apron and looking as tempting as a pot of honey.

In the end, since Brasi couldn't make up his mind to eat that honey, she herself had to do the grabbing. "Listen, Compare Brasi," she said, "why are you robbing me of my peace? I know that I'm not for you. It's about time you stopped walking past here, because the more I see you the more I want to see you, and by now I'm the talk of the whole village. Venera Zuppidda rushes to her door every time she sees you walk by, and then she goes and tells everybody about it. But she'd do better to keep an eye on her daughter Barbara, that flirt, who's lured so many men down here that she's turned the street into a piazza. But you can bet that she won't tell people how many times Don Michele walks up and down to see Barbara at her window!"

After this little talk, Brasi didn't budge from her street, not even a clubbing would have driven him away, and he was always there, prowling about, with his arms dangling, his nose in the air and his mouth agape, just like a puppet in a puppet show. As for the Mangiacarrube girl, she was always at her window, and every day she wore a new silk kerchief and a necklace of glass beads, like a queen. "Everything she has she puts on show at her window," Venera Zuppidda went around saying. And that oaf Brasi took it all for solid gold and became so frantic that he wasn't even afraid his father might come and give him a few whacks. "It's the hand of God," the people said, "punishing Master Fortunato for his pride and arrogance." Yes, it would have been a hundred times better if he'd given his son the Malavoglia girl, who at least had a bit of dowry and didn't spend it on kerchiefs and necklaces. But Mena didn't even stick her nose out of the window, because now that her mother had died, it wasn't proper and she wore a black kerchief; and besides, she also had to take care of her little sister and be a mother to her, and she didn't have anyone to help her with the chores around the house and had to go to the wash shed and the fountain and carry the bread to the men when they hired out; so now she was no longer like Saint Agatha, as she'd been when nobody ever saw her and she was always at the loom. Now she had little time to work at the loom. For ever since the day Venera Zuppidda had stood on her landing, distaff in hand, to announce that she would use it to gouge out Don Michele's eyes if he ever came buzzing around there for her Barbara, Don Michele walked up and down Black Lane ten times a day, just to show that he wasn't afraid of La Zuppidda or her distaff; and when he reached the Malavoglia house he slowed down and looked inside, to see the pretty girls who were growing up in there too.

When the men returned in the evening, they found everything ready; the pot was boiling, and the cloth was spread on the table; but now the table was too large for them and they felt lost at it. Then they'd close the door and eat in sainted peace. Afterwards they sat in front of the house, their arms around their knees, and rested from the day's work. At least they had all they needed, and they no longer used the money for the house. Master 'Ntoni always had the house before his eyes, right across the way, with its windows shut and the medlar tree showing above the wall of the yard. Maruzza hadn't been able to die in that house, and perhaps he wouldn't die there either, but the money was again being put away, and one day his children would return to it, now that Alessi was also becoming a man, and he was a good boy, made of the real Malavoglia stuff. If, after having married off the girls and bought back the house, they could buy a boat too, then all their wishes would be fulfilled and Master 'Ntoni could die content.

After the evening meal, Nunziata and Cousin Anna also came to sit on the stones and talk with those poor people, who were alone and deserted now, and it seemed they were part of the family. Nunziata behaved as if she were in her own house, and took all her little ones along with her, like a mother hen. Alessi, who was sitting next to her, said: "Did you finish your weaving today?" or "Are you going to pick grapes at Massaro Filippo's on Monday? Now, with the olive harvest, you'll be able to earn a day's pay, even if you don't get any laundry to wash; and you can take your little brother with you, because now they'll pay him two soldi a day." Nunziata, very serious, would tell him about all her plans and ask for his advice, and they sat to one side, talking things over, as though they already had white hair. "They've learned early, because they've seen so much trouble," Master 'Ntoni said. "Good judgment comes with misfortune."

Alessi, his arms around his knees, exactly like his grandfather, asked Nunziata: "Will you marry me when I'm grown up?"

"There's still time for that," she replied.

"Sure, there's time, but it's best for us to think of it now, so I'll know what I must do. First we must marry off Mena, and then Lia, when she'll also be grown up. Lia's starting to wear long dresses and kerchiefs with roses on them, and then you too have to get your children settled. First of all we must buy a boat; then the boat will help us to buy the house. My grandfather would like to get the house by the medlar tree again, and I'd like that too, because there even at night I know where to go with my eyes shut, without even stumbling. And it has a big yard for the gear, and you take just two steps and you're at the sea. Then, after my sisters are married, Grandfather will come to live with us and we'll put him in the big room on the yard, where the sun shines. That way, even when he no longer can go out to sea, poor old man, he can sit by the door in the yard and in the summer he'll have the medlar tree nearby to give him shade. We'll take the room on the garden, would you like that? And right next to it you'll have your kitchen. So you'll have everything handy, isn't that right? When my brother 'Ntoni comes back, we'll give the room to him and we'll go up in the attic. And you'll just have to go downstairs to get to the kitchen or the garden."

"The hearth in the kitchen needs fixing," Nunziata said. "The last time I cooked the soup there, when poor Comare Maruzza hadn't the heart to do a thing, I had to put stones under the pot to hold it up."

"Yes, I know!" replied Alessi, nodding his head, his chin on his hands. His eyes stared spellbound, as if he saw Nunziata at the hearth and his mother weeping beside the bed. "You, too, could find your way through the house by the medlar in the dark, you've been there so many times. My mother always said that you're a good girl."

"Now they've planted onions in the garden, and they've come up as big as oranges."

"Do you like onions?"

"I've got to like them. They help you eat your bread and they're cheap. When we don't have any money for soup, my little ones and I always eat them."

"That's why they sell so many onions. Uncle Crocifisso didn't plant cabbages and lettuce at the house by the medlar and has sown only onions, because he has another garden at his own house. But we'll plant broccoli and cauliflowers, too. . . . They're good, aren't they?"

The young girl huddling on the doorstep with her arms around her knees was also staring far away; and then she started to sing, and Alessi listened intently.

At last she said: "But there's still time."

"Yes," Alessi agreed. "First we have to marry Mena and Lia too, and then your children have to be settled. But it's best to make plans now!"

"When Nunziata sings," said Mena, coming to the door, "it means that the next day the weather will be good and she'll be able to go to the wash shed." It was the same for Cousin Anna, because the wash shed was her farm and vineyard, and plenty of clothes to wash was her holiday, especially now that her son Rocco celebrated at the tavern from one Monday to the next, trying to wash down the bitter taste that Mangiacarrube flirt had left in his mouth.

"Some misfortunes are a blessing," Master 'Ntoni said to her. "Maybe in this way your son Rocco will settle down at last. My 'Ntoni will also learn a lesson by being far from home. So when he comes back, he'll be tired of traveling about the world and everything here will look good to him, and he'll no longer complain about everything. And if we once again manage to have boats on the water and to set up our beds in that house over there, you'll see how fine it will be to rest next to that doorway in the evening when we come home tired and have had a good day's fishing, and to see the lamp in that room where we've seen it so often, and where we've seen the faces of all those who were dear to us in this world. But now so many of them have gone one by one and will never return, and the room is dark and the door is shut, as though those who left had carried away the key in their pockets forever."

After a while the old man added: " 'Ntoni shouldn't have left! He should have known that I'm an old man, and that if I die these children will be left all alone."

"If we buy back the house by the medlar tree while he's gone, he won't believe it when he comes back," Mena said. "And he'll come looking for us here."

Master 'Ntoni shook his head sadly.

"But there's still time!" he finally said, just like Nunziata; and then Cousin Anna added: "If 'Ntoni comes back rich, he'll buy back the house."

Master 'Ntoni did not reply; but the whole village was saying that 'Ntoni was bound to come back rich, since he'd left so long ago to seek his fortune, and many people already envied him and wanted to drop everything and go in search of their fortunes too, as he had done. After all, they were right, because all they left behind were a few whining women; and the only ones who hadn't the heart to leave their women were that lout La Locca's son—and you know what sort of mother he had—and Rocco Spatu, who was tied body and soul to the tavern.

But, luckily for the women, all of a sudden it got around that Master 'Ntoni's 'Ntoni had returned at night, on a ship from Catania, and that he was ashamed to show his face because he didn't even have shoes on his feet. He was so ragged that if it was true that he'd come back rich he certainly had no place to put his money. But his grandfather, his brother, and his sisters gave him a warm welcome, as though he had really returned loaded with money, and his sisters clung to his neck, laughing and crying, and Lia had grown so big that 'Ntoni could hardly recognize her. And they said to him: "Now you won't leave us again, isn't that so?"

His grandfather blew his nose and muttered: "Now that these children won't be left alone and out in the middle of the street, I can die in peace."

But for eight days 'Ntoni didn't have the courage to set foot in the street. As soon as they saw him, they all laughed in his face, and Piedipapera went around saying: "Did you see all the wealth that Master 'Ntoni's 'Ntoni brought home?" And those who'd taken their time to prepare their bundles of shoes and shirts before venturing on that foolish journey away from home, laughed so hard their bellies ached.

When a man fails to grab his fortune, he's a fool—we all know that. Don Silvestro, Uncle Crocifisso, Master Cipolla, and Massaro Filippo were not fools, and everybody looked up to them, because those who have nothing gape at the rich and fortunate, and work for them for a fistful of straw, like Compare Mosca's donkey, instead of kicking out, smashing the cart to pieces and lying down on the grass with their bellies in the sun. The pharmacist was right when he said that the world as it was now should be given a good kick and made all over again from scratch; but even he, with his big beard and all his preaching about starting from scratch, was one of those who'd seized his fortune, and he kept it in those glass jars and enjoyed God's bounty standing at the door of his shop, chatting with this fellow and that, and after he'd pounded some dirty water in his mortar, his day's work was done. What a fine trade his father had taught him, making money out of water from the cistern! But 'Ntoni's grandfather had taught him a trade in which all day long he broke his arms and his back, and risked his skin, and died of hunger, and

never had a single day when he could lie in the sun, like
Alfio Mosca's donkey. A thief of a trade that ate up your
soul, by the Madonna! And he had it up to his eyes and
preferred doing like Rocco Spatu, who at least did nothing
at all. Yes, he didn't give a rap now for Barbara Zuppidda
and Comare Tudda's Sara, and all the other girls in the
world. All they wanted was to hook a husband who
would work like a dog to give them food and buy them
silk kerchiefs so that they could stand at the doorway on
Sundays, their hands clasped over their full bellies. Instead, he wanted to stand there with his hands over his
belly on Sundays and Mondays and all the other days too,
because there's no point in toiling for nothing.

So 'Ntoni had become a preacher, like the pharmacist.
At least he'd learned that on his travels and now he'd
opened his eyes, like kittens do forty days after they're
born. "The chicken that goes for a stroll comes home
with its belly full." If nothing else, he had filled his belly
with good sense, and he told what he'd learned on the
piazza, in Pizzuto's store, and also in Santuzza's tavern.
Now he no longer went to Santuzza's tavern on the sly,
because he'd grown up and when all was said and done
his grandfather couldn't pull his ears for it; and he'd know
how to tell them off if they reproached him for seeking
what little pleasure he could find.

His grandfather, poor old man, instead of pulling his
ears, tried to talk him around. "You see," he said, "now that
you're here we'll soon be able to put together the money
for the house." He was always harping on that same old
tune—the house. "Uncle Crocifisso has promised not to
give it to anyone else. Your mother, poor woman, wasn't
able to die there! The house will also give us a dowry for
Mena. Then, with God's help, we'll fit out another boat,
because I must tell you that at my age it's hard to hire
out and be ordered around, when you've been the master.
You boys were born to be masters too. Do you want us
to buy the boat first, with the money for the house? Now
you're a man and you must also have your say, because
I'm old and you should have better judgment. What do
you want to do?"

'Ntoni didn't want to do anything. What did he care

about the house and the new boat? Then another bad year would come, another cholera epidemic, another disaster, and eat up both house and boat, and they'd go right back to scrounging, like ants. A fine outlook! And when they had the house and the boat, did that mean they wouldn't work anymore? That they'd eat pasta and meat every day? But in the cities, where he'd been, there were people who rode about in their carriages all the time, that's what they did. Compared to them, Don Franco and the town clerk worked like donkeys, smearing ink on paper and pounding dirty water in the mortar. At least he would like to know why there must be people in the world who have a good time without doing a lick of work and were born with a fortune in their laps, and other people who have nothing and drag their load all their life long—and with their teeth at that.

Besides, this business of hiring out didn't suit him at all, for he had been born a master, as his grandfather had said. To be ordered around by people who had sprung up from nothing when everybody in the village knew how they'd made their money, penny by penny, toiling and sweating—! He hired out only because his grandfather forced him to, and he still didn't have the heart to say no. But when the master kept after him like a dog and yelled at him from the stern: "Hey you, over there! What do you think you're doing?" he felt like breaking his oar over his master's head, and he'd rather repair the lobster pots and mend the nets, sitting on the beach with his legs stretched out and his back leaning against the stones; because then nobody said a word, even if he rested for a moment with his arms crossed.

Rocco Spatu also came down to the beach to stretch his arms, and Vanni Pizzuto, when he had an idle moment between one shave and the next, and Piedipapera too, for chatting with everybody to drum up a deal was his trade. And they talked about what had happened in the village and about how, when there'd been the cholera, Donna Rosolina, under the seal of the confessional, had told her brother that Don Silvestro had cheated her out of twenty-five onze, and she couldn't take it to court because Donna Rosolina herself had stolen the twenty-five onze from her brother the priest, and everybody would have known, to her shame, why she had given that money to Don Silvestro!

"Anyway," Pizzuto said, "where did Donna Rosolina get those twenty-five onze? You see, stolen goods don't last!"

"At least they were still in the house," Spatu replied. "If my mother had twelve tarì and I took them, would that make me a thief?"

One thief led to another, and so they started talking about Uncle Crocifisso, who, they said, had lost more than thirty onze because so many people had died of the cholera and left him holding their pledges. And now Dumbbell, since he didn't know what to do with all those rings and earrings he had on his hands, was getting married to La Vespa; it was all arranged because they'd even seen him go to the Town Hall to put his name down in Don Silvestro's presence. "It's not true that he's marrying her because he's stuck with all those earrings," said Piedipapera, who knew what he was talking about. "After all, the earrings and chains are solid gold and silver and he could have sold them in Catania. In fact, he could have made twice what he loaned out. If he's marrying La Vespa, it's only because she showed him as clear as day that she was set on going to the notary with Rocco Spatu for the marriage contract, now that the Mangiacarrube girl has lured Brasi Cipolla into her house. No offense meant, Compare Rocco."

"Never mind, never mind, Compare Tino," Rocco replied. "I don't care. Anyone who trusts women, those bitches, is a pig. My sweetheart is Santuzza, who gives me credit when I ask her for it, and with that bosom she's got you'd have to put two Mangiacarrube girls on the scale to equal her, am I right, Compare Tino?"

"A beautiful woman behind the counter spells a big bill!" said Pizzuto, spitting.

"They look for a husband so he can work and support them!" said 'Ntoni. "They're all the same!"

And Piedipapera went on: "Then Uncle Crocifisso ran to the notary so fast his lungs nearly burst. So now he's finally taking La Vespa."

"It's a stroke of luck for that Mangiacarrube girl, isn't it?" 'Ntoni exclaimed.

"God willing, a hundred years from now, when his father dies, Brasi Cipolla will be as rich as a pig," said Rocco Spatu.

"Right now his father is raising the devil, but in time he'll bow his head. He has no other sons, and if he doesn't want the Mangiacarrube girl to get fat on his property despite him, the only thing he can do is get married himself."

"Now that's what I like to hear," 'Ntoni said. "The Mangiacarrube girl doesn't own a thing. Why should only Master Cipolla be rich?"

At this point the pharmacist, who came down to smoke his pipe on the beach after dinner, joined in the conversation and began as usual pounding at the water in his mortar, saying that the world wasn't being run right and that everything should be blown up and started all over again from scratch. But talking to people like that was indeed like pounding water in a mortar. The only one who understood anything was 'Ntoni, who'd seen the world and had opened his eyes, like the kittens. In the navy they'd taught him to read, and so he went to the pharmacy too and stood at the door to hear what the newspapers said, and to talk with the pharmacist, who was friendly to everyone and didn't put on airs like his wife, who yelled at him: "Why do you stick your nose into affairs that don't concern you?"

"You've got to let the women talk, and then go ahead and do what you want," Don Franco would say, as soon as the Signora went up to her room. He had nothing against discussing things even with people who didn't wear shoes, provided they didn't put their feet on the chair rungs; and he explained to them word by word what the newspaper said, showing them in black on white that the world should be run exactly the way they said in the newspaper.

When Don Franco got to the beach where the men were talking, he winked at 'Ntoni Malavoglia, who was mending the nets with his legs outstretched and his back propped against some stones. Then Don Franco nodded his head, shaking his beard in the air. "There's no justice!" he said. "Some have to break their backs against the stones while others warm their bellies in the sun, smoking their pipes, and instead all men should be brothers—Jesus, the greatest revolutionary there ever was, said so, and nowadays his priests are policemen and spies!" Didn't they all know that what went on between Don Michele and Santuzza had been found out by Don Giammaria under the seal of the confessional?

"What are you talking about, Don Michele! Santuzza has Massaro Filippo, while Don Michele is always buzzing around Black Lane, not the least afraid of Comare Zuppidda and her distaff! He's got his pistol."

"Santuzza has both of them, I tell you! These women who go to confession every Sunday have a big sack to collect their sins in; that's why Santuzza wears the holy medal on her breast! To cover the filth underneath it!"

"Don Michele is wasting his time with Barbara. The town clerk has said that he's going to make her fall with his feet, like a ripe pear."

"Of course! Meanwhile Don Michele is amusing himself with Barbara and with all the other girls who live on the lane. I know what I'm saying," and he motioned on the sly to 'Ntoni. "He has nothing to do and every blessed day he gets his pay of four tarì."

"That's what I always say!" the pharmacist repeated, pulling at his beard. "The whole system's like that; pay out money to a bunch of idlers to do nothing and chase our women, when we're the ones who are paying them! That's how things stand. People who get four tarì to stroll under Barbara's window; and Don Giammaria who gobbles up his lira a day to confess Santuzza and listen to all that filthy stuff she tells him; and Don Silvestro who . . . well, I know what he does! And Mastro Cirino who's paid to pester us with his bells, but then he doesn't light the street lamps and puts the oil he saves in his own pocket, because over there, at Town Hall, there are more dirty deals, you can believe me! Once they talked about cleaning out the whole bunch, but now they've gotten together again, Don Silvestro and the rest of them, and they never mentioned it again. . . . Exactly like those other thieves in Parliament who talk and talk among themselves; but do you know anything about what they say? They foam at the mouth and you'd think that at any minute they're going to tear each other's hair out, but then they laugh right under the noses of the idiots who fall for it. It's all bluster to fool the people who pay the thieves and pimps and spies like Don Michele."

"That's a fine life," said 'Ntoni. "Four tarì a day to go strolling about. I'd like to be a customs guard."

"There, you see!" cried Don Franco, his eyes starting out of his head. "You see the results of the system! The result is that everyone turns into scum. Don't be insulted, Compare 'Ntoni. The fish rots at the head first. I would be like you, too, if I hadn't studied and didn't have my profession to earn my living."

In fact people said that it was a fine profession his father had taught him, pounding in the mortar and making money out of dirty water, while there were other folks who had to roast their skulls under the sun and wear out their eyes mending nets, and get cramps in the legs and back, just to earn a few pennies. And so then they left the nets and the talk and went back to the tavern, spitting on the street as they walked.

CHAPTER THIRTEEN

When his grandson came home drunk at night, Master 'Ntoni did his best to get him into bed before the others noticed it, because among the Malavoglia there'd never been a thing like this, and he felt like crying. Before dawn, when he got up and called Alessi to go out to sea, he let his brother sleep, since he wouldn't be much help anyway. At first 'Ntoni was ashamed of it and as soon as he saw them coming back, he went to wait for them on the shore, with his head hanging. But gradually he got used to it and said to himself: "So tomorrow I'll have another holiday."

The poor old man tried in every way to touch his heart, and even had Don Giammaria bless his shirt without his knowing, and spent three tarì on it. "Now see here," he said to 'Ntoni, "this has never happened to the Malavoglia before. If you go down that evil path like Rocco Spatu, your brother and your sisters will follow you. One rotten apple spoils the whole barrel, and all the money we've put together with so much toil and effort will go up in smoke. One fisherman can sink the boat, and then what will we do?"

'Ntoni hung his head or muttered under his breath, but the next day he started all over again and once he even said to his grandfather: "What do you want from me! At least when I'm not in my senses, I don't think of my bad luck."

"What bad luck? You're healthy, you're young, and you know your trade. What do you lack? Your brother, who's still a boy, and I, an old man, we've pulled ourselves out of the ditch. And if you'd help us now, we'd once again be what we were, and if we won't be as happy because those who've died will never come back, at least we won't have any other worries; and we'd all be united, like the fingers of the hand must be, and we'd have bread in the house. If I die now, what will become of all of you? Now, you see, I have to be afraid every time we sail far out from shore. And I'm an old man! . . ."

When his grandfather succeeded in touching his heart, 'Ntoni broke down and cried. His brother and sisters, who knew all about it, crept into the corners as soon as they heard him coming, as if he were a stranger, or they were afraid of him; and his grandfather, holding his rosary beads, muttered: "Oh blessed soul of Bastianazzo! Oh soul of my daughter-in-law Maruzza, help me, bring us this miracle!" When Mena saw 'Ntoni come home with his face pale and his eyes glittering, she said to him: "Come in this way. Grandfather's there!" And she made him come in through the small kitchen door; then she started sobbing softly, sitting next to the hearth. And at last 'Ntoni said: "I'm through going to the tavern! I won't go, not even if they kill me!" And he went back to work with as good a will as before; he even got up before the others and went to wait for his grandfather on the shore, two hours before the dawn, when the Three Kings were still shining high above the church tower and you could hear the crickets trilling in the vineyards as if they were right there next to you. His grandfather could scarcely fit into his shirt, he was so happy; and he kept talking to 'Ntoni to show how much he cared for him, and said to himself: "It's the blessed souls of 'Ntoni's mother and father who've brought us this miracle."

The miracle lasted the entire week, and on Sunday 'Ntoni didn't even go to the piazza, so that even from a distance he wouldn't see the tavern or hear his friends calling him. But all day long he broke his jaw yawning, because he had nothing to do and the day seemed to drag on and on. He was no longer a boy who could spend his time picking broom on the lava field and singing like his brother Alessi and Nunziata, or sweeping the floors like Mena, nor was he an old man like his grandfather, who got pleasure out of fixing the broken barrels and lobster pots. He sat next to the door on Black Lane, where not even a chicken passed by, and listened to the shouts and laughter coming from the tavern. Finally he went to sleep, because he didn't know what else to do, and on Monday he began looking glum again. His grandfather said to him: "It would be better for you if Sunday never came; because the next day you're like a madman." Sure, that would be better for him—if Sunday never came! And his heart sank into the ground at the thought that all the days could be Mondays, and in the evening when he came back from the sea, he didn't even feel like going to sleep and roamed restlessly about the streets, alone with his bad luck. In the end, he wound up at the tavern again.

Before, when he came staggering home, he slipped in very quietly, making himself small and stammering excuses, or at least he didn't open his mouth. But now he began to raise his voice, argued with his sister if she was waiting by the door with her face pale and her eyes swollen, and if she told him in a low voice to come in through the kitchen because grandfather was home, he yelled: "I don't give a damn!" The next day he got up wild-eyed and in a bad temper; and he shouted and cursed from morning till night.

One time there was an ugly scene. His grandfather, no longer knowing what he could do to touch his heart, had drawn him into a corner of the room and, with the doors shut so the neighbors shouldn't hear, said to him, crying like a child: "Oh, 'Ntoni, have you forgotten that your mother died here? Why do you want to give your mother this sorrow of letting her see you turn out like Rocco Spatu? Don't you see how poor Cousin Anna has to toil and sweat for that drunken son of hers? And how she cries sometimes when she has no bread to give her other children, and then, with all her cheerful heart, she doesn't feel like laughing? 'He who goes with wolves turns into a wolf,' and 'he who goes with the lame limps within the year.' Don't you remember the night of the plague when we were all gathered around that small bed, and your mother begged you to take care of Mena and the children?" 'Ntoni cried like a calf and said that he wanted to die too; but then, slowly but surely, he found his way back to the tavern and at night, instead of going home, he knocked about the streets with Rocco Spatu and Cinghialenta, stopping in front of the doorways, leaning against the walls dead tired, and then, to chase away the melancholy, he sang along with them.

At last Master 'Ntoni was so ashamed he no longer dared show his face on the street. But his grandson, to escape all that preaching, came home looking grim; that way, they wouldn't spoil his fun with the usual sermons. In fact he preached to himself all the time, under his breath, putting the blame on his bad luck which had caused him to be born a poor man.

And he went to complain to the pharmacist and all the other people who had a bit of free time to discuss the damned injustice which is in everything in this world. If, for example, a man goes to Santuzza's to forget his troubles, he's called a drunkard, but what about all those who get drunk at home on good wine and don't even have any troubles to forget?—nobody ever reproaches them or preaches to them to go to work, for they have no work and are rich enough for two; and yet we're all God's children in the same way, and each should get his equal share. "That boy there has talent!" the pharmacist told Don Silvestro, Master Cipolla, and anyone else who'd listen. "He sees things crudely and a bit confusedly, but he's got the gist of it. It's not his fault if he isn't able to express himself better. It's the fault of the government which leaves him in ignorance."

To educate him, Don Franco brought him the *Secolo* and the *Gazzetta di Catania*. But 'Ntoni felt that reading was a nuisance; first of all, because it was hard work, and they'd forced him in the navy to learn how to read; but now he was free to do whatever he chose and pleased, and had nearly forgotten how all those written words fit together. Besides, all that printed gabble didn't put a penny in his pocket. What did he care? Don Franco explained to him why he ought to care; and when Don Michele walked across the piazza, the pharmacist winked and pointed at him with his big beard, whispering that he was strolling by to see Donna Rosolina, now that he'd heard she had money and gave it to people so they'd marry her.

"We've got to start out by making a clean sweep of all those fellows with the gold-braided caps. We've got to make a revolution. That's what we've got to do!"

"And what will you give me if I make this revolution?"

Then Don Franco, greatly irritated, shrugged and went back to pounding dirty water in his mortar; anyway, talking to such people, he'd say, was worse than pounding water in the mortar. And as soon as 'Ntoni turned his back, Piedipapera added in a low voice:

"If he wants to murder Don Michele, he should murder him for something else; because he's trying to steal his sister, but that 'Ntoni is worse than a pig. Why, he even lets Santuzza support him." Piedipapera had his belly full of Don Michele, ever since he had started watching him, Rocco Spatu, and Cinghialenta with a grim look in his eye; and so he wanted to get rid of him.

By now those poor Malavoglia girls were being talked about by everybody, that's how low the Malavoglia had fallen, and it was all 'Ntoni's fault. Now the whole village knew that Don Michele strolled up and down Black Lane to spite La Zuppidda, who was guarding her daughter, distaff in hand. In the meantime, so as not to waste his stroll, he had set his eyes on Lia, who'd also become a pretty girl and had nobody to guard her, except for her sister, who would blush for her and say: "Let's go inside, Lia. Now that we're orphans, it doesn't look right for us to stay at the door."

But Lia was as light-headed as her brother 'Ntoni, and worse, and she liked to stand in front of the door to show off her kerchief with the roses on it, because everybody said: "How pretty you look with the kerchief on, Comare Lia!" And Don Michele devoured her with his eyes.

Poor Mena, as she stood there at the door, waiting for her brother to come home drunk, felt terribly weary and disheartened. And then, when she tried to pull her sister into the house because Don Michele had come strolling by, and Lia answered her, "Are you afraid he'll eat me up? Why nobody wants us, now that we haven't a thing. Don't you see what's happened to my brother? Even the dogs don't want him!" She didn't know where to turn and gave up entirely.

"If 'Ntoni had any guts," Piedipapera went about saying, "he'd get rid of that Don Michele."

But 'Ntoni had another reason for wanting to get rid of Don Michele. After having broken with Don Michele, Santuzza had become fond of 'Ntoni, because of the way he wore his cap tilted over his ear and that strut he'd picked up in the navy, rolling his shoulders as he walked. She saved all the leftovers from the dishes of her customers, putting them under the counter for him; and by taking a drop here and a drop there, she also filled his glass. This was how she kept him around the tavern, fat and greasy as the butcher's dog. 'Ntoni returned the courtesy by using his fists on the malcontents who start splitting hairs when they see the bill, cursing and swearing before they fork out the money. But with the good customers he was gay and talkative, and he also kept an eye on the counter when Santuzza went to confession. So everybody liked him and made him feel at home, except for Uncle Santoro, who glowered at him and kept grumbling about him, between one Hail Mary and the next, because he was living off his daughter, like a canon priest. Santuzza replied that if she wanted to let 'Ntoni Malavoglia live off her, fat as a canon priest, nobody could stop her. It was the proof that she liked it and no longer needed anyone else.

"Yes, yes," muttered Uncle Santoro, when he could grab her for a minute to talk in private. "But you'll always need Don Michele. Massaro Filippo has told me over and over that it's about time to stop this nonsense, because he can't keep the new wine in his cellar any longer, and you'll have to smuggle it into town."

"Massaro Filippo is grinding his own ax. But even if I have to pay the customs twice over, and the smugglers too, I don't want to have anything to do with Don Michele! And that's that!"

She couldn't forgive Don Michele for having played her that dirty trick with Barbara Zuppidda after all the time he'd been treated like a canon priest at the tavern for the sake of his gold braid; and 'Ntoni Malavoglia, without the gold braid, was worth ten Don Micheles; what she gave to him, she gave with her whole heart. So this was how 'Ntoni earned his bread, and when his grandfather reproached him for not working, and his sister stared at him sadly, he replied: "Do I cost you anything? I'm not taking any of the money for the house, and I don't come to you for my bread."

"It would be better if you died of hunger," his grandfather said. "If we all died this very day!" In the end they stopped talking and sat there, turning their backs to each other. Master 'Ntoni had to keep his mouth shut if he didn't want to have a fight with his grandson; and 'Ntoni, when he was fed up with the sermon, left the company to its whining and went looking for Rocco or Compare Vanni, fellows with whom you could always be gay and think up something new to pass the time.

The night Uncle Crocifisso married La Vespa, 'Ntoni and his friends got the idea of serenading him. They gathered under his window all the people to whom Uncle Crocifisso would no longer lend a penny, and made a hellish din until midnight with broken crockery and cracked pots, cattle bells and cane whistles. The next morning La Vespa got up looking greener than ever, and took it out on that slut Santuzza, in whose tavern that piece of roguery had been hatched out of jealousy because *she* had found herself a husband and could now live with God's blessing, while other women were always in mortal sin and committed all sorts of filth, hiding beneath the Madonna's scapular.

People laughed right in Uncle Crocifisso's face when they saw him, a bridegroom in the piazza, all dressed up in a new suit, and as yellow as a corpse from the fright La Vespa had given him, making him buy that suit which had cost so much. La Vespa was always spending and squandering, and if he'd let her have her way she'd have put him in the poorhouse inside of a week. She said that she was the mistress now, and so every single day there was a devil of a row at Uncle Crocifisso's house. His wife scratched his face and screamed that she wanted to hold the keys, and didn't want to be hankering after a piece of bread or a new kerchief, as she had before, and even worse; for if she had known what she was going to get out of marriage with that fine husband she'd hit on, she would rather have kept her plot of land and her Daughter of Mary medal! And, anyway, from the way things had gone between them, she could still be wearing her Daughter of Mary medal! And he shrieked that he was ruined; that he was no longer master of his own property; that he still had the cholera in his house; and that they wanted to make him die of a broken heart before his time so they could gaily fritter away the property which he had toiled so hard to scrape together! He too, if he'd known all this, would have sent both plot and wife to the devil, because he didn't need a wife, and they had seized him by the throat, making him believe that La Vespa had gotten her claws into Brasi Cipolla and was all set to slip through his fingers, together with her plot! That accursed plot!

Just then it was found out that Brasi Cipolla had let himself be hooked by the Mangiacarrube girl, like a booby, and Master Fortunato went searching for them on the lava field and the inlet and under the bridge, his mouth frothing, swearing up and down that if he found them he would give them both a good kicking and pull his son's ears until they came off. When he heard this, Uncle Crocifisso began tearing his hair too, and said that the Mangiacarrube girl had ruined him by not carrying off Brasi a week earlier. "It was the will of God," he went around saying, beating his breast. "It was the will of God that I should take La Vespa as a punishment for my sins!" And he must have sinned a great deal, because La Vespa poisoned the bread in his mouth and made him suffer the torments of purgatory night and day. On top of all this, she boasted that she was faithful to him, and that she wouldn't look at another man for all the gold in the world, even if he were as young and handsome as 'Ntoni Malavoglia or Vanni Pizzuto; while the men were always hanging around her to tempt her, as if she had honey on her skirts. "If it were true, I would go and bring him here myself!" Uncle Crocifisso muttered. "Provided he took her out of my sight!" And he even said that he was willing to pay something to Vanni Pizzuto or 'Ntoni Malavoglia if they'd present him with a pair of horns, since 'Ntoni was in that trade anyway. "Then I could throw out that witch I've dragged into my house!"

But 'Ntoni plied his trade where it paid well, and he ate and drank so much he was a pleasure to look at. Now he carried his head high, and he laughed if his grandfather tried to scold him. And now it was his grandfather who slunk around, almost as though he were in the wrong. 'Ntoni said that if they didn't want him in the house, he knew where he could go, he could sleep in Santuzza's stable; and anyway at home they weren't spending a cent to feed him. As for all the money Master 'Ntoni, Alessi, and Mena earned by fishing, weaving, washing, and doing all their odd jobs, they could set it aside to buy that miraculous Saint Peter's boat, and with it they'd have the pleasure of breaking their backs every day for a *rotolo* of fish. Or to buy the house by the medlar tree, and then go there to starve merrily to death! Because he didn't want a penny from them. If he had to be a poor devil, he preferred to enjoy a little rest while he was still young and didn't moan all night long, like his grandfather. The sun was there for everyone, and the shade of the olive trees to cool you off, and the piazza to stroll in, and the church steps to sit on and chat, and the highway to see the people go by and to hear the latest news, and the tavern to eat and drink in together with your friends. Then if you felt bored, you could play cards, *mora* or *briscola;* and when at last you got sleepy, there still was the pasture where Compare Naso's rams grazed, to lie down to sleep in during the day, and there was Sister Mariangela's stable at night.

"Aren't you ashamed to live this kind of life?" his grandfather finally asked him. He had come on purpose, all bent over and with his head hanging, to see his grandson. And as he said it he cried like a child, pulling 'Ntoni by the sleeve behind Santuzza's stable so that nobody should see them. "Don't you think of your home? Don't you think of your brother and sisters? If only your father and La Longa were both here now! 'Ntoni! 'Ntoni!"

"But are you people living any better than I am, with all your working and useless struggling?" 'Ntoni retorted. "It's our cursed lot, that's what it is! You see how worn out you are, you look like a fiddle bow, and you've grown old always living the same life! And now, what have you got? You people don't know the world, you're like kittens with their eyes still closed. Do you eat the fish you catch? Do you know for whom you work, from Monday to Saturday, and for whom you've worn yourself out so that they wouldn't even take you in at the hospital? For the people who never do a lick of work and have piles of money. That's who you're working for!"

"But you don't have any money, and neither do I. We've never had any, and we've earned our bread as God has willed. That's why we have to keep our hands busy, so we can earn it. If we didn't, we'd die of hunger."

"As the devil has willed, you should say. Because our misfortune is all the devil's work. Do you know what is in store for you when you'll no longer be able to keep your hands busy because they'll be all twisted by rheumatism like vine roots? The ditch under the bridge, so you can die there!"

"No! No!" the old man cried hopefully, and threw his arms, gnarled like vine roots, around his neck. "We always have the money for the house, and if you help us . . ."

"Ah, the house by the medlar tree! You've never seen anything, but you think it's the most beautiful palace in the world!"

"I know it isn't the most beautiful palace in the world. But you shouldn't be the one to say so, for you were born there, and all the more since your mother couldn't die there."

"My father didn't die there either. We leave our skins out at sea, in the mouths of sharks, that's our trade. And at least as long as I've still got my skin, I want to enjoy what little pleasure I can find, since it's useless to wear it out for nothing! When you've got the house and the boat, what then? What about Mena's dowry? And Lia's dowry? . . . Ah, by the blood of the thieving Judas, what a miserable fate!"

All hunched over and miserable, the old man left, shaking his head. His grandson's bitter words had crashed down on him like a huge rock. He had lost all his courage, he felt completely helpless and all he wanted to do was cry. All he could think of was that Bastianazzo and Luca had never had ideas like 'Ntoni's and had always done what they had to do without complaining; and he kept telling himself over and over that it was useless to think about a dowry for Mena or Lia, for they'd never be able to manage it.

Poor Mena was so downcast that it seemed she knew it,

too. Now the women passed the Malavoglia door without stopping, as if they were still afraid of the cholera, and they left her all alone, sitting beside that sister of hers with the rose-adorned kerchief. Or beside Nunziata or Cousin Anna, when they took pity on her and came over to chat for a while. Because Cousin Anna had that other drunkard, Rocco, to worry about, and by now the whole village knew about it; and Nunziata had her share of troubles, because she was just a little girl when her father, that rascal, had deserted her and gone elsewhere to seek his fortune. That's why the three of them, poor things, understood each other as they sat there talking in low voices, their heads lowered and their hands under their aprons, and even when they were silent and didn't look at each other, each thinking of her own troubles. "When a family is as bad off as we are," said Lia, who talked like a grown-up woman, "each one's got to help himself and look out for his own interests."

Now and then Don Michele stopped to say hello or to tell them a few jokes; and so the women became familiar with that gold-braided cap and were no longer frightened by it; indeed, Lia had even gone so far as to tell a few jokes herself and giggle over them. Nor did Mena dare to scold her or go into the kitchen and leave her alone, now that she no longer had a mother. But she just stayed there, huddled up in herself, looking up and down the street with weary eyes. Now that they saw how the neighbors had forsaken them, their hearts swelled with gratitude each time that Don Michele, even though he wore that gold-braided cap, deigned to stop and chat for a while at the Malavoglia door. And if Don Michele found Lia alone, he would gaze into her eyes, pulling at his mustaches and with his braided cap set at a dashing angle; then he would say: "My, what a pretty girl you are, Comare Malavoglia!"

Nobody had ever said that to her, and she got red as a beet.

"How is it that you're not married yet?" Don Michele asked.

She shrugged and said that she didn't know.

"You should have a dress of wool and silk and long earrings, because, then, on my word of honor, you'd look much prettier than many ladies in Catania."

"Dresses of wool and silk are not for me, Don Michele,"
she replied.

"Why not? Doesn't Barbara Zuppidda wear one? And
the Mangiacarrube girl, now that she's grabbed Master
Cipolla's Brasi, won't she get one, too? And La Vespa, if
she wants it, won't she get it like the others?"

"But they're rich!"

"Cruel fate!" cried Don Michele, beating his fist against
his saber. "I wish I could win in the lottery, I swear it,
Comare Lia, then you'd see what I would do!"

At times, when he had nothing else to do, Don Michele
went on to say: "May I?" touching his cap with his hand,
and then sat down on the stones near her. Mena thought
that he had come there on account of Barbara Zuppidda,
and so she didn't say a word to him. But to Lia, Don
Michele swore that he wasn't there for Barbara, and that
he had never even given her a thought, on his holy word
of honor! He was thinking of someone else entirely, and
Comare Lia ought to know that! . . .

And he rubbed his chin or stroked his mustaches, staring
at her like a basilisk. And she blushed all colors and got
up to leave. But Don Michele seized her hand and said:
"Why do you insult me like this, Comare Malavoglia?
Stay here, nobody's going to eat you!"

That was how they passed the time, waiting for the men
to come back from the sea; Lia standing in the doorway
and Don Michele sitting on the stones, idly snapping a
twig between his fingers.

And he asked her: "Would you come to live in
Catania?"

"What would I come to Catania for?"

"Oh, that's the place for you! You're not made to live
here among these clodhoppers, on my word of honor! You
are fine stuff, of the best quality, and you were made to
live in a lovely little house and stroll along the harbor and
in the park when the band's playing, elegantly dressed, as
I understand it. With a beautiful silk kerchief on your head
and an amber necklace. Here it's like living among the
pigs, on my word of honor! and I can hardly wait to be
transferred, because they've promised to call me back to
Catania after the New Year."

Lia laughed at the joke and shrugged her shoulders,

because she didn't even know what amber necklaces and silk kerchiefs looked like. And one day Don Michele, with an air of great mystery, pulled out a beautiful yellow and red kerchief, all nicely wrapped, which he had gotten from some smuggler, and he wanted to give it as a present to Comare Lia.

"No! No!" she cried, blushing. "I won't take it even if you kill me!" And Don Michele kept on insisting: "I didn't expect this, Comare Lia. I don't deserve it, honestly!" But he had to wrap up the kerchief again and thrust it back in his pocket.

From then on, whenever she saw Don Michele's cap appear at the end of the lane, Lia ran and hid in the house for fear he might try to give her the kerchief. No matter how many times Don Michele walked up and down the lane, trying to make Comare Zuppidda grumble and rave, and no matter how often he craned his neck to get a look through the Malavoglia door, he couldn't catch a glimpse of anyone. So at last he decided to walk right in. When the girls saw him suddenly standing there, they were dumbfounded and trembled as though they had a fever, and didn't know what in the world to do.

"You didn't take the silk kerchief, Comare Lia," he said to the girl, who had turned red as a poppy, "but I've come back anyway because I like you people so much. Now tell me, what is your brother 'Ntoni doing?"

When people asked her what her brother 'Ntoni was doing, Mena became flustered because he wasn't doing anything. Then Don Michele went on: "I'm afraid that your brother 'Ntoni will make all of you unhappy. I'm a friend of yours and so I shut my eyes. But when another sergeant comes to take my place, he may want to know what your brother's doing at night with Cinghialenta, out at the Rotolo, together with that other fine fellow Rocco Spatu, when they all go strolling on the lava field as if they had shoe leather to waste. Open your eyes wide about what I'm telling you now, Comare Mena; and you can also tell him that he shouldn't hang around so much in Pizzuto's shop with that swindler Piedipapera, because we know everything, and if trouble comes, he'll get the worst of it. The others are old foxes, and it might be a good idea for your grandfather not to let him go strolling on the lava

field, because the lava field isn't a place for strolls, and
even the rocks at the Rotolo have ears, tell him that, and
they don't need binoculars to see the boats which at dusk
come coasting along the shore on the sly, as if they were
fishing for bats. You tell him this, and you might also tell
him that the person who's giving him this warning is a
friend who wishes you people well. As for Cinghialenta
and Rocco Spatu, and even Vanni Pizzuto, they're all
being watched. Your brother trusts Piedipapera, and he
doesn't know that the customs guards get a percentage on
all the contraband they seize, and the way to seize it is to
offer one of the smugglers part of that percentage and get
him to spill the beans. As for Piedipapera, just remind
your brother that Jesus Christ said to John: 'Beware of
marked men.' Also the proverb says so."

Mena opened her eyes wide and went white, without
understanding too well what he was saying. Yet she was
already terrified that her brother might get into trouble
with those men who wore the braided caps.

Then Don Michele took her hand to reassure her and
said: "If anybody got to know that I came to tell you this,
I'd be in for it. I'm risking my gold-braided cap for the
friendship I have for you Malavoglia. And I don't want
any harm to come to your brother. No, I wouldn't like to
meet him some night in the wrong place, not even if it
meant seizing one thousand lire worth of contraband, on
my word of honor!"

After Don Michele had put that flea in their ear, the
girls didn't have a moment's peace. At night they couldn't
sleep and waited up till late for their brother, sitting behind
the door, trembling from cold and fear, while he was singing in the streets, together with Rocco Spatu and the others
in the band, and the poor girls always thought they heard
screams and rifle shots, just like that time people had said
there had been a hunt for quails with shoes on.

"You go to sleep," Mena kept saying to her sister.
"You're too young, and there are things you shouldn't
know about!"

She didn't say anything to her grandfather, to spare him
this new heartbreak, but when she saw that 'Ntoni had a
quiet moment, sitting sadly by the door, his chin on his
hand, she got up the courage to ask him: "What are you

always doing with Rocco Spatu and Cinghialenta? Beware, because they've seen you on the lava field and near the Rotolo. And beware of Piedipapera. You know what Jesus said to Saint John: 'Beware of marked men!' "

"Who told you that?" said 'Ntoni, leaping to his feet as if the devil were in him. "Tell me who said that to you!"

"Don Michele said it!" she replied, with tears in her eyes. "He told me that you should beware of Piedipapera, because when they want to seize contraband, they give a share to one of the gang."

"And he didn't say anything else?"

"No, he didn't say anything else."

'Ntoni swore that it was all a lie and told her that she shouldn't tell it to his grandfather. Then he got up brusquely and went to the tavern to throw off his gloom, and if he met any of those gold-braided caps, he gave them a wide berth so he wouldn't have to see hide nor hair of them. He was sure that Don Michele didn't know anything and was just talking to give him a fright, because he had it in for him on account of Santuzza, who had thrown him out like a mangy dog. When all was said and done, he wasn't afraid of Don Michele or his gold braid, a man who got good pay to suck the blood of the poor. Don Michele was so fat and well fed that he didn't have to round out his pay like that. But it seemed he had nothing better to do than get his hands on some poor devil who tried to earn a twelve tarì piece as best he could; and it was pure tyranny that you had to pay customs duty to land goods from other parts of Italy, as though they were stolen! And then Don Michele and his spies had to stick their noses into it! They could lay hands on anything and take whatever they wanted; but if other people, at the risk of their skins, tried to land their goods in their own way, they were considered thieves and hunted down with pistols and carbines, like wolves. But stealing from thieves has never been a sin. Don Giammaria himself had said so in the pharmacy. And Don Franco had approved of that statement, nodding his head and his big beard and saying with a sneer that there wouldn't be any such dirty goings-on after the republic was founded. "And the clerks, too, those devils!" the priest had added. Don Giammaria was still rankling over those twenty-five onze which had slipped out of his house.

Now Donna Rosolina had lost her head, together with those twenty-five onze, and she was chasing Don Michele, so he could gobble up the rest. When she saw him walking down Black Lane, she thought he was coming by to see her on the balcony, and so she was always there with her tomato paste or her jars of peppers, to show what she could do as a housewife; because not even a pair of pincers could pry it out of her head that Don Michele was looking for a good, sensible housewife—and she knew what that meant—especially now that he'd gotten rid of his mortal sin with Santuzza. So she took his part when her brother cursed the government and the loafers who were paid by it, and she answered: "Loafers like Don Silvestro, I agree entirely! People who devour a whole town without lifting a finger. But customs duties are needed to pay the soldiers, who look so nice in their full-dress uniforms, and without soldiers we'd all be eating each other like wolves!"

"Idlers who are paid to carry around a rifle, that's all they are!" sneered the pharmacist. "Just like the priests, who take three tarì for a Mass. Tell the truth, Don Giammaria, what sort of capital do you invest in the Mass, that they should pay you three tarì?"

"And what sort of capital do you put in that dirty water which a man has to pay for with his blood?" the priest came back at him, furious.

Don Franco had learned to laugh like Don Silvestro, just to drive Don Giammaria into a frenzy; and he went right on, not even answering him, because he had discovered the perfect way to make the priest lose his head completely: "In a half hour they earn their day's pay, and then they spend the rest of the day strolling around; just like Don Michele, who looks like a lazy crow and is always underfoot since he's stopped warming Santuzza's benches."

"That's why he's got it in for me!" 'Ntoni said. "He's as mad as a dog, and he thinks he can tell everybody what to do, just because he's got a saber. But some day, by the blood of the Madonna, I'll break that saber over his snout, to show him that I don't give a damn!"

"Good!" cried the pharmacist. "That's what you should do! The people must show its teeth. But not in here, because I don't want any trouble in the pharmacy. The government would like nothing better than to drag me by the hair into some sort of imbroglio, but I don't intend to have anything to do with judges and all that government scum."

'Ntoni Malavoglia raised his fists to heaven and cursed and swore by Christ and the Madonna that he really meant to put an end to it, even if he had to go to jail. He had nothing to lose anyway. Santuzza was no longer so fond of him, after all the things her father, that leech, had said to her, whining it out between one Hail Mary and the next, when Massaro Filippo had stopped sending his wine to the tavern! He had told her that the customers were beginning to thin out like flies after Saint Andrew's Day, since they could no longer get Massaro Filippo's wine, to which they were as accustomed as a baby to the breast. And each time Uncle Santoro said to his daughter: "What do you expect to do with that beggar 'Ntoni Malavoglia? Can't you see that he's eating up everything you've got, and all for nothing? You fatten him up better than a pig, and then he runs after La Vespa or the Mangiacarrube girl, now that they're rich. The customers are leaving us, because he's always tied to your skirt and doesn't even leave you for a minute so they can tell you a joke." Or he would say to her: "It's a dirty shame to have such a ragged, filthy fellow hanging around the tavern. Why it looks like a stable, and the people are sick to the stomach, and they won't even drink from these glasses. Don Michele, though, looked fine in his gold-braided cap. People who pay for their wine want to drink it in peace and quiet, and they're happy when they see a man with a saber posted outside. Besides, everyone tipped his hat to Don Michele, and no-body would have dared refuse to pay you a penny he owed you, after it was written on the wall with the charcoal. Now that Don Michele's no longer here, Massaro Filippo doesn't come either. The last time he came by I tried to get him to come in. But he said that there's no point in coming here, because, now that you're angry with Don Michele, he can't smuggle in his new wine anymore! This is good neither for soul or body. And because Massaro Filippo doesn't come here anymore, people are even starting to whisper that you're being so nice to 'Ntoni for your own reasons, and you'll see how it'll all end! You'll see—it'll come to the ears of Don Giammaria and they'll take away your Daughter of Mary medal."

Santuzza didn't give in for a while, because she wanted to be the mistress in her own house; but her eyes began to be opened, for she took everything her father said as Gospel truth, and she no longer coddled 'Ntoni as she'd done in the past. If there were some leftovers to put aside, she no longer gave them to him, and she filled the bottom of his glass with dirty water. So in the end 'Ntoni began to look sour, and then Santuzza told him that she had no use for idlers, that she and her father earned the bread they ate and that's what he should do, helping a little in the house, splitting wood and keeping the fire ablaze, instead of hanging around like a big lout, shouting and sleeping with his head on his arms, or spitting on the floor, all over it, like a sea, so you couldn't walk without stepping in it.

'Ntoni chopped wood for a while, grumbling, or kept the fire ablaze because that was easier. But it was hard on him, working all day long like a dog, even harder than he worked at home, and then to be treated worse than a cur, with rudeness and insults, for the sake of those dirty dishes they gave him to lick. At last one day, when Santuzza was coming back from confession, rosary in hand, he made a scene for her, complaining that all this was happening because Don Michele was prowling around the tavern again, and even waited for her on the piazza when she went to confession; and Uncle Santoro shouted greetings after Don Michele when he heard his voice, and went to look for him even all the way to Pizzuto's shop, tapping his cane against the wall to find his way. At that La Santuzza began to raise the devil and replied that he had come on purpose to make her sin, while she still had the Host in her mouth, and to ruin her communion. "If you don't like it, leave!" she said. "I don't want to damn my soul on account of you; and I didn't say anything when I found out that you were running after sluts like La Vespa and the Mangiacarrube girl, now that they're married and regret it. Go to them, because now they have a full trough in the house and they're looking for a pig." But 'Ntoni swore that it was all a lie and that he had no interest in such things; he no longer thought about women, and she could spit in his face if she ever saw him talking to another woman.

"No, that's not the way to get rid of him," Uncle Santoro kept saying. "Can't you see how he's holding on to the bread he takes from you? To fix the pot you've got to break it. He's got to be kicked out. Massaro Filippo has told me that he can't keep the new wine in the casks anymore, and he'll sell it to somebody else if you don't make peace with Don Michele and can't smuggle it in as before!" And he went looking again for Massaro Filippo at Pizzuto's shop, tapping the walls with his cane. His daughter played the high and mighty, declaring that she would never bow her head to Don Michele, after the way he had behaved to her. "Leave it to me. I'll fix it up!" Uncle Santoro assured her. "I'll do it the right way. I won't let you look as though you were running after Don Michele to lick his boots. Am I or am I not your father, God in heaven?"

Since Santuzza was mistreating him, 'Ntoni had to find some way to pay for the food they gave him at the tavern, particularly since he didn't dare to show his face at home. And all along his poor family thought of him every time they ate their soup listlessly, as though he were dead too, and didn't even set the table but ate scattered through the house, holding their bowls on their knees. "This is the last blow, for an old man like me," his grandfather repeated; and those who saw him walk past with his nets on his back on his way to work, said: "This is the last winter for Master 'Ntoni. It won't be long, and then all those orphans will be out in the middle of the street." And if Mena told Lia to come inside when Don Michele sauntered by, she opened a big mouth and said: "Sure! I've got to get inside, like some treasure! Don't worry your head, not even the dogs want treasures like us!"

"Oh, if your mother were here, you wouldn't talk like that!" Mena murmured.

"If my mother were here, I wouldn't be an orphan and I wouldn't have to think about helping myself. And 'Ntoni wouldn't be roaming the streets, so that it's a disgrace to be his sisters, and nobody is going to take the sister of 'Ntoni Malavoglia for a wife."

Now that he was down and out, 'Ntoni had no scruples about being seen together with Rocco Spatu and Cinghialenta, on the lava field and out towards the Rotolo, or whispering with them, dark looks on their faces, like famished wolves. Don Michele said to Mena again: "Your brother is going to bring you grief, Comare Mena!"

And Mena had to go looking for her brother on the lava field and out towards the Rotolo, or at the door of the tavern. And then sobbing and crying she pulled at his shirt sleeve. But he replied: "No! Don Michele has it in for me, I told you. He's always plotting against me, together with Uncle Santoro. I heard them in Pizzuto's shop, when that spy said to him: 'And how would I look if I went back to your daughter?' And Uncle Santoro answered: 'That again! I'm telling you, the whole village would die of envy!'"

"But what are you trying to do?" repeated Mena, with a pale face. "Think of Mama, 'Ntoni, and think of us who no longer have anyone!"

"Forget it! I want to shame Don Michele and Santuzza before the whole village, when they go to Mass! I want to tell them off and make everybody laugh at them. There's nobody in the world who scares me. And then even that pharmacist over there will hear me."

Mena was wasting her breath begging and pleading, because he went right on saying that he had nothing to lose and that other people had more to worry about than he, for he was fed up with the life he led and wanted to put an end to it, just as Don Franco said. And since he wasn't welcome at the tavern, he hung around the piazza, especially on Sundays, and sat down on the church steps to watch the faces of all those shameless swindlers coming to fool the world and to cheat Our Lord and the Holy Virgin under Their very eyes.

Since she began meeting 'Ntoni on guard at the church door, Santuzza went to Aci Castello for Sunday Mass, very early in the morning, so as to stay out of temptation's way. 'Ntoni saw the Mangiacarrube girl walk past, her nose hidden in her shawl, and not looking at a soul now that she had hooked herself a husband. And La Vespa, all decked out and holding a big rosary, went to pray to the Lord to deliver her from her husband, that wrath of God. And 'Ntoni sneered: "Now that they've caught a husband they don't need anything else. They've got someone who worries about feeding them!"

Ever since he had saddled himself with La Vespa, Uncle

Crocifisso had lost his piety too and didn't even go to church, so at least for the time it took to say Mass he wouldn't see his wife. And that way, he damned his immortal soul.

"This is my last year!" he whimpered; and now he ran to see Master 'Ntoni and other wretches like himself. "It hailed on my vineyard, and I myself won't live to see the grape harvest."

"You know, Uncle Crocifisso," Master 'Ntoni said, "whenever you want to go to the notary for that business of the house, I'm ready and I have the money here." That's all *he* thought ever about, and he didn't give a rap about other people's troubles.

"Don't talk to me about the notary, Master 'Ntoni! When I hear talk of the notary, I remember the time I let La Vespa drag me there; cursed be the day I set foot in that place!"

But Compare Piedipapera, scenting a deal, said to him: "If you die, that witch La Vespa is quite capable of giving him the house by the medlar tree for a pittance; and I'd advise you to take care of the business yourself, so long as you're still here and alive and kicking."

At that Uncle Crocifisso said: "Yes, yes, let's go to the notary; but you've got to let me make something from this deal. You know yourself how many losses I've had!" And, pretending to go along with him, Piedipapera added: "If your wife, that witch, finds out that you're getting back the money for the house, she's quite capable of strangling you to spend it on necklaces and silk kerchiefs." And he also said: "At least the Mangiacarrube girl doesn't buy necklaces and silk kerchiefs anymore, now that she's landed a husband. You see how she comes to Mass, wearing just a cotton dress!"

"I don't give a rap for the Mangiacarrube girl, but they should have burned her alive too, with all the other women who are in this world just to make us damn our immortal souls. Do you believe she doesn't buy things anymore? It's all a fraud to make a fool of Master Fortunato, who goes around yelling that he'd rather take a woman off the streets than let that beggar, who's robbed his son, enjoy his property. For my part, I'd willingly give him La Vespa, if he wanted her. They're all the same! And woe to him who falls into their clutches, because then Our Lord takes his wits from him. Look at Don Michele, who walks down Black Lane to make eyes at Donna Rosolina—what does the man lack? Respected, well paid, with a big belly! . . . Well, he chases after the women too, looking for trouble with a lantern. Hoping to get his hands on the priest's few pennies."

"Oh no, he doesn't come for Donna Rosolina!" Piedipapera said, winking at him on the sly. "Donna Rosolina can strike root on her terrace among her tomatoes, and gaze at him like a dead fish, but Don Michele doesn't care about Don Giammaria's money! I know what he's walking down Black Lane for!"

"So, how much do you want for the house?" Master 'Ntoni asked again.

"We'll talk about it, we'll talk about it when we go to the notary," Uncle Crocifisso replied. "Now let me listen to the Holy Mass." And that's how he sent Master 'Ntoni away, crestfallen.

"Don Michele has other things on his mind," Piedipapera repeated behind Master 'Ntoni's back, glancing significantly at his grandson 'Ntoni, who was going over to lie on the wall with a rag of a jacket over his shoulders, and flashing nasty looks at Uncle Santoro, who had started coming to Mass to hold out his hand to the faithful, mumbling Hail Marys and Glorias. As the crowd filed out of church he recognized them one by one, and to this person he said: "May the Lord bless you with wealth!" and to another: "May the Lord keep you in good health!" and as Don Michele passed by he added: "Go, she's waiting for you in the garden, behind the shed! *Santa Maria, ora pro nobis!* Oh Lord God, forgive me! . . ."

As soon as Don Michele began showing up at Santuzza's, the people said: "The cats and dogs have made peace! Which means they had a good reason for falling out."

And since Massaro Filippo had also returned to the tavern, they all said: "The other one, too! Can't he get along without Don Michele? It proves he's in love with Don Michele, not with Santuzza. Some people can't live alone even in Paradise!"

Then 'Ntoni Malavoglia's mouth filled with bile, seeing

himself kicked out of that filthy tavern like a mangy dog, without even a penny in his pocket so he could go and drink right under Don Michele's nose and stay there all day long with his elbows planted on the table so both of them would eat their hearts out. Instead, he had to stay out on the street like a mongrel, his tail between his legs and his muzzle to the ground, grumbling: "Blood of Judas! Some day soon I'll put on a real tragedy here, don't you worry!"

Rocco Spatu and Cinghialenta, who always had a few cents, laughed at him from the tavern door and gave him the sign of the cuckold; and then they came out and whispered to him, pulling him by the arm towards the lava field, talking into his ear. But he couldn't decide to say yes, like the boob he was. Then they taunted him: "You deserve to die of hunger, out there in front of the tavern, and watch Don Michele as he cuckolds you right under your eyes."

"By the blood of Judas, don't talk like that!" 'Ntoni shouted, lifting his fist in the air. "Because one of these days I'll put on a real tragedy, don't you worry!"

But they sneered and left him standing there. So, in the end, they really got his blood up. He went straight to the tavern and stood right in the middle of the floor, yellow as a corpse, his fist on his hip and his old jacket hanging from his shoulders, posing as though he were dressed in velvet, and throwing fierce glances in all directions to provoke his enemy. Don Michele, for the sake of his gold braid, pretended he didn't see him and tried to leave; but now that Don Michele was acting the coward, 'Ntoni felt his rage boil up in him, and started laughing and sneering in his and Santuzza's faces, and he spat in the wine he was drinking, saying that it was poison, the poison they'd given to the blessed Jesus on the cross! And on top of that it was baptized, because Santuzza had watered it, and it was real idiocy to come and let yourself be robbed of money in that filthy tavern; and that's why he didn't come there anymore! Touched on the raw, Santuzza couldn't contain herself any longer, and she told him that he no longer came there because they were tired of keeping him out of charity, and that they'd been forced to chase him out the door with a broom, that's how hungry he'd been. . . . At this 'Ntoni began to brawl, breaking glasses and yelling that they'd thrown him out to drag in that other sheepshead with the gold braid on his cap. But if he felt like it, he could make the wine Don Michele was drinking spurt through his nose, because he wasn't afraid of anybody. Don Michele, yellow too, and with his cap askew, stammered: "By my holy word of honor, there'll be hell to pay!"—while Santuzza threw glasses and bottles at both of them. So, at last, they jumped at each other and began fighting, rolling under the benches, ready to fight to the finish, while the customers kicked and punched them to pull them apart. Peppi Naso finally managed to do it—with his leather belt, which he'd taken off his pants, and wherever it landed it took off a piece of hide.

Don Michele brushed the dust off his uniform, picked up his saber, which he'd lost in the scuffle, and walked out muttering to himself. Just for the sake of his gold braid, they all said. But when 'Ntoni Malavoglia, whose nose was streaming blood, saw him slip away, they couldn't stop him from pouring a flood of insults after him from the tavern door, showing him his clenched fist and using his sleeve to dry the blood that dripped from his nose. He promised that he would give him the rest the next time they met.

CHAPTER FOURTEEN

There was hell to pay when 'Ntoni Malavoglia met Don Michele to give him the rest—it was at night, the rain came down in torrents and it was so dark that even a cat couldn't find its way—at the corner of the lava field towards the Rotolo, where the boats coasted along on the sly, pretending to be fishing for mullet at midnight, and where 'Ntoni, Rocco Spatu, Cinghialenta, and other rascals went to prowl, with their pipes in their mouths; and the customs guards, flattened on their bellies among the rocks and holding their carbines, knew each of those dots of fire by heart.

"Comare Mena," Don Michele had said once again, passing through Black Lane, "tell your brother not to go to the Rotolo at night with Rocco Spatu and Cinghialenta."

But 'Ntoni had turned a deaf ear because a "hungry belly won't listen to reason"; and anyway, he was no longer afraid of Don Michele, after they had rolled under the tavern benches, mauling and punching. Besides, he had promised to give him the rest when he met him, and he didn't want to look like a coward and braggart in the eyes of Santuzza and of all the others who'd been there when he'd made his threat. "I told him I'd give him the rest wherever I meet him; and if I meet him at the Rotolo, I'll give it to him at the Rotolo!" he kept saying to his friends. And now they'd dragged La Locca's son into it too. They had spent the evening at the tavern, drinking and brawling, because a tavern is like a seaport, and Santuzza couldn't send 'Ntoni packing now that he had money in his pocket and bounced the coins on his hand. Don Michele had passed on his rounds, but Rocco Spatu, who knew the law, spat and said: "So long as there's a lamp at the door, we have the right to stay here!" and he leaned against the wall to make himself more at home. 'Ntoni Malavoglia enjoyed keeping Santuzza up, seeing her half asleep behind her row of glasses, lolling her head on those pillows on which the Daughter of Mary's medal rested. "That medal is more comfortable there than on a sheaf of .fresh grass!" cried 'Ntoni, whose tongue had been loosened by the wine; while Rocco, as full as a barrel, his shoulders against the wall, couldn't get a word out.

Meanwhile Uncle Santoro, groping his way, had taken in the lamp and was shutting the door. "Now get out of here, because I'm tired," Santuzza said.

"I'm not tired!" 'Ntoni answered. "Massaro Filippo doesn't keep me up all night."

"I don't care whether he keeps you up or not; but I don't want to get fined because of you, if they find the door still open at this hour!"

"Who'll fine you? That spy, Don Michele? Tell him to come here and I'll give him a fine! Go and tell him that 'Ntoni Malavoglia's here, by the blood of the Madonna!"

Santuzza had seized him by the shoulders and was pushing him out through the door. "Go and tell him yourself; and go and look for trouble somewhere else. I don't want to have the police on my neck because of your lovely eyes."

'Ntoni, seeing himself thrown out like that into the street, in the mud and the pouring rain, pulled a knife and started to curse and swear, saying that he wanted to prick both of them, her and Don Michele! Cinghialenta was the only one there who still had his senses about him, and he pulled 'Ntoni by his jacket and said: "Let it go for tonight! Don't you know what we have to do?"

And suddenly, in the dark, La Locca's son began bawling.

"He's drunk!" cried Rocco Spatu, who was standing under the rainspout. "Bring him over here. It'll do him good."

'Ntoni, a bit calmed by the water showering on him from the spout, let himself be led away by Cinghialenta; he was still blustering as he slogged through the puddles, swearing that if he met Don Michele he'd give him what he'd promised him. All of a sudden he actually found himself face to face with Don Michele, who was prowling around there too, his pistol on his belly and his pants stuffed into his boots. That took the wind out of 'Ntoni's sails there and then, and all three of them slunk away very quietly, towards Pizzuto's shop. When they got to the door, now that Don Michele was far away, 'Ntoni wouldn't move a step until they listened to what he had to say.

"Didn't you see where Don Michele was going? And Santuzza said that she was tired! What will they do if Massaro Filippo is still in the stable?"

"Let Don Michele alone," Cinghialenta said, "and he'll let us alone to go about our business."

"You're just a pack of cowards!" cried 'Ntoni. "You're afraid of Don Michele."

"You're drunk tonight! But I'll show you if I'm afraid of Don Michele! Now that they made me sell my mule, I don't want anyone to come asking how I earn my bread, blood of a dog!"

Then they huddled against the wall and began whispering to each other, and the splashing of the rain covered their words. Suddenly the clock struck the hour and all four fell silent and listened.

"Let's go into Compare Pizzuto's," said Cinghialenta. "He can keep his door open as long as he wants to, and without a lamp lit outside."

"It's so dark you can't see a thing!" La Locca's son said.

"With this kind of weather we've got to have a drink," replied Rocco Spatu. "If we don't we'll break our necks on the lava field."

Cinghialenta began grumbling: "We're not going out there to play! Now I'll get Mastro Vanni to give you some lemon water."

"I don't need any lemon water!" 'Ntoni snapped, "and you'll see that I can handle myself better than all of you!"

Compare Pizzuto didn't want to open the door at that

late hour and he answered that he was in bed; but since they went on banging and threatened to rouse the whole village and bring the guards running to see what they were up to, he changed his mind and came down in his underwear to open the door.

"Are you crazy, banging on the door like that?" he exclaimed. "I just saw Don Michele go by."

"Yes, we saw him too. Right now he's saying the rosary with Santuzza."

"Do you know where Don Michele's coming from?" asked Pizzuto, staring into his eyes. 'Ntoni shrugged and Vanni, as he stepped aside to let them come in, winked at Rocco and Cinghialenta.

"He's been at the Malavoglia's," he whispered in their ears. "I saw him come out myself!"

"Good for him," Cinghialenta said, "but we ought to tell 'Ntoni to make sure his sister keeps Don Michele there all night, when we're busy . . ."

"What's that? What do you want me to do?" 'Ntoni asked with a thick tongue.

"Nothing. It's not for tonight."

"If it's not for tonight, why did you make me leave the tavern and get all soaked in the rain?" Rocco Spatu asked.

"Cinghialenta and I are talking about something else," Pizzuto said. Then he added: "Yes, the man from Catania came and said that the goods will be there tonight, but it won't be a joke unloading them in this weather."

"All the better. This way, nobody will see us unload them."

"Yes, but the customs guards have sharp ears. And watch out, because I've seen them snooping around here and looking inside too!"

Then there was a moment of silence and Compare Vanni, to put an end to it, went to fill three glasses with anise.

"I don't give a damn for the customs guards!" said Rocco Spatu, after he'd knocked off his drink. "All the worse for them if they come and stick their noses into my business. I have my knife right here and it doesn't make as much noise as their pistols."

"We earn our bread as we can, and we don't want to

hurt anyone!" Cinghialenta added. "Can't a person unload his goods where he wishes any longer?"

"They stroll around like thieves, making you pay duty on every handkerchief you want to bring ashore, and nobody shoots at them," said 'Ntoni Malavoglia. "Do you know what Don Giammaria said? He said that it's not a sin to steal from thieves. And the biggest thieves of all are those fellows with the gold braid, who eat us alive!"

"We'll make tuna hash of them," concluded Rocco Spatu, his eyes glittering like a cat's.

But when he heard that, La Locca's son set down his glass without even bringing it to his lips, yellow as a corpse.

"What, are you drunk already?" Cinghialenta asked him.

"No," he answered. "I didn't drink anything."

"Let's get out. The fresh air will make us all feel better. Good night to all who stay!"

"Wait a minute," said Pizzuto, his hand against the door. "I'm not talking about the money for the anise. That I gave you for nothing, because you're my friends. But just remember, eh! If the deal comes off, my house is here waiting for you. You know that I've got a room in the back where you could store a shipful of stuff, and nobody ever puts his nose in there, because I and Don Michele, together with all his guards, get along like bread and cheese. But I don't trust Piedipapera, because last time he did me dirty and took the stuff to Don Silvestro's house. Don Silvestro would never be satisfied with the share you'd give him, because he says he's risking his post; but with me you don't have such fears, and you can give me what's coming to me. And yet I've never denied Piedipapera his percentage and I give him a glass every time he drops in here, and I shave him for nothing. But, by the holy devil! if he does me dirty again, I'm not going to be the fool and I'll tell Don Michele all about this smuggling!"

"No, no, Compare Vanni. There's no need to tell Don Michele! Did you see Piedipapera around this evening?"

"Not even on the piazza! He was over there in the pharmacy, building the republic together with Don Franco. Every time they bring in some goods, he steers clear, just to prove that no matter what happens, he's got nothing to do with it. He's an old fox and the guards' bullets will never hit him, even though he's as lame as the devil himself. Then tomorrow morning, when everything's over, he'll come to collect his percentage, brazen as can be. But he leaves the lead for the others."

"It's still raining," said Rocco Spatu. "Is it going to go on all night?"

"There won't be anybody at the Rotolo in this rotten weather," La Locca's son said. "So we'd better go home."

'Ntoni, Cinghialenta, and Rocco Spatu stood in the doorway watching the rain that spluttered and hissed like a fish in a frying pan. They kept quiet for a moment, staring into the dark.

"You're a fool!" cried Cinghialenta, to give him courage; and Vanni Pizzuto closed the door very quietly, after having whispered:

"Now listen, if anything goes wrong, you didn't see me tonight, remember! I gave you a glass of anise just because I'm a friend, but you were never in my house! Don't betray me, because I'm all alone in this world!"

They walked away dispiritedly, under the rain, hugging the walls. "There's another one," grunted Cinghialenta. "He says he's all alone in this world, and then he throws dirt at Piedipapera for playing it safe. At least Piedipapera has a wife to take care of. And I've got a wife, too. But I'm one of the fellows who get shot at!"

Just then they were slinking past Cousin Anna's door, and Rocco Spatu said that he had his mother who, the lucky woman, was sleeping at that time of night.

"Who'd want to go out in this rotten weather if he could stay in bed?" said Compare Cinghialenta.

'Ntoni made a sign to keep quiet and turn down the path to avoid passing in front of his house, because Mena or his grandfather might be waiting for him and would hear them.

"Don't you worry, your sister isn't waiting for you," said Rocco Spatu, that drunkard. "But maybe she's waiting for Don Michele!"

At that 'Ntoni threatened to tear his heart out, because he had his knife right there in his pocket. And Cinghia-

lenta asked: "Are you drunk? Fighting over such foolishness, when we're on our way to do this together?"

In fact Mena was waiting for her brother behind the
door, her rosary beads in her hand, and Lia too, not saying a word about what she knew, though she looked as
pale as death. And it would have been better for all of
them if 'Ntoni had gone up Black Lane instead of turning
into the path. Don Michele had actually been there an
hour after sunset and had knocked at the door.

"Who is it at this time of night?" asked Lia, who was
secretly edging a silk kerchief Don Michele had finally
convinced her to accept.

"It's me, Don Michele! Open the door because I've got
to talk to you right away!"

"I can't open it because everyone is in bed and my sister
is in the other room, waiting for 'Ntoni behind the door."

"It doesn't matter if your sister hears you open it. The
fact is, it's about 'Ntoni, and it can't wait. I don't want
your brother to go to jail. So open the door quick, because
if they see me here I'll lose my daily bread."

"Oh, Holy Virgin!" the girl began to whimper. "Oh,
Holy Virgin!"

"Lock your brother in tonight, when he comes home!
But don't tell him I've been here. Tell him that he'd better
stay at home. Don't forget!"

"Oh, Holy Virgin! Holy Virgin!" Lia repeated, her
hands clasped together.

"He's at the tavern now, but he has to go by here. Wait
for him at the door; it'll be better for him."

Lia was crying softly, her face covered by her hands so
that her sister wouldn't hear, and Don Michele, his pistol
on his belly and his pants stuffed into his boots, watched
her cry.

"There's nobody who's anxious about me, or cries over
me tonight, Comare Lia, but I'm in danger too. So, if
something happens to me, remember that I came to warn
you and risked losing my daily bread for your sake."

Lia lifted her face from her hands and gazed at him
with eyes full of tears. "God will reward you, Don Michele, for your kindness!"

"I don't want to be rewarded, Comare Lia; I did it for you, because I like you so much."

"Go now, because they're all asleep! Go away, Don Michele, for the love of God."

Don Michele left and she stayed behind the door, telling her rosary beads for her brother, and begging the Lord to send him that way.

But the Lord did not send him. All four of them, 'Ntoni, Cinghialenta, Rocco Spatu, and La Locca's son, crept quietly along the walls down the paths, and when they reached the lava field they took off their shoes and stopped to listen for a moment, anxiously, their shoes in their hands.

"Can't hear a thing," said Cinghialenta.

The rain continued to come down, and there on the lava ledge all you could hear was the sea grumbling below.

"You can't even see enough to curse!" said Rocco Spatu. "How will they be able to find the Doves' Rock in this darkness?"

"They know the place," Cinghialenta replied. "They know the whole coastline, inch by inch, with their eyes shut."

"But I can't hear anything!" 'Ntoni said.

"It's true, you can't hear anything!" said Cinghialenta. "But they must have gotten here some time ago."

"So let's all go home," La Locca's son said.

"Now that you've had enough to eat and drink, all you can think about is going home," said Cinghialenta. "But if you don't stop whining, I'll kick you into the sea!"

"Well, anyway, I hate spending the night here for nothing," Rocco Spatu muttered.

"Now we'll see whether they're here or not," said Cinghialenta. And he began to screech like an owl.

"If Don Michele's guards hear that," 'Ntoni said, "they'll come running, because on a night like this the owls stay home."

"So let's go home," whined La Loeca's son, "since nobody answers."

All four of them looked at each other, although they couldn't see in the dark, and they were thinking of what Master 'Ntoni's 'Ntoni had said.

"What are we going to do?" La Locca's son kept on.

"Let's go down to the road," Cinghialenta proposed. "If nobody's there, it means they didn't come."

While they walked down to the road, 'Ntoni said: "Piedipapera wouldn't think twice about selling us all for a glass of wine."

"Now that you don't have a glass in front of you," Cinghialenta said, "you're afraid too."

"Come on, by the blood of the devil! I'll show you whether I'm afraid."

As they carefully climbed down the rocks, holding on tightly so as not to break their necks, Spatu whispered: "Right now Vanni Pizzuto is in his bed, the same fellow who threw dirt at Piedipapera because he grabs his percentage without lifting a finger."

"All right! If you don't want to risk your skin, you should have stayed in bed," Cinghialenta said curtly.

They all fell silent, and as he groped about to see where to put his feet, 'Ntoni thought that Compare Cinghialenta shouldn't have talked like that, because at such moments everybody has his home before his eyes, and his bed, and Mena dozing behind the door.

Rocco Spatu, that drunkard, finally said: "Our skins aren't worth a penny!"

Suddenly they heard somebody shout from behind the wall on the road: "Who goes there! Halt! All of you! Halt!"

"We've been betrayed, betrayed!" they began to yell, running off across the lava field, no longer caring where they put their feet.

But 'Ntoni had already clambered over the wall and found himself face to face with Don Michele, who was pointing his pistol at him.

"By the blood of the Madonna!" shouted Malavoglia, pulling out his knife. "I'll show you what I think of that pistol!"

Don Michele's pistol shot into the air, but he crashed down like an ox, stabbed in the chest. 'Ntoni tried to run away, leaping like a goat, but the guards jumped on him and threw him to the ground, while all around the bullets were rattling like hailstones.

"Now what will my Mama do!" whimpered La Locca's son, as they tied him up worse than Christ.

"Don't pull so tight, by the blood of the Madonna!" 'Ntoni cried. "Can't you see that I can't even move?"

"Quiet down, Malavoglia!" they answered. "You're fixed for good now!" And they prodded him forward with the barrels of their carbines.

As they were taking him to the barracks, bound and tied like Jesus too, and were carrying Don Michele behind him on the guards' shoulders, 'Ntoni kept looking around to see if he could find Cinghialenta and Rocco Spatu. "So they got away with it!" he said to himself. "And they've nothing to be afraid of now, just like Vanni Pizzuto and Piedipapera, who are sleeping safely in their beds. But they aren't sleeping in my house, since they heard the shots."

True enough, the poor people weren't sleeping, and stood in front of the door under the driving rain, as though their hearts had warned them; while their neighbors turned over on their sides and went back to sleep, yawning: "Tomorrow we'll find out what's happened."

Later on, when dawn was beginning to break, a crowd gathered in front of Pizzuto's shop, where the lamp was still lit, and they all talked excitedly about what had happened during that uproar last night.

"They caught both the contraband and the smugglers," Pizzuto was saying. "And Don Michele got himself stabbed." Then people looked towards the Malavoglia's door, pointing their fingers. At last Cousin Anna arrived at the Malavoglia's all disheveled and white as a rag and she didn't know what to say to them.

"What about 'Ntoni? Do you know where he is?" Master 'Ntoni asked her, as if his heart had warned him.

"They arrested him last night for smuggling, together with La Locca's son," replied Cousin Anna, who'd lost her head. "They've killed Don Michele!"

"Ah, my God, my God!" the old man cried, tearing at his hair; and Lia begain tearing at her hair too. Master 'Ntoni, still clutching his head, just said over and over: "My God, my God!"

Later that morning Piedipapera came to see them, clapping his forehead with his hand, his face anguished. "Did you hear about it, Master 'Ntoni, what a terrible misfortune! I was struck dumb when I heard about it." His wife, Comare Grazia, was crying real tears, poor woman, at seeing how one disaster after another crashed down on the Malavoglia household. "What did you come here for?" her husband whispered, pulling her aside. "You have no business here. Hanging around this house now will bring us to the attention of the police!"

That's why the people didn't even stop and look into the Malavoglia doorway. Only Nunziata, as soon as she'd heard the news, had entrusted her children to the eldest and asked a neighbor to keep an eye on her house, and had rushed over to Comare Mena, to weep with her, like someone who doesn't yet know what life is like. The other people stayed on the street to watch the spectacle from a distance, or massed like flies in front of the barracks to see what Master 'Ntoni's 'Ntoni looked like behind bars, after he'd stabbed Don Michele. Or they rushed to Pizzuto who was selling anise and shaving people, and was telling the story of what had happened, word for word.

"You want to know who gets caught?" the pharmacist proclaimed. "The fools get caught!"

"There'll be hell to pay!" Don Silvestro added. "They won't cut away that jail sentence, even with a razor!"

And then Don Giammaria gave it to him, smack in the face: "The people who ought to go to jail never get there!"

"You're right! They don't!" replied Don Silvestro, unruffled, coming right back at him.

"Nowadays," Master Cipolla said, as yellow as bile, "the real thieves rob you blind in broad daylight and right in the middle of the piazza. They worm their way into your house, without breaking down either the windows or the doors."

"Which is just what 'Ntoni Malavoglia wanted to do in my house," said La Zuppidda, who had joined the group to spin her hemp.

"Didn't I always say that, by God!" her husband began.

"You keep quiet, because you don't know what you're talking about! Just look at the sort of day that was in store for my daughter Barbara if I hadn't kept my eyes open!"

Her daughter Barbara was at the window, waiting to see 'Ntoni pass by, surrounded by the police taking him to Catania.

"He'll never get out of there," they were all saying. "You know what's written over the Vicaria jail in Palermo? 'Just go on running, I'm here waiting for you!' and 'Bad metal wears out on the grindstone.' The poor devils!"

"Decent folk don't work at such trades!" La Vespa ranted. "Trouble comes to those who look for it! You see who goes in for such things? Fellows without a trade, scoundrels, like that 'Ntoni Malavoglia and La Locca's son!" Everyone agreed with her and said that if you get a son like that, the best thing is for the house to fall on his head. But La Locca went looking for her son and posted herself in front of the customs guards' barracks, screaming that they should give him back to her, and refused to listen to reason. And when she went to pester her brother Dumbbell, standing on the steps of his landing for hours on end, her white hair flying wildly, Uncle Crocifisso told her: "I've got a jail right in my own house. I wish I were in your son's place! What do you want from me? He wasn't giving you any bread anyway!"

"La Locca will gain from it," Don Silvestro remarked. "Now that she no longer has somebody to support her, they'll send her to the poorhouse and she'll eat meat and pasta every day. If they don't, the Commune will have to take care of her."

And each time that they wound up by saying that "bad metal wears out on the grindstone," Master Fortunato would add:

"It's a good deal for Master 'Ntoni, too. Do you think that good-for-nothing grandson of his didn't eat up plenty of money? I know what it means to have a son who turns out like that! Now the King will support 'Ntoni for him."

But instead of saving that money, now that his grandson was no longer eating it up, Master 'Ntoni went on throwing it away on him, on lawyers and ink-slingers; all that money which had cost him so much sweat and which was meant for the house by the medlar tree. "Now we no

longer need the house or anything else!" the old man said,
his face as pale as 'Ntoni's when they had led him off to
Catania between the police guards and the whole village
had gone to see him with his hands bound, and clutched
under his arm the bundle of shirts which Mena, weeping
bitterly, had brought him in the evening when nobody
could see her. His grandfather had gone to the lawyer,
the one who talked so well, because now that he'd seen
Don Michele leave too, taken to the hospital in a carriage, his face yellow and his uniform jacket unbuttoned,
the poor old man had become frightened and didn't
look too closely at the lawyer's fine talk. All he wanted
was that they free his grandson's hands and let him come
back home; because he felt that after that catastrophe
'Ntoni would come home and live with them for the rest
of his life, just as he did when he was a boy.

Don Silvestro did him the kindness of going with him
to the lawyer, saying that when a man is struck by the
misfortune that had struck the Malavoglia, you must help
him with your hands and feet even if he is a criminal, and
do everything in your power to get him out of the hands
of the law, because that's why we're Christians and must
help our brothers. And after he had listened to the whole
story and had understood what it was all about, thanks to
Don Silvestro, the lawyer said that it was a fine case, good
for a life sentence if it weren't for him, and he rubbed his
hands. Hearing this talk about life sentences, Master
'Ntoni went as limp as a rag; but Dr. Scipioni patted him
on the back and said that he hadn't earned his diploma if
he couldn't get 'Ntoni off with no more than four or five
years of prison.

"What did the lawyer say?" Mena asked, as soon as she
saw her grandfather coming in with that look on his face;
and she began to cry even before she heard his reply. The
old man tore out the few white hairs he had left, wandering frantically through the house, repeating over and over:
"Oh, why didn't we all die!" And Lia, white as a sheet,
stared with great round eyes at anyone who talked to her,
unable to say a word. Soon after that, summonses arrived
for Barbara Zuppidda, Grazia Piedipapera, and Don
Franco, the pharmacist, to appear as witnesses, and for

all those who gossiped in the piazza and at Pizzuto's barber shop. So the whole village was in a commotion, and the people gathered, summonses in hand, swearing that they didn't know a thing, as true as there's a God! because they didn't want to have anything to do with the law. Damn that 'Ntoni and all the Malavoglia who were dragging them into their mess. La Zuppidda shrieked like a soul possessed: "I don't know anything. After the Ave Maria, I shut myself in my house, and I'm not like those people who slink about to do what they do, or who stand at their doorways and chat with police spies."

"Stay away from the government!" Don Franco cried. "They know that I'm a Republican, and they'd be only too glad to get a pretext to make me vanish from the face of this earth."

People wore out their brains trying to figure out what La Zuppidda and Comare Grazia and the others could say as witnesses, since they had seen nothing and had heard the rifle shots from their beds while they were fast asleep. But Don Silvestro rubbed his hands like the lawyer and declared that he knew why they'd been summoned, and that it would help the lawyer. Every time that the lawyer went to talk with 'Ntoni Malavoglia, Don Silvestro, if he had nothing to do, accompanied him to the prison; nobody came to the Town Council these days, and the olives had already been harvested. Also Master 'Ntoni had tried to go two or three times; but faced by those barred windows and the soldiers with rifles who guarded them, and inspected all who came in, he felt sick, and so he'd waited outside, sitting on the sidewalk, surrounded by the chestnut and prickly pear venders, and he couldn't believe that his 'Ntoni was in there, behind those bars and with those soldiers guarding him. Then the lawyer would come back from his talk with 'Ntoni, as fresh as a rose, rubbing his hands; and he told him that his grandson was well, in fact had put on weight, and then the poor man felt as though his grandson were one of those soldiers.

"Why don't they let him go?" he asked each time, like a parrot, or a child that won't listen to reason, and he also wanted to know if they kept his hands tied. "Let him stay where he is," Dr. Scipioni replied. "In a case like this, the more time goes by, the better it is. He doesn't lack for anything, I told you, and he's getting as fat as a capon. Things are going well. Don Michele's wound has almost healed, that's a good thing for us, too. Don't worry about it, I tell you, go back to your boat, because this is my business!"

"I can't go back to the boat, now that 'Ntoni is in jail; I can't go back. Everybody would look at us when we walked by, and besides my head isn't working right, now that 'Ntoni is in jail."

And he kept on saying the same thing over and over again, while the money flowed away like water, and the whole family spent their days shut up in the house, with the door closed.

At last the day of the summonses arrived, and those who had their names listed had to go to court on their own steam, if they didn't want to be dragged there by the carabinieri. Even Don Franco went, leaving his big black hat behind for his appearance in court, and he was paler than 'Ntoni Malavoglia, who sat there behind those bars, like a wild beast, between the carabinieri. Don Franco had never had any dealings with the law, and having to appear for the first time before that bunch of judges and police spies who can clap you behind the bars as quick as a flash, like 'Ntoni Malavoglia, really put him off his feed.

The whole village had gone to see how Master 'Ntoni's 'Ntoni looked between the carabinieri. He was as yellow as a candle and didn't dare to blow his nose, afraid he'd see all those friends and neighbors devouring him with their eyes, and he kept turning and twisting his cap in his hands, while the president of the court, wearing a big black robe and a white napkin under his chin, reeled off to him all the crimes he had committed, which were all written down on that paper, without missing a single word. Don Michele was there, looking yellow too, sitting on a chair facing the judges, who were yawning and fanning themselves with their handkerchiefs. And in the meantime 'Ntoni's lawyer was chatting in a low voice to the man next to him, as though the whole thing didn't concern him.

"This time," La Zuppidda murmured into her neighbor's ear, after hearing all the dirty tricks 'Ntoni had pulled, "this time he won't get away with it. Nobody can save him from jail!"

Santuzza was there too, to tell the court where 'Ntoni had been and had spent that evening.

"What a question to ask Santuzza!" La Zuppidda muttered. "I'm anxious to hear what she'll answer so she won't have to tell the law all her private business."

"But what do they want to know from us?" asked Comare Grazia.

"They want to know if it's true that Lia had something going with Don Michele, and that her brother 'Ntoni tried to kill him to get revenge. The lawyer told me so."

"The cholera on both of you!" the pharmacist whispered, glaring at them. "Do you want us all to go to jail? Remember that with the law we've always got to say no, that we don't know a thing."

Comare Venera Zuppidda shrunk into her shawl, but continued to mutter: "It's the truth. I've seen them with my own eyes, and the whole village knows it."

That morning there had been a tragic scene at the Malavoglia house. When he had seen the whole village leave to go and watch 'Ntoni being sentenced, Master 'Ntoni had wanted to rush after them, and Lia, with disheveled hair, wild eyes, and a shaking chin, wanted to go too, and looked all through the house for her shawl with an anguished face and trembling hands, but without saying a word. But Mena, who was pale too, seized her hands and said: "No, you mustn't go! You mustn't go!"— and that's all she said. Also the old man said that they should stay at home and pray to the Madonna; and you could hear their wailing all over Black Lane.

As soon as the poor old man got to Catania, hidden behind the corner of a building, he saw his grandson walk past between the carabinieri. And then with legs that buckled under him at every step, he had to go and sit on the steps of the courthouse, among the feet of the people who were going up and down, tending to their business. But at the thought that all those people were going to hear his grandson being sentenced, in there between the soldiers, before the judges, he felt as if he had deserted 'Ntoni in the middle of the street, or on a stormy sea, and he walked up with the crowd, standing on tiptoe to see, up there, the top of the cage's bars, and the carabinieri's hats and their glittering bayonets. But he couldn't see 'Ntoni among all those people, and the poor old man still thought that he must be one of the soldiers.

Meanwhile the lawyer talked and talked, and his words whined and whined like a pulley on a well. He said it wasn't true, he said that 'Ntoni Malavoglia hadn't committed all those crimes, that the president of the court had dug them out just to get a poor young man into trouble, because that was his profession. And, after all, how could the president say anything? Had he perhaps seen 'Ntoni Malavoglia on that night, dark as it was? "In a poor man's house, the first person who walks in, is right" and "The gallows were built for the unfortunate!" The president watched him through his glasses, his elbow resting on some dusty books, and all those words went in one ear and out the other. And Doctor Scipioni declared again that he would like to know where all that smuggled stuff was. Since when couldn't an honest man go for a stroll any time he chose and pleased, especially if he had a bit of wine in him to walk off? At that Master 'Ntoni nodded his head and said, "That's right! that's right!" with tears in his eyes, and at that moment he felt like embracing the lawyer who was calling 'Ntoni a drunkard. Then suddenly his head came up. Now the lawyer was saying something really good, something that all by itself was worth fifty lire: he said that since they were trying to push him up against the wall and were trying to prove, like two and two make four, that they'd caught 'Ntoni red-handed with the knife in his hand, by bringing Don Michele in there looking like a dummy because of that knife he'd gotten in his belly—"How do you know he got it from 'Ntoni Malavoglia?" the lawyer declaimed. "Can anyone prove it? And who knows whether Don Michele didn't give himself that stab in the belly on purpose, so he could send 'Ntoni Malavoglia to jail?"—very well, did they want to know the truth? Contraband had absolutely nothing to do with it! There was an old grudge between Don Michele and Master 'Ntoni's 'Ntoni, on account of a woman. And

Master 'Ntoni again nodded his head, because if they'd made him swear on the crucifix he would have sworn it, and the whole village knew it, that story between Santuzza and Don Michele, who had gone wild with jealousy after Santuzza had taken a fancy to 'Ntoni, and 'Ntoni and Don Michele had met at night after his boy had had a lot to drink; and everybody knows what can happen when you can no longer see straight. And the lawyer went on: "They could ask Barbara Zuppidda again, and Comare Venera, and a hundred thousand witnesses, whether it was true or not that Don Michele was having an affair with Lia, 'Ntoni Malavoglia's sister, and hung around Black Lane every evening because of the girl. They'd even seen him there on the night of the stabbing!"

And this was the last Master 'Ntoni heard because his ears began to whistle, and for the first time he saw 'Ntoni, who had stood up in the cage and was tearing at his cap, his eyes frenzied, and wanted to speak and kept shaking his head, as though to say "No! No!" The people next to him carried the old man away, thinking that he'd had a stroke; and the carabinieri laid him on a wooden bunk bed in the witnesses' room and threw water in his face. Later on, while they were helping him down the stairs, tottering, the crowd poured out in a flood and he heard them say: "They've sentenced him to five years' hard labor." Just at that moment 'Ntoni came out of the other small door, his face white, between the carabinieri and handcuffed like Christ.

Comare Piedipapera rushed back to the village and arrived before any of the others, because bad news flies as fast as a bird. As soon as she saw Lia, who was waiting at her door like a soul in purgatory, she grabbed her by the hands and, completely beside herself, shrieked:

"What have you done, you wretch! They've told the judge that you are having a love affair with Don Michele, and your grandfather has had a stroke!"

Lia didn't say a word, as though she hadn't heard or didn't care. She just stared at her dumbstruck. Then she slowly slumped on the chair, and it seemed that at one blow both her legs had been broken. And after she had stayed like that for a long time without moving or saying a word, while Comare Grazia was throwing water in her face, she began to stammer: "I want to go away! I don't want to stay here anymore!" And she said it to the chest of drawers, and to the chairs, like a crazy woman; and in vain her sister followed her through the house crying, "I told you! I told you!" and trying to seize her hands. In the evening, when they brought their grandfather home on a cart and Mena ran to meet him, for by now she no longer cared what people would say, Lia walked out through the yard and into the street, and she really left, and they never saw her again.

CHAPTER FIFTEEN

People said that Lia had gone to live with Don Michele; but by this time the Malavoglia had nothing more to lose, and at least Don Michele would feed her. Now Master 'Ntoni really looked like a graveyard crow, and all he did was wander about, broken in two, with a face as white as clay, declaiming proverbs without head or tail: "For the felled tree, get the ax! the ax!" or "He who falls in the water must surely get wet!" or "The skinny horse draws the flies." And if someone asked him why he was wandering about all the time, he'd answer that: "Hunger drives the wolf out of the woods" and "A famished dog isn't afraid of the stick"; but now that he was reduced to such a pitiable state, they didn't want to listen to him. Everyone had something to say to him, and asked him what he was waiting for there, his back against the wall under the church tower, looking like Uncle Crocifisso when he waited to lend money to people, or sitting next to the boats drawn up on the beach as though he had a trawler like Master Cipolla's out at sea; and Master 'Ntoni replied that he was waiting for death, which didn't want to come and take him, for "the miserable have long, long days." At home none of them ever spoke about Lia, not even Saint Agatha, who, if she felt like crying, did it in secret in front of her mother's little bed, when she was alone in the house. Now the house was as wide as the sea itself, and they felt lost in it. All the money had gone, together with 'Ntoni; Alessi was always away, earning his bread in one place or another; and Nunziata did Mena the kindness of coming to light the fire when, at vespers, she had to go and fetch her grandfather, leading him by the hand like a child, because he could no longer see at night, worse than a chicken.

Don Silvestro and other people in the village said that the best thing that Alessi could do was to send his grandfather to the poorhouse, now that he was completely useless; but this was the one thing that still frightened the old man. Every time Mena took him out into the sun, leading him by the hand, and he sat there all day waiting for death, he thought that they were taking him to the poorhouse, that's how foolish he'd become, and he used to mumble: "Death never comes!" so that some people came and asked him, laughing: "Well, where is it now, that death of yours? At Catania?"

On Saturdays Alessi came home and counted out the week's earnings in front of his grandfather, as though the old man still had his wits about him. Master 'Ntoni kept saying "Yes, yes" to everything, nodding his head; and then Alessi had to go and hide his few pennies under the mattress, and to make the old man happy he'd say that it wouldn't take much to put together the money for the house by the medlar tree once more, and in a year or two they'd do it.

But the old man shook his head stubbornly and replied that they no longer needed the house now; and that since the Malavoglia were scattered everywhere now, it would have been better if there'd never been a house of the Malavoglia in this world.

Once, when nobody was there, Master 'Ntoni drew Nunziata aside under the almond tree, and it seemed he had something very important to say to her; but he kept moving his lips without speaking, looking here and there, searching for the words. At last he said: "What they said about Lia, is it true?"

"No," replied Nunziata, crossing her hands on her breast. "No! By the Madonna of Ognina, it's not true."

He began shaking his head, his chin sunk on his chest. "Then why did she run away, too? Why did she run away?" And he looked for her all through the house, pretending he'd lost his cap; he touched the bed and the chest of drawers and sat down at the loom, but he didn't say a word. "Do you know," he finally asked, "do you know where she's gone?" But he didn't say anything to Mena.

Nunziata didn't know, honestly she didn't, nor did anyone else in the village.

One evening Alfio Mosca stopped in Black Lane with his cart, which was drawn by a mule now, and to get the money to buy it he had caught the fever at Bicocca and he'd almost died, and in fact his face was yellow and his belly was as swollen as a wine skin; but the mule was fat and had a glossy coat.

"Remember when I left for Bicocca?" he said. "You still lived in the house by the medlar tree! Now everything's changed, because the world is round, and some swim and some sink to the bottom." This time they couldn't even offer him a glass of wine in welcome. Compare Alfio knew where Lia was; he had seen her with his own eyes, and it had been as if he had seen Comare Mena when they used to talk from window to window. That's why he kept looking at the furniture and the walls, as if his loaded cart were weighing on his stomach, and he too didn't say a word as he sat at that table, which was bare and where nobody ate in the evening.

"Now I'll go," he kept repeating, seeing that they didn't have anything to say to him. "When a man leaves his village, he'd better not come back, because while he's away everything changes, and even the faces that look at him are changed, and he feels that he has also become a stranger."

Mena still kept silent. And Alessi told him that he was going to marry Nunziata after he'd put together a little money, and Alfio said that he was doing right, if Nunziata had a bit of money too, because she was a good girl and everyone in the village knew her. That's how things are: even the family forgets those who have gone, and everyone in this world has to drag the cart that God has given him, like Compare Alfio's donkey, which was now God knows where, since he'd passed into other people's hands.

Now that her younger brother had begun earning some money, Nunziata had her dowry too, and she'd bought neither gold nor linens, because she said that such things are for the rich, and besides, there was no sense in buying linens while she was still growing.

She had in fact grown into a tall girl, as thin as a broomstick, with black hair and eyes so soft and gentle that when she sat at the door with all those children around her, it seemed she was still thinking of the day her father had deserted them, and of all the troubles she had tripped through until then, with her little brothers clinging to her skirts. And seeing how she'd pulled herself and her brothers out of the mire, weak as she was, and thin as a broomstick, everyone greeted her and was glad to stop and chat with her.

"We've got the money," she said to Alfio, whom they'd known so long that he was almost like a relative. "At All Saints' Day, my oldest brother is going to start work as an apprentice for Massaro Filippo, and the youngest will get a job with Master Cipolla. When I've settled Turi too, I'll get married; but we've got to wait until I am old enough and my father gives his consent."

"Do you think your father knows that you're still alive!" said Alfio.

"If he came back now," Nunziata replied in that soft, calm voice of hers, with her hands resting on her knees, "he would never go away again, because now we have money."

Then Compare Alfio said again to Alessi that he was doing the right thing to marry Nunziata, if she had a bit of money.

"We'll buy the house by the medlar tree," Alessi added, "and grandfather will live with us. When the others come back, they'll also live there; and if Nunziata's father comes back there'll be room for him too."

They didn't say a word about Lia; but all three of them were thinking about her as they sat there looking at the lamp, their arms resting on their knees.

At last Compare Mosca got up to leave, because his mule was jangling his bell-collar, as though he too had known the girl Compare Alfio had met on the street, the girl for whom there was no longer a place in the house by the medlar tree.

Uncle Crocifisso, though, had been waiting anxiously for the Malavoglia to come to him about the house by the

medlar tree which nobody wanted, as though it were
cursed, and so he was stuck with it. And as soon as he
heard that Alfio Mosca had returned to the village—the
same Alfio whose bones he had wanted to break when he
was jealous of La Vespa—he went to ask him to talk to
the Malavoglia and settle that deal for him. Now when he
met him on the street, he greeted him, and even tried to
send La Vespa to talk to him about the deal, and perhaps, who knows? they might also remember their old
love and Compare Alfio Mosca would take that cross off
his back, too. But now that she had her own husband
and was the mistress of her own house, that bitch La
Vespa didn't want to hear any talk of Compare Alfio
Mosca or anyone else, and she wouldn't have exchanged
Uncle Crocifisso for King Victor Emmanuel in person,
not even if they dragged her by the hair. "All the misfortunes come my way!" Uncle Crocifisso wailed; and he
poured his heart out to Compare Alfio, and he beat his
breast as though he were before his confessor for ever
having thought of paying ten lire to get someone to break
Alfio's bones.

"Ah, Compare Alfio, if you only knew the ruin that has
descended on my house. I can't sleep or eat anymore, and
all I do is store up bile, and I'm no longer the master of a
cent of my own property, after having sweated all my life
and taken the very bread out of my mouth to put it together penny by penny. And now I must watch that viper,
building up and tearing down just as she pleases! And I
can't even get rid of her through the courts, because she
wouldn't be tempted even by Satan himself! And she loves
me so much that I'll never get her off my neck until I
croak, if I don't die from heartbreak!

"I was just telling Compare Alfio here," Uncle Crocifisso continued, seeing Master Cipolla, who dawdled
about the piazza all day like the butcher's dog, ever since
that other shrew Mangiacarrube had come into his house,
"if we don't want to burst from rage, we've got to stay out
of the house. They've chased us out of our own houses,
those sluts! They're the ferrets and we're the rabbits.
Women are put in this world as a punishment for our sins.
Without them, we'd all live much better. Who would ever
have said it, eh, Master Fortunato? We who had the peace

of the angels! You see how the world is made! There are
people who go searching for a marriage deal with a lantern, while the ones who are married would like to get out
of it."

Master Fortunato rubbed his chin for a while, and then
he burst out: "Marriage is like a rattrap; those who are in
it want to get out, while the others snoop around it trying
to get in."

"They're crazy, that's what I think! Just look at Don
Silvestro, what does he lack? And they say he's got it into
his head to make Barbara Zuppidda fall with his feet; and
if Comare Venera can't find anyone better, she'll have to
let her fall."

Master Cipolla continued to rub his chin and didn't say
anything else. "Listen, Compare Alfio," Dumbbell went
on, "help me wind up that sale of the house to the Malavoglia, while they still have the money, and I'll buy you
a new pair of shoes for the leather you'll wear out."

Compare Alfio talked to the Malavoglia again; but
Master 'Ntoni shook his head and said no. "What use
would we have for the house now, for Mena can't get
married and there isn't a Malavoglia left! I'm still here
because the miserable have long, long days. But after I've
closed my eyes, Alessi will take Nunziata and he'll leave
the village."

Master 'Ntoni too, was ready to leave. He spent most
of the time in bed, like a shrimp under the rocks, growling
worse than a dog. "What have I got to do here?" he muttered; and he felt that he was stealing the soup they gave
him. Alessi and Mena tried in vain to dissuade him. He
replied that he was stealing their time and their soup, and
he made them count the money under the mattress, and
when he saw it was disappearing little by little, he grumbled: "At least if I weren't here you wouldn't spend so
much. Now I can no longer do anything here, and I might
as well leave."

Don Ciccio, who came to feel his pulse, said that it
would be better if they took him to the hospital, because
here he was uselessly consuming his own substance and
that of his family. And with lifeless eyes the wretched old
man waited anxiously to hear what they'd answer, and was
afraid that they'd send him off to the poorhouse. But

Alessi wouldn't hear any talk of sending him to the poor-house and said that so long as there was bread, there was enough for all; and Mena, for her part, agreed with him and took the old man out in the sun on the fine days and sat alongside him with her distaff, when she didn't have to go to the wash shed, spinning and telling him stories as though he were a child. To cheer his heart, she also talked about what they would do when a little good fortune came to them. She told him that they were going to buy a calf on Saint Sebastian's Day, and she herself would gather the grass and fodder for the winter. In May they'd sell it at a profit; and she also showed him the broods of chicks she had raised, and the chicks came to cheep around their feet, in the sun, fluttering their wings in the dust of the road. With the money from the chicks they would also buy a pig, so as not to waste the hulls of the prickly pears and the water they used to cook the pasta, and at the end of the year it would be like having put money in the money box. The old man, with his hands on his cane, looked at the chicks and nodded his head in approval. He listened to her so carefully, poor old man, that he even said that when they had the house by the medlar tree, they could raise the pig in the yard, for surely they could sell it to Peppi Naso at a profit. In the house by the medlar tree there was also a stall for the calf, and the shed for the fodder, and every-thing they needed; and he remembered all these things one by one, looking about here and there with his spent, dead eyes, his chin on his cane. Then he whispered to his grand-daughter: "What was it Don Ciccio said about the hos-pital?" At this Mena scolded him like a child and said: "Why do you think about such things?" He kept silent and listened meekly to all that the girl said. But then he said again: "Don't send me to the hospital, because I'm not used to it!"

Finally he couldn't leave his bed at all, and Don Ciccio said that this was really the end, and that they didn't need him anymore, because the old man might even lie in that bed for years, and Alessi, Mena, and even Nunziata would just waste their days watching over him; and if they didn't, the pigs might eat him, if they found the door open.

Master 'Ntoni understood very well what was being said, because he kept looking at all their faces one by one, with eyes that hurt you just to see them; and as soon as the doctor left, as he was still talking at the door with Mena, who was weeping, and Alessi, who kept saying no and stamping his foot, the old man made a sign to Nunziata to come to the bed and said to her in a low voice:

"It will be better for you if you send me to the hospital. Here I eat up your earnings every week. Send me away when Mena and Alessi aren't at home. They would say no, because they have the good hearts of the Malavoglia. But I'm eating up your money for the house, and besides the doctor said that I could lie here for years. And I've got nothing more that I can do here. But I wouldn't like to go on living for years there in the hospital."

Nunziata began crying and also said that she wouldn't do it, and the neighbors talked about them, saying that they wanted to be so high and mighty when they didn't even have enough bread to eat. They were ashamed to send their grandfather to the hospital, while all the others in the family were scattered everywhere, and some fine places, too!

And Santuzza kissed the holy medal she wore on her breast, to thank the Madonna for having protected her from the peril into which Saint Agatha's sister had fallen, like so many other girls. "They ought to send that poor old man to the hospital, so he won't suffer the agonies of purgatory before he dies," she said. Her father at least didn't lack for anything now that he was an invalid, and she kept him at the door of the tavern. "And he even helps you!" Piedipapera added. "That invalid is worth his weight in gold! He seems just made to sit at the tavern door, blind and shriveled up as he is! And you should pray to the Holy Virgin that he lives for one hundred years. After all, what does he cost you?"

Santuzza had plenty of reason to kiss the holy medal. Nobody could gossip about her. Since Don Michele had left, Massaro Filippo didn't come around either, and people said that he couldn't manage things without Don Michele's help. Now the wife of Cinghialenta came every so often to raise the devil in front of the tavern, her hands on her hips, screaming that Santuzza was stealing her husband, and when Cinghialenta went home, she got a beating with the mule's halter, because Cinghialenta had sold his mule and didn't know what to do with the halter, and she shrieked so much at night that their neighbors couldn't fall asleep.

"That's not right!" said Don Silvestro. "The halter is meant for the mule. Compare Cinghialenta is a coarse man." He made these remarks when he could be heard by Venera Zuppidda, who, since the army was taking away the young men, had finally become a bit tamer towards him.

"Everybody knows what goes on in his own home," answered La Zuppidda. "If you're saying this because evil tongues say that I beat my husband, I must tell you that you may know how to read and write but you don't know a thing. Besides, everyone does as he pleases and chooses in his own house. In my house, my husband is the master."

"Let them talk," her husband said. "They all know that if they get my blood up, I'll make tuna hash of them!"

Now La Zuppidda proclaimed that her husband was the master in her house, and that he was free to marry Barbara off to whomever he liked, and if he was going to give her to Don Silvestro, it meant he had promised her to him and had bowed his head; and when her husband had bowed his head, he was worse than an ox.

"That's right!" Don Franco declared, his beard in the air. "He has bowed his head because Don Silvestro is one of the people who hold the ladle."

Since he'd been in court surrounded by all those police spies, Don Franco was more enraged than ever, and he swore that he wouldn't go back to court even if the carabinieri dragged him there. And when Don Giammaria raised his voice to argue, he almost scratched the priest's eyes out, rearing up on his little legs, as red as a rooster, and he pushed him to the rear of the shop. "You're doing this on purpose to compromise me!" Don Franco spat at him, frothing at the mouth. And if two people quarreled in the piazza, the pharmacist rushed to close his door so that they couldn't call him as a witness. Don Giammaria was triumphant; that green asparagus had the courage of a lion, because he wore a soutane to protect him, and criticized the government, gobbling up his lira a day, and said that they all deserved that government, for they'd made the revolution, and now strangers from all over were coming to steal their women and the people's money. He knew what he was talking about, he'd even gotten jaundice he'd been so angry, and Donna Rosolina had grown thin as a stick from bile, especially after Don Michele had left town and his dirty deals had come out in the open. Now all she did was go in search of masses and confessors, here, there, and everywhere, all the way to Ognina and Aci Castello, and she neglected her tomato paste and tuna jars in order to give herself to God.

Then Don Franco relieved his feelings by cackling like a hen, irritating Don Silvestro, and rearing up on his toes with the door flung wide open, since there was no danger of going to prison for that; and he said that so long as there would be priests, things would always be the same, and that one had to make a clean sweep—and he had definite ideas about whom—and he'd slash the air, left and right, with the side of his hand.

"I myself would like to see them all burned alive!" replied Don Giammaria—and he also had definite ideas.

Now the pharmacist no longer mounted the podium; and when Don Silvestro came around he disappeared to pound his unguents in the mortar, to avoid compromising himself. Everybody knows that those who are in cahoots with the government and eat the King's bread are people to beware of. And he complained to Don Giammaria and Don Ciccio, the doctor, who left his donkey at the pharmacy to go and feel Master 'Ntoni's pulse and never wrote out any prescriptions, because he said that they wouldn't be of any help to those poor people who didn't have money to throw away.

"Then why don't they send that old man to the hospital?" the people said again. "Why do they keep him in the house, so he can be eaten up by the fleas?"

And they kept pounding away and pounding away, and the doctor kept saying that he was going back and forth on a fool's journey for nothing, and when the neighbors gathered around the sick man's bed, Comare Grazia, Cousin Anna, or Nunziata, he always declared that the fleas were eating the old man up alive. Master 'Ntoni, his face white and haggard, did not dare to say a word. And since the neighbors went on chirping like sparrows, and even Nunziata didn't know what to do, one day when Alessi wasn't there, the old man said:

"Call Alfio Mosca, because he'll do me the charity of taking me to the hospital in his cart."

So Master 'Ntoni went to the hospital in Alfio Mosca's cart, on which Alfio had put his mattress and pillow. But when they carried him out, holding him up under his armpits, though he didn't say a word, the poor sick man kept looking everywhere. Alessi had gone to Riposto and they'd found some excuse to send away Mena, for those two would never have let him go. All down Black Lane, passing the house by the medlar tree and crossing the piazza, Master 'Ntoni kept looking around him, to stamp it all on his mind. Alfio was leading the mule on one side, and Nunziata, who had left Turi in charge of the calf, the turkeys, and the chickens, walked on the other, with the bundle of Master 'Ntoni's shirts under her arm. Seeing the cart go past, everyone came to the door and stood there to watch; and Don Silvestro said that they had done right, that's why the Commune paid its regular share to the hospital; and Don Franco would have blurted out his sermon, which he had all nicely prepared in his head, if Don Silvestro hadn't been there. "At least that poor devil will be living in peace," Uncle Crocifisso concluded.

"Nobility gives way to necessity," Master Cipolla replied, and Santuzza said a Hail Mary for the poor man. Only Cousin Anna and Comare Grazia Piedipapera dried their eyes with their aprons as the cart slowly drove away, jolting on the stones. But Compare Tino snapped at his wife: "Why are you crying? Did I die, perhaps? What does it matter to you?"

As he led the donkey, Alfio Mosca told Nunziata how and where he had seen Lia, who was the picture of Saint Agatha, and he still couldn't believe that he had seen her with his own eyes, and his voice failed him as he talked to pass the time while they went down the dusty road. "Ah, Nunziata, who would have thought it, when we used to talk from door to door, and the moon was shining, and the neighbors were gossiping out in front, and you could hear Saint Agatha's loom thwacking all day long, and those chickens which knew her just by the way she opened the latch of the gate, and La Longa calling her from the yard, because from my house I could hear everything, as though it were right there with me! Poor La Longa! Now, you see, when I have a mule and everything I longed for—though I wouldn't have believed it then, even if an angel from heaven had come to tell me—now I am always thinking of those evenings when I used to hear your voices while I was grooming my donkey, and I saw the lamp shining in the house by the medlar tree, which is shut up now, and when I came back I no longer found anything the way I had left it, and even Comare Mena didn't seem the same to me. If a man leaves his village, he'd better never come back again. You see, now I also think of that poor donkey who worked with me for so long a time and always kept going, rain or shine, with his head hanging low and his long ears. Now who knows where he's being driven, and with what loads and on what roads, and his ears must be even lower now, so that he too is sniffing the earth that must receive him. He's getting old too, poor beast!"

Master 'Ntoni, stretched out on the mattress, didn't hear any of this, and they had put a blanket on poles over the cart, so that it looked as though they were carrying a dead man. "It's better for him if he doesn't hear any more," Compare Alfio went on. "He already knows about 'Ntoni's troubles, and sooner or later he'd also find out how Lia has ended up."

"He often asked me about her," Nunziata said. "He wanted to know where she was."

"She went the same way as her brother. We poor people are like sheep, and we always go one after the other with our eyes shut. You mustn't tell him, or anyone in the village, where I saw Lia, because it would be like the stab of a knife for Saint Agatha. I'm sure that she recognized me as I passed the door, because she went white and then red, and I whipped the mule to go by fast, and I'm sure that the poor girl would rather have had the mule walk on her belly and be carried off stretched out on the cart, as we're now carrying her grandfather. Now the Malavoglia family is destroyed, and you and Alessi must start it up again."

"The money for the things we need is already there. And on Saint John's Day we'll also sell the calf."

"You're right! This way, when you'll put the money aside, there's no danger that it'll go up in smoke in a single day, as it would if the calf should die, God forbid! These are the first houses of the city, and you can wait for me here, if you don't want to come all the way to the hospital."

"No, I want to come too. Then at least I'll see where they put him, and he will also see me till the last moment."

Master 'Ntoni did see her to the very last moment, and as Nunziata went away with Alfio Mosca, walking slowly through the huge room, so slowly they seemed to be walking in a church, he followed them all the way with his eyes; then he turned on his bed, and didn't move anymore. Compare Alfio and Nunziata got up on the cart again, rolled up mattress and blanket, and returned over the long dusty road, without once saying a word.

When he didn't find his grandfather in bed and saw them bringing back the rolled-up mattress, Alessi began beating his head and tearing at his hair; and then he began yelling at Mena, as though she'd been the one to send him away. But Compare Alfio said to him: "What could you do? The house of the Malavoglia is destroyed now, and it's for you to start it up again."

And Alfio kept trying to talk about the money they'd saved and what they'd get for the calf, which he and Nunziata had discussed on the road; but Alessi and Mena didn't listen to him; with their heads clasped in their hands and their eyes staring and bright with tears, they sat at the door of the house where they were really alone now. And all the time Alfio tried to comfort them by reminding them of what the house by the medlar tree had been before, when they used to talk from door to door, with the moon shining, and all day long you could hear the thwacking of Saint Agatha's loom, and the chickens clucking, and the voice of La Longa, who was always busy. Now everything was changed, and when a man leaves his town, it's better that he never come back again, because even the road didn't look the same since all those people had stopped strolling back and forth to see the Mangiacarrube girl, and even Don Silvestro didn't show up anymore, waiting to make Barbara Zuppidda fall with his feet; and Uncle Crocifisso had shut himself up in his house to guard his property or to fight with La Vespa; and there wasn't so much arguing in the pharmacy as there used to be, ever since Don Franco had seen the law face to face, and nowadays he hid in a corner to read his newspaper and blew off steam by pounding his mortar all day, and that's how he made the time pass. Even Master Cipolla no longer sat on the church steps, ever since he too had lost his peace.

For one fine day the news got around that Master Fortunato was getting married so that the Mangiacarrube girl shouldn't enjoy his property, whether he liked it or not. That's why he wasn't sitting on the church steps anymore, because he was getting married to Barbara Zuppidda. "And he used to tell me that marriage is like a rattrap!" Uncle Crocifisso went about grumbling. "Now how can you trust men?"

The girls who were jealous said that Barbara was marrying her grandfather. But levelheaded people, like Peppi Naso, Piedipapera, and even Don Franco, murmured: "Comare Venera has defeated Don Silvestro. It's a great blow for Don Silvestro, and the best thing he can do is leave the village. Strangers should be thrown out anyway! No stranger has ever put down roots here. Don Silvestro won't dare start anything with Master Cipolla."

"What did he think?" Comare Venera blared, her hands on her hips. "Did he think he could get my daughter by famine? This time I give the orders! And I made that clear to my husband! A good dog feeds in his own trough! We don't want any strangers in our house! There was a time when the village was well off, when these people from outside hadn't come to write down on a piece of paper every mouthful you ate, like Don Silvestro, or to pound mallow blossoms in a mortar and get fat on the blood of the people who live here. In those days we all knew each other, and we knew what our neighbor was doing, and what his father and his grandfather had always done, and even what they ate, and when we saw somebody walk by we knew where he was going, and the plots belonged to the people who were born on them, and the fish didn't let themselves be caught by the first comer. In those days folks didn't go straying all over the place, and they didn't go to die in the hospital."

Since everyone was getting married, Alfio Mosca would have liked to take Comare Mena, whom nobody wanted anymore now that the house of the Malavoglia had gone to pieces, and Compare Alfio, with the mule he owned, could be considered a good match for her. So on Sundays, as he kept her company, sitting in front of the house, his back leaning against the wall, snapping twigs from the hedge between his fingers to pass the time, he brooded over all these reasons to give himself courage. She too watched the people go by, and that's how they enjoyed their Sundays.

"If you still want me, Comare Mena," he said at last, "I'm here."

Poor Mena didn't even blush at hearing that Compare Alfio had guessed she had wanted him when they were marrying her to Brasi Cipolla; it all seemed so far away now, and she herself no longer felt the same person. "I'm old now, Compare Alfio," she replied, "and I won't get married anymore."

"If you're old, I'm old too, because I was years older than you when we used to talk from window to window, and it seems like yesterday, because my heart has never forgotten. But more than eight years must have passed. And now when your brother Alessi gets married, you'll be left out in the street."

Mena shrugged her shoulders, for she was used to bowing to God's will, like Cousin Anna. And seeing this Compare Alfio went on:

"Then that means you don't care for me, Comare Mena, and you must forgive me for asking you to marry me. I know that you were born better than I was, and that you are the daughter of people with property. But now you no longer own anything, and if your brother Alessi marries, you'll be left out in the middle of the street. I have my mule and my cart, and you'll never lack for bread, Comare Mena. Now forgive me for the liberty I've taken!"

"No, Compare Alfio, you haven't insulted me. And I would have told you yes even when we had the *Provvidenza* and the house by the medlar tree, if my family had wanted it, because God knows I had you in my heart when you went away to Bicocca with your donkey cart, and I still can see that lamp in the stable, and you putting all your belongings on the cart in the yard. Do you remember?"

"Yes, I remember! Then why don't you say yes, now that you've lost everything, and I have a mule instead of a donkey in front of my cart, and your family couldn't say no?"

"I'm not a girl that can marry," Mena repeated, with her face lowered, snapping twigs from the hedge between her fingers, too. "I'm twenty-six, and the time when I could get married has passed."

"No, that's not why you won't say yes!" said Alfio, his face lowered, like hers. "You don't want to tell me the reason!" And so they sat there in silence, snapping twigs and not looking at each other. After a while he got up to leave, his shoulders hunched and his chin sunk on his chest. And Mena followed him with her eyes as long as she could see him, and then she stared at the wall across the way and sighed.

Just as Alfio Mosca had said, Alessi married Nunziata and bought back the house by the medlar tree.

"I'm not a girl that can marry," Mena kept saying. "You get married, because you still can." And so she had gone to live in the attic of the house by the medlar tree, like an old pot put away on the shelf, and had set her heart at rest, waiting for Nunziata's children so she could mother them. They had chickens in the coop, and a calf in the stable, and firewood and fodder stored under the shed, and nets and all kinds of gear hanging in the yard—everything as Master 'Ntoni had said; and Nunziata had again planted broccoli and cabbages in the garden with those delicate arms of hers, so delicate that you couldn't believe that she had washed so much laundry, and had given birth to those fat, rosy babies, whom Mena carried in her arms all over the neighborhood, mothering them as though she herself had brought them into the world.

Whenever he saw her walk past, Alfio Mosca shook his head and looked away with heavy shoulders. "You didn't think me worthy of such an honor!" he said to her at last, when he could bear it no longer, with a heart heavier than his shoulders. "I wasn't worthy of hearing you say yes!"

"No, Compare Alfio, that's not the reason!" said Mena, feeling the tears coming to her eyes. "I swear it by this pure soul I hold in my arms! It's just that I can't get married anymore."

"But why can't you get married, Comare Mena?"

"No! No!" repeated Comare Mena, who was almost weeping. "Don't make me say it, Compare Alfio! Don't make me speak! If I got married now, people would start talking about my sister Lia again, because after what's happened nobody would dare to marry a Malavoglia girl. You'd be the first one to regret it. Leave me alone, because I can't get married, and set your heart at rest."

"You're right, Mena!" said Compare Mosca. "I never thought of that. Cursed be the fate that brought so many troubles on us!"

So Compare Alfio set his heart at rest, and Mena continued to carry Nunziata's babies around in her arms, as though her heart were at rest too, and to sweep and tidy the attic, preparing for the day when the others, who'd been born there too, would return. "Just as if they've gone on a journey and were coming back any day!" Piedipapera remarked.

But Master 'Ntoni had gone on a long journey, farther away than Trieste and Alexandria in Egypt, that journey from which no one ever returns; and when his name came up, while they were resting, reckoning up the week's accounts and making plans for the future, sitting in the shadow of the medlar tree with their soup bowls between their knees, the talk would suddenly die out, and they all felt that they had the old man right before their eyes, as they'd seen him the last time they'd gone to visit him—in that huge, ugly room with the beds all lined up in long rows, so many beds that you had to search to find him. And grandfather was waiting for them like a soul in purgatory, his eyes fastened on the door, although he could hardly see, and he had to touch them to make sure it was really they, and then afterwards he didn't say a word, though you could see from the look on his face that he had so many things he wanted to say, and he broke your heart because you could see that sorrow on his face but he could not say it. And then when they told him that they had bought back the house by the medlar tree, and that they wanted to take him back to Trezza, he said yes! yes! with his eyes, which began to shine again, and he almost smiled, the smile of those who no longer smile, or smile for the last time—a smile that remains stuck in your heart like a

knife. And on Monday when the Malavoglia returned with
Alfio Mosca's cart to fetch their grandfather, he was no
longer there.

Remembering all these things, they let their spoons drop
in their soup bowls and they thought about all that had
happened, which seemed dark, very dark, as though the
deep shadows of the medlar tree hung over it. And now
when Cousin Anna came to spin for a while with the Malavoglia women, her hair was white, and she said she had
lost the smile from her mouth because she had no time to
be cheerful, with that family she had to take care of. And
every day she had to go searching for Rocco through the
streets and in front of the tavern, and chase him home like
a stray calf. Also the Malavoglia had their two strays; and
Alessi racked his brain trying to figure out where they
could be, on what roads burned dry by the sun and white
with dust, because after all this time they would never
come back to the village again.

One evening, late, the dog began barking behind the
door to the yard, and Alessi himself went out to open it,
and he didn't recognize 'Ntoni, who had come back with
his bag under his arm, so much had he changed. He was
all covered with dust and had a heavy beard. After he
came in and sat down in a corner, they were almost afraid
to say how happy they were to have him back. He no
longer seemed the same man, and kept looking around the
room as though he had never seen it; even the dog growled
at him, for he didn't know him. They put a bowl of soup
between his knees, because he was hungry and thirsty, and
he ate it in silence, his nose in his plate, as if he hadn't
seen God's bounty for a week. But the others lost their
appetite, they had such a pang in their hearts. Then 'Ntoni,
when he had eaten and rested a while, took his bag and
got up to leave.

He had changed so much that Alessi was afraid to say
anything to his brother. But when he saw him pick up his
bag, he felt his heart leap in his breast, and Mena said,
trembling: "Are you going away?"

"Yes," answered 'Ntoni.

"And where will you go?" asked Alessi.

"I don't know. I came to see you. But since I've been
here the soup has turned to poison in my mouth. Besides

I can't stay here, because everybody knows me, and that's why I came at night. I'll go far away, where I'll find some way to earn my bread, and nobody will know who I am."

The others didn't dare to breathe a word, because their hearts were gripped in a vise, and they realized that 'Ntoni was right to speak as he did. 'Ntoni kept looking everywhere, and stood in the doorway, and could not make up his mind to leave. "I'll let you know where I'll be," he said at last, and when he was in the yard under the medlar tree, where it was dark, he also said: "And what about grandfather?"

Alessi did not reply; and 'Ntoni fell silent too. Then after a while, he said: "And what about Lia? I didn't see her."

And since he didn't get an answer, he added in a shaky voice, as though he had a chill: "Is she dead too?"

Alessi did not answer this time either; and then 'Ntoni, who was under the medlar tree with his bag in his hand, started to sit down, because his legs were trembling, but he straightened up abruptly, muttering: "Goodbye! Goodbye! Don't you see that I must go away?"

But before he left, he wanted to go through the house, to see whether everything was in its place, as before; but though he had had the heart to leave home and stab Don Michele and go through so much trouble, he did not have the heart to walk from room to room unless they asked him. Alessi saw the yearning in his eyes, and he took him into the stable, on the excuse of showing him the calf Nunziata had bought; and it was fat and had a shiny coat, and in a corner was the mother hen with her chicks. And then Alessi took him into the kitchen, where they had built a new oven, and into the room alongside it, where Mena slept with Nunziata's children, and you'd think she'd given birth to them herself. 'Ntoni looked at everything, and nodded his head approvingly, and said: "Grandfather would have also put the calf here; and this is where the hens used to stay, and that's where the girls used to sleep, when the other one was here too. . . ." But then he said no more and silently looked around him, his eyes bright with tears. At that moment La Mangiacarrube walked past, scolding Brasi Cipolla out on the street, and 'Ntoni said:

"Well, that one's found a husband. And when they're through fighting, they'll go home and go to sleep."

The others kept silent, and all through the village there was a great silence, and all you could hear was now and then the slamming of a door, but at 'Ntoni's words, Alessi got up the courage to say:

"If you want it, there's a home for you too. Your bed is in the next room."

"No," 'Ntoni answered, "I must go away. Mother's bed used to be in there, and she soaked it with tears when I wanted to go away. Do you remember the fine talks we used to have in the evening while we were salting the anchovies? And Nunziata explained the riddles? And Mama and Lia were there, all of us sitting in the moonlight, and you could hear people talking all over the village, as though we were one large family? I didn't know anything then, and I didn't want to stay here, but now when I know everything I've got to go away."

He spoke with his eyes staring at the ground, and his head sunk between his shoulders. Then Alessi threw his arms around his neck.

"Goodbye!" 'Ntoni repeated. "You see that I'm right to go away! I can't stay here. Goodbye, and forgive me, all of you!"

And he left with his bag clutched under his arm. And when he was out of their sight, in the middle of the piazza, dark and deserted because all the doors were shut, he stopped to hear whether they were shutting the door of the house by the medlar tree, while the dog barked after him, and its barking told him that he was all alone in the village. Only the sea was grumbling the same old story, down below there among the Fariglioni rocks, because the sea is homeless too, and belongs to all those who listen to it, here and there, wherever the sun rises and sets, though at Aci Trezza it grumbles in a special way, and you can recognize it at once when it gurgles and breaks among those rocks, and it seems the voice of a friend.

Then 'Ntoni stopped in the road to look back at the village, which was all black, as though, now that he knew everything, he hadn't the heart to tear himself away from it. And he sat down on the low stone wall around Massaro Filippo's vineyard.

He sat there like that for a long time, thinking of so many things, gazing at the darkened village and listening to the sea grumbling below.

And he stayed there until he began to hear certain familiar sounds, and voices calling to each other behind the closed doors, and shutters slamming, and footsteps down the darkened streets. The lights began to swarm on the shore at the end of the piazza. He lifted his head to look at the Three Kings, glittering in the sky, and the Pleiades which announce the dawn, as he had seen them do so many times. Then he bent his head again, and thought of his whole story. Little by little the sea began to grow white and the Three Kings faded, and the houses rose up, one by one, from the dark streets, with their doors still shut, and he could see them all, and only in front of Pizzuto's shop there was a small light, and Rocco Spatu, his hands in his pockets, coughing and spitting. "Soon Uncle Santoro will open the door," 'Ntoni thought, "and he'll huddle down beside it and begin his day too." And he looked at the sea again, which had turned purple, and was all sown with boats which had also started their day. He picked up his bag and said: "Now it's time to go, because soon people will start coming down the road. But Rocco Spatu was the first to begin the day's work."